TWAYNE'S WORLD AUTHORS SERIES
A Survey of the World's Literature

Sylvia E. Bowman, Indiana University
GENERAL EDITOR

SOUTH AFRICA

Joseph Jones, University of Texas, Austin
EDITOR

Roy Campbell

TWAS 439

Photo by Jane Bown,
courtesy of The Observer

Roy Campbell

ROY CAMPBELL

By JOHN POVEY
University of California at Los Angeles

TWAYNE PUBLISHERS
A DIVISION OF G. K. HALL & CO., BOSTON

Library of Congress Cataloging in Publication Data

Povey, John.
  Roy Campbell.

  (Twayne's world authors series ; TWAS 439 : South Africa)
  Bibliography: p. 227-30.
  Includes index.
  1. Campbell, Roy, 1901 - 1957. 2. Poets, South
African—20th century—Biography. I. Series.
PR9369.3.C35Z85   821.912   77-1358
ISBN 0-8057-6277-9

Contents

About the Author

John Povey was born in London and educated in England and South Africa. He is at present Professor of English and Director of the Center for African Studies at the University of California at Los Angeles.

He has written several articles on South African writing and guest edited a special number of *The Literary Review* on this subject. He has been particularly closely involved with the development of the teaching of various African literatures in this country and was the first chairman of the Literature Committee of the African Studies Association. He has also written extensively on the new second-language literatures from the independent countries of Africa; collaborating in such books as: *Africa in the Wider World, African Literature Today, Critical Approaches to African Literature, Black African Writing in English, African Protest, Contemporary Nigerian Literature* and *World Literatures in English* and has published numerous articles and reviews in professional journals on this topic. For the ten years since its founding he has edited the magazine *African Arts* which is aimed at rectifying the false image of Africa held by so many.

He is at present working on a study of black South African poetry and a collection of South African writing.

Preface

It has always been difficult to find an impartial interpreter of Roy Campbell. My own efforts at detachment were often rent by exasperation (along with irresistible admiration at his supreme lyric gift) at the provocation of Campbell's bellicose and irrational lines. Yet I do not think the poet himself, who so savaged indifference and apathy, would have much appreciated too bland an assessment.

I first encountered Campbell's work at school when, as politically self-conscious adolescents, we urgently took sides over the Spanish Civil War with a vehemence we had usually reserved for partisan support of the varsity boat race. In our common room it was unquestioned that Campbell was on the "wrong" side, for we all had our idealistic dreams when reading of the heroics of the International Brigade. It was not politics alone that called for his rejection. His poetry, so impassioned, so virulent, so lurid, seemed only gross and excessive, even vulgar, if contrasted with the prosy rationalism of the poets who were our heroes: T. S. Eliot, W. H. Auden. Yet all the arguments I advanced then were not quite sufficient to dismiss from memory Campbell's impassioned lines. It was impossible not to respond to some of those magnificently surging lines, even if one did read them privately to keep that lamentable literary self-indulgence a close secret.

It was only after the war when I emigrated to South Africa that I returned to his work and to the new context supplied by Campbell's own native land. South Africa affected me, as it has done so many visitors, with its extraordinary beauty and its lavish color, the "beloved country" of Alan Paton transposed into an exhilarating and lovely landscape. Reading *Adamastor* again I saw how it matched the environment that had occasioned its brilliant lines. In this new perception I read Campbell's work through and found much to admire in his poetic skill; yet there remained much to exasperate in his political posturing.

Campbell is not an easy poet to read, just as he was not the easiest man to know. There is so much deplorable posing, such frustrating pretensions, so many unbecoming petulances, and yet there is also supreme poetry. Against such extensive output, to assess a dozen or so highly successful lyrics seems little enough. Yet there are few modern poets who can lay claim to so many undeniable masterpieces. Campbell has achieved this with an apparently casual air that masks intense technical skill.

This study attempts to trace the bewildering convolutions in Campbell's itinerant, exiled life and his muddled, vicious, untenable philosophies. Above all, it concentrates on poetry, indicating, as it must, how regularly Campbell's intrusive political and personal antagonisms seem likely to destroy a remarkable poetic talent, but pointing, too, at the rich lyric achievements of his poems of intimate personal sincerity, where diction and feeling meld in that supreme union where poetry rests. It is just because there is no middle ground with Campbell that none should be attempted. We do not wish to assess some commonplace average to a poet whose production ranges from the inferior to the sublime, but to distinguish between the two extremes and admire and enjoy the finest.

Whatever else Campbell might be accused of being, he remains a fiery spirit, a poet, and a man still capable of moving the reader to admiration and excitement. Alan Paton reveals much by his tone of amazement when, on meeting Campbell in London, he made the rediscovery "that human beings could still explode and crackle in such a dreary world." A reader may rejoice in the opportunity to meet, even at second hand through books, a man who loved life so ardently, who consistently through his poetry praised God "for letting me loose in such a world."

JOHN POVEY

University of California at Los Angeles

Chronology

1952-
1957   Settles in Portugal on a farm at Sintra near Lisbon.
1953   Lecture tour in Canada and United States (repeated in 1955).
1954   Visits Durban to receive doctor of literature degree from the University of Natal.
1957   April 23, death in car crash in Portugal. Volume II of *Collected Poems* published in London.
1960   *Collected Poems*, Volume III.

CHAPTER 1

Light on a Dark Horse

I *Family Background*

ROY Campbell was born in Durban, the major city and port of the province of Natal, on October 2, 1901. Natal is the most British area of South Africa, for there, because of a series of British military and political maneuvers, the Dutch-speaking Afrikaaner settlers made the least degree of penetration. Campbell's family was mostly Scottish, as may be seen not only from his own surname Campbell but from the name of his mother's family which he retained as his own middle name, Dunnachie. His ancestors appeared generally to have been poor tenants working the farms of local squires, though one legendary ancestor of whom Campbell was inordinately proud, eloped with the daughter of a landlord. She had developed a passion for him while he was playing his fiddle at a village dance.

It was Campbell's grandfather William who decided upon emigration, choosing Natal in preference to the dubious possibilities offered by the convict-settled areas of Australia. William Campbell became entangled with a well-known con man named Byrne who formed an emigration party and then stole the entire investment of the group. Bryne himself was later to become quite a legendary figure for undertaking a whole series of these schemes to fleece such emigrant groups: he would extract from the emigrants substantial deposits of their funds which he claimed would be transferred to his agent on the spot. In this way there would be both capital and know-how available to them for the arduous task of beginning to farm. Naturally enough the gullible immigrants found neither agent nor money awaiting their arrival; Bryne had simply pocketed their contributions. Campbell's grandfather's group totaled one hundred and twenty-seven people. When they landed in Natal they soon realized that they had been swindled, but they equally recognized that they now lacked both the resources and the opportunity to return to England. Even without the valuable capital on which they had counted, they determined, rather than admit failure, to develop a major port at Durban. Because of his enterprise in difficult circumstances, in 1850 William Campbell found himself an important member of a rapidly developing new town, admired and prosperous.

Among his other (and many) peculiarities Roy Campbell records that his grandfather used to write letters in verse. He calls these missives "tolerable doggerel," but their agreeable rhyming couplets are not so far removed from some of the more banal lines which his grandson occasionally permitted to be printed as examples of his own writing. His remarks on Byrne may be taken as a brief example:

> "One day," said old Byrne, "when I journeyed out there
> I was taking a jaunt and enjoying the air:
> My stick, as I wandered, got stuck in a sluit
> And I found it next morning all covered with fruit:"[1]

William Campbell's energy and determination set up the opportunity for Roy Campbell's own father Samuel to become one of the most distinguished men in Natal. His personal distinction was reinforced for the family by the many achievements and honors earned by Roy Campbell's uncle, Sir Marshall Campbell, who owned a very large house outside Durban. There are tales of the usual, perhaps obligatory, series of disasters, as the settlers claimed and pacified the colonial wilderness. Both his uncle and his father were involved in the Matebele War and the so-called Zulu rebellion. But Campbell's father was an intelligent man, ambitious for more intellectual endeavors than the role of a hardy colonial settler. He decided to become a doctor. A loan from his brother permitted him to go to Scotland to study at Edinburgh. He took a medical degree and returned to practice medicine in Durban.

On his return, he became a doctor of some distinction, and although, according to Campbell, his medical practice was marked by a high degree of individual benevolence, he advanced in his studies beyond the role of ordinary general practitioner. He later studied further at the Pasteur Institute in Paris and received another medical degree from Vienna. But if he was avowedly loved for his medical dedication, he was also something of an eccentric. One might perhaps wonder at this point whether the remarkable and unexpected elements of behavior in Campbell's relations are evidence of an exhibitionist tendency that seems to have been established genetically within the whole family. However, we must consider that we are in fact gleaning our information from Campbell's own biographical viewpoint. His interpretation of his own family might well be colored by that need to discover the exotic and the unexpected that constituted such a basic element in his own nature.

Regardless of their possible exaggeration—or even invention—the tales he tells of his family are engaging and amusing. His father apparently always loved speeding and when called out upon a case he would drive fanatically. In the words of Campbell: "He always took advantage of urgent calls in order to stage 'Ben Hur' chariot races and Jehu stampedoes in his flying buggies, to the consternation of pedestrians and poultry alike. He stood on the board with the reins in his left hand, whirling a whip round and round with his right hand in the position of a Roman charioteer, and took the corners on one wheel, so that he was always in trouble with the police"(*L*, 32). Such an activity was relatively harmless while he was dependent on two horsepower, as it were, but he soon advanced to engine power. By 1916 he had acquired a Ford motor car and not long after this, one of his calls for medical attention left him crushed between a tram and a lampost and he was carried home with five broken ribs and a concussion. In spite of these oddities of behavior, he was undoubtedly an intelligent and able man. He was responsible for founding the major technical college of Durban and participated in the formation of the University College of Durban. It is difficult to know what part he played in the shaping of his son's own nature. He exemplified intelligence, ardor, industry, and a flamboyant nature that attracted many. These indeed were the influential aspects of Roy Campbell's early training, judging by the later demonstration of similar behavior in his adult life.

II   *Childhood*

Roy Campbell was brought up in Durban. The town was developing at this time, but it was still very easy to escape into the local countryside, which was largely the territory occupied by the Zulu people. In his autobiography, Campbell records a particularly significant event. Again, it is one of those moments when one is not truly sure whether the fact is true or whether the symbolic truth of the issue is so important that it must necessarily be invented. In either case, it is utterly appropriate that the first thing he recalls in his child memory is a view of the sea. As if that were not enough, the vision is coupled with that of a horse. He recalls, "The first thing I remember distinctly was seeing the sea. That first remembered glimpse of the sea was symbolical of my subsequent life, since I actually saw it first *through the legs of a horse!*" He describes the curious incident:

A horse had its head over the wire fence, and as we rounded the hedge and surprised it, it reared up and turned away: and I, looking down from the grassy slope through its legs, saw a huge living expanse of glittering azure, like a peacock's tail, electrified with winds and solar fire. It took my breath away, and Catherine told me what it was, that Zulu word for the sea, "Lwandhla," which, in two syllables, Homerically expressed the pride and glory of the ocean and the plunge of its breakers, struck my mind with a force which no other word or line in prose or poetry has ever had for me since. (*L.*, 27-28)

The vision of the child is reinforced by the maturity of the subsequent experience of the poet, as is obvious from the very word choice. Nevertheless, the fact that he chooses to lend such emphasis to this event is in itself an important issue. Psychologically, out of the mass of child experiences, the adult memory selects those which subsequently turn out to be of major significance. The sea and the horse and their implicit challenge to manhood are Campbell's metaphors as well as his memories. The brilliant description of the sea, "peacock's tail electrified," is most characteristic of Campbell's poetic vision in its color and in its deliberately frenetic verb. The terms he chooses for the ocean, "pride and glory," are in themselves judgments of his subsequent personal attitude.

The young boy grew up in circumstances which, if not perhaps quite so wild as he would choose to aver later, allowed him many experiences with the African animals. These impressions became a significant part of his poetry. While at school, he used to collect snakes and sell them to the zoo for pocket money. He learned to ride early. Naturally, it is characteristic of Campbell that he would not learn to ride in the usual type of riding school. He learned it by trying to sit on bucking calves in cattle kraals. When ejected off their backs, he fell on the trampled dung which he claims was soft enough to prevent broken bones. After riding bareback on a bucking steer, apparently riding a horse proved a simple task. Not that

Campbell would be content with such relatively simple and efficient maneuvers. Before long he had developed an exhibitionist display of riding: "I developed this faculty of standing on the saddle after seeing a film of desert Arabs, till I could stand barefoot going at a full gallop firing my rifle over my head to show off to girls." (*L*, 63). It seems a remarkable prowess, though we only have Campbell's own assertion of its total success. Although "showing off" is common in many young boys, it seems to presage more coming from Campbell.

III *Schooling*

Campbell's description of his actual school life also stands in that curious middle ground between the initial event, that is in essence probably true, and the deliberate selection and overemphasis of these elements which, in retrospect, could be seen to have such a remarkable effect upon his character. In 1910, he began schooling at Durban High School. This had been taken over by a determined and ambitious new headmaster, A. S. Langley. According to Campbell, Langley was angered by the fact that Campbell's father founded the technical school. He felt it to be an inferior version of the education which was possible at his own grammar school, and snobbishly scorned the opportunities that the technical college provided for the poor. Langley consequently resented Campbell's family, and out of this antagonism he generated an immense dislike for the young boy. Campbell insisted that "Langley would try to break my spirit" by retarding his promotion academically and refusing to allow him to demonstrate his prowess on the sports field.

There are several anecdotes recorded in Campbell's memoirs to indicate how he handled the situation. They are much as we would expect. When, for example, Langley called upon Campbell to battle the seniors in the boxing ring, in the expectation that he would be knocked about, he triumphed by a display of determination and valor. His victories made him renowned throughout the school. He thus proved his physical prowess. More importantly, he demonstrated a direct and vehement response to challenge. Rather than bow to an established and powerful hierarchy, he would bluntly assault it with unsubtle and open antagonism. This was to become his characteristic approach to similar adversity when it assumed a social and literary dimension in London.

He remarks on the superior quality of the other masters. Even for

Langley, he has some curiously sentimental affection, since he exposed young Campbell's determination to resist persecution. Although he is equivocal, arguing, "I owe him the best half of my character, and a sound knowledge of Latin," (*L*, 71), he goes on in his autobiography to remark in a significant way of the development of his character at Langley's hands. Again, there is no accurate way of assessing whether Langley truly influenced the character or whether the character that Campbell maintains as an adult must sift through the experiences of the past in order to justify its present existence.

The mere fact that he chooses to assert the relationship with his oppressive, vindictive, and occasionally vicious headmaster in the same context as he remarks upon the battles he fought to establish himself in European literary society is of major significance in understanding the disposition of Campbell the writer: "In the end, Langley's training had some very great compensations, for it made me completely insensible to literary boycotts, or unfair criticism, either from bullfighting critics, South African political writers, or literary reviewers: things that would break the hearts of other writers only made me laugh!" (*L*, 71). Again this is mere bravado. There is no evidence that he laughed when assaulted by the literary reviewers; rather, he became like a bull at the mercy of the matador, charging in savage and doomed attack. Yet the link between Roy Campbell as a schoolboy and Roy Campbell as a poet supplied by these memories is an important one and one that must be balanced with greater issues which generate the later poetry.

However disastrous the school days may have been, they were not the entire life of the young boy. There were holidays, many of which he spent in Rhodesia where his uncle was a district officer. An interesting element of his autobiography concerning this period of his life is the way he describes the animals encountered on these visits. It foreshadows the attitude which one notices in his verse. Such accuracy of description and vividness of perception establish a particularly intimate association with the animals and the environment in which they live. At one level, one can argue that he is simply showing off a questionable familiarity with the techniques of big game hunting. This reminds us of his similar enjoyment in bandying specialized knowledge concerning the Spanish bullfight, a topic on which he enjoyed posing as an expert. Yet, even if the information is not as accurate and full as he pretends, the desire to express it becomes evidence of a determination to establish a relationship with the animals as part of that environment in which his spirit, and subsequently his poetry, would flourish.

There were other holiday adventures. He records diving for the coins which passengers threw from tourist boats as they were anchored in Durban harbor. He characteristically depreciates the achievement by recording, with his regularly averred professionalism, the fact that large silver coins drop slowly in the water and are therefore fairly easily collected by the young divers. He records another profitable exhibition of vigorous skill. He and his friends would search in the harbor until they discovered an octopus. They would throw the octopus into the swimming pool of one of the major Durban resort hotels much patronized by the rich Johannesburgers during the winter season. The boys would scream that an octopus was in the pool. When the swimmers jumped out in horror, Campbell and his friends would go in and make a great show of wrestling with the beast, and finally kill it by turning it inside out. Apparently even after the spectators had realized that the octopus was not very dangerous and had been artificially introduced into their pool, they still enjoyed this display which got more and more dramatic with artificial blood brought into the water in the form of red ink. The holiday spectators would contribute with enthusiasm when the boys passed around the hat.

There is the risk of pressing this kind of character analogy too far. It is irresistible to point out that the showmanship this anecdote indicates always existed in Campbell's nature, and to consider its implication in evaluating his poetry. The elements are very revealing. Bold action turns out to be more theatrical display than dangerous involvement. There is such open pride and delight in this flamboyant prowess, however, that even when it is acknowledged as mere deception it still receives applause for the delight such exhibition can give. David Wright has a similar anecdote to record from Campbell's later years, when he was visiting London from Spain:

I was trying to crack a walnut with the usual implement when Campbell took it from me and placing it in the massive crook of his elbow, set his biceps to work to split it in two. He went through a formidable pantomime of effort, veins bulging from his forehead and sweat pouring down, while the rest of us watched appalled and, wondering if he was going to burst a blood vessel. After thirty excruciating seconds of terrifying exertion, he produced the nut neatly cracked. Overwhelmed by his spectacular demonstration I thought "My word the old man's even stronger than he says he is."

But later he took me aside and, after swearing me to secrecy, explained it was a parlor trick (you hold the nut in a certain way so that the slightest pressure cracks it).[2]

Campbell remarks in passing upon the profits he made from this kind of boyhood venture: "I always wondered where the point came, between my boyhood and my majority at which I lost this amazing faculty of money-getting, so that between twenty and forty-five, I was completely poor."(L, 173). Between twenty and forty-five, he was, of course, struggling to establish himself as a man and a poet in Europe, far from this benign and exciting Africa of his youth. It is difficult to know how long this kind of youthful adventuring might have continued, but 1914 brought the war in Flanders. Campbell was too young to enlist but he began immediately to think of the excitements of serving as a soldier in Europe. It was characteristic that as soon as the war broke out he would immediately attempt to become involved in the battle, in spite of the fact that he was clearly underage. He apparently volunteered in 1916 and nearly managed to get himself accepted in 1917 until they checked his birth certificate. He then reluctantly stayed in South Africa as an army cadet and never had the chance to join the fighting as all his spirit wished. He finally arrived in England in late 1918, by which time the war was over.

IV   *Europe: The Voyage*

Campbell made his way to England in what was already a typical fashion, by working his passage on a freighter. He takes a great delight in recording his superior prowess as a seaman on board the ship and in describing how he won the admiration of those who thought him merely a bookish egghead. This theme of the triumph of his physical prowess haunts his autobiography. He records one incident which appears so much a parable that one is perhaps tempted to set too great a store by it. His anecdote concerns the third mate, under whom he had to work. When this sailor came in the cabin one day and found that seaman Campbell was carrying a number of books of poetry, he was suitably indignant. He cried out, "Wot's this? Classics, hey? Never done no good to nobody since they was first invented. They'll never get you anywhere, they won't."(L, 173). He was a man of action, and Campbell records, "Whereupon he pushed Shakespeare, Milton, Keats, Dryden, Pope,

Marlowe, and all my painting and drawing materials out of the porthole into the sea."(*L*, 175).

David Wright in repeating this anecdote suggests that if he had taken the elimination of Dryden and Pope from his library to heart, he might well have become a more satisfactory writer. Without the influence of these poets he would not have practiced so incompetently the hammering heroic couplets of those great masters of satire. Unconcerned with such stylistic questions, Campbell himself merely records that when he finally got to England and stayed with his relatives, a gift from his grandfather, James Dunnachie, was used to replenish his library with copies of the drowned books.

He does assert the temporary advantage of this deprivation to the development of his nature. He insists that during the voyage the absence of these books and the lack of opportunity to read left him more time to contemplate the excitement of the elements, the sea, the sky: "Yes. The third mate was right. . . . to chuck those good books out of the porthole, so that I spent my spare time with the sun, stars and moon and the winds and the spray. He not only meant well, but did well, because I was getting too studious." (*L*, 175).

One can see the experience of this voyage in Campbell's first poem, *The Flaming Terrapin*. With his usual honesty Campbell also remarks the obvious fact that he used familiar classic writers in planning the construction of *The Flaming Terrapin*. This poem "would have been impossible without all the chunks of ore stolen from Marlowe, Keats, Dryden, Pope and Milton." (*L*, 176). Campbell is sometimes a derivative poet and he is willing to admit it, yet even ore needs processing if it is to shine with its true beauty.

Apart from this incident, the voyage to Europe was uneventful, though it is interesting to have evidence of the standard South African reactions which Campbell brought to his new experiences. The boat calls in at Dakar, Senegal; Campbell observes the native quarter of Dakar was "dirtier than Kensington with the excrement of dogs." (*L*, 176). His racial prejudice is repeatedly shocked. He learns that a British soldier is being kept by a Negress in the native quarter, and observes for the first time "whites philandering with blacks." He compares this to the more acceptable apartheid separation of his own country with the instinctive reaction of the South African, supported by some untenable anthropology: "I had never thought of coloured women as being anything but the concern of coloured men; and white women as the concern of white men. That seemed to me to be the very reason of their colouration so that they could keep to their own people. Hybrids between negro and white do not seem to justify the mixture, as they are neither hardy, strong, nor intelligent as a general rule." (*L*, 183).

He finally arrived at the London station and was unable to acquire a taxicab for the last part of his trip. With that curious flamboyance of Campbell which is initially half accidental, and in retrospect appears so deliberate, he rented a small donkey cart and was driven around London in this vehicle. This conveyance permitted him later to look back with delighted memory at the unusual and unexpected entrance he had made into this city that he was so determined to conquer.

V *Oxford*

Campbell went first to Scotland, arriving after eight thousand miles "with only sixpence to spare." He stayed for a time with his grandfather, James Dunnachie. There he was able to see something of his brother George, who was on leave and was to be a student at the University of Edinburgh. Then in 1919, he went on south to Oxford, the university city, where he had a number of introductions to people, supplied by his distinguished father. There does not seem to have ever been expectation or desire on Campbell's part that he should formally become a student at Oxford. His casual attitude toward preparatory studies and his indifference to the required Greek denied him regular entrance to the university. Nevertheless, during his residence there, which lasted nearly a year, he was in fact able to make many of those acquaintances of which he is so proud to remark. In particular, he met "a real genius," William Walton, the English composer, and with him began what was to be a long-term friendship that allowed Campbell important literary introductions.

Campbell realized that his own attitudes would not fit the accepted outlook required by the Oxford students' training. It is difficult to say whether this realization is something that he really discovered there or is the result of his subsequent boast of deliberate colonial noncomformity. He was proud of his South African background, and it is true that a conventional education would not have shaped the direction of his subsequent poetry. He recognized, again with the contributory arrogance that persists through the calculated humility, "The sort of knowledge I required, before I could exploit my minor talent, was only to be acquired by travel, adventure, and rubbing shoulders with all sorts of people." (*L*, 183).

At Oxford he apparently read widely; at least he rather boastfully observed he read more than twenty other students would read in that period. He also made friends with those significant names in the world of English letters who were later to support him so loyally and with an affection and enthusiasm which was only equaled in intensity by the rancor and antagonism that he generated among others. Those who defended Campbell as both a poet and a man included in particular Wyndham Lewis, who was his especial friend and supporter in subsequent years, and the three Sitwells: Edith, Osbert, and Sacheverell. Dame Edith Sitwell, as she was later to be, always respected and admired his work, and was both a loyal and responsible devotee of Campbell and a critical advocate of his poetic achievement. Less well known abroad perhaps was Thomas Earp, who played a very significant part in Campbell's development. Earp was an important figure at Oxford, and it was he who took Campbell to France on his first visit. He introduced Campbell to the French symbolist poets who were to become a substantial influence upon the development of his poetic style. As Campbell appreciatively puts it, "Earp's unofficial tuition saved me years of trial and error: and it was through him that I found the French symbolists who have since influenced me most—if we discount my own basic self-immersion in the English Elizabethans and metaphysical poets." (*L*, 183-4)

While asserting this initial influence upon his work, Campbell also makes a more generalized statement about the nature of poetry, which is somewhat more disconcerting: "One cannot improve upon the original meters of English verse: one can only bring the language more up to date. If you attempt to eliminate rhyme and grammatical structure, you have to fall back on the far more artificial aid of Whitman's rhetorical repetitions at the beginnings of lines." (*L*, 187). This is obviously an either/or approach which does not follow from the data. Certainly Campbell himself did not eliminate rhymes or grammatical structure. His constant attachment to somewhat heavy and strained end-rhymes, particularly when they terminate those end-stopped lines he too repeatedly uses, were not successful in the control of his rampant poetic imagination. Campbell is fertile and facile in rhyming poetry as others were in uninhibited blank verse.

The period when Campbell was at Oxford was a flourishing era for English letters. Claiming to have met most of the major and literary figures of England at this time, he particularly mentions Robert Graves, Edmund Blunden, L. A. G. Strong, L. P. Hartley, and others. These men undoubtedly were at Oxford at the time, and possibly this rather brash but interesting young South African did attract their attention. Nevertheless, Campbell is a great one for name-dropping, and it is not clear whether the friendship with these people which he claims was in every case more than the most passing of public acquaintances at this date. However limited the actual intimacy of such friendships may in fact have been, Campbell was pleased and excited to be some part of this gathering of literary talent. The miraculous feeling of walking into a famous university from the bush and being accepted on a much higher intellectual level than he was allowed at home was very exhilarating. It was understandable that Campbell should be so enthusiastic, so impressed at being taken for one of this literary set. It paves the way for the extraordinary resentment and disappointment which he was later to exhibit when the Georgian poets in the London literary salons refused to accept him either as a poet or a man; it supplied the sense of letdown that motivated that outburst of vitriolic satire included in *The Georgiad.*

VI *Provence*

However impressed he was with this intellectual milieu in which he so delightedly found himself, coming from Natal, from the color and brilliance and light and sun of South Africa, he found England's cold understated grey increasingly difficult to support over a longer period. As he says, "Though London fascinated me, I wearied for a flash of the clear pagan sunlight to which I was used, and, hearing from Augustus John of the beauties of Provence, I decided to have a holiday down there." (*L*, 187).

This was the beginning of an emotional association with the Mediterranean which was to continue through the rest of his life. In particular, it was Provence, that poetic area of troubadours and minstrels, of horses, of cattle, of bold people, which was to be, by choice, his spiritual home after he broke from South Africa. Here it was, as in Barcelona and the other Iberian areas in which he later resided, that he could feel identification with a world of men who were physical, confident, flamboyant, simple. Although it may seem to many a little naive of him, there is something most revealing and totally appropriate in the incident Campbell later selects as being one of the greatest distinctions of his life. It was not, by deliberate paradox, the appreciation of any poetic recognition. In 1950, after thirty years of association with Provence, he tells how he was made the guest of honor at the bullfighting at Arles. It is very characteristic that his delight should be the more excessive because, as he points out, his poetry had not been translated into Provençal and therefore the appreciation was not given to him as a poet but as a man, a bullfighter, a horseman, a rider. He writes with pride, "This proves me to be a true citizen of the equestrian nation, as we call it." (*L*, 294). The mutually inclusive first person plural pronoun is especially indicative of his attitude.

Thus began the first stage of his long-continued Mediterranean residence. All the things that he was later to love and admire in the Provençal and Iberian scene were suddenly exposed to his delighted gaze. He saw rodeos and bullfights. As he traveled widely, he described the different types of bullbaiting and bullfighting, making technical distinctions about the varieties; a subject which he develops at much greater length and mystical depth in his prose book *Taurine Provence* (1932). This book is a curious mixture: explanation of bullfighting technique, some shabby political prejudice, and a kind of poetic evocation of what he feels is the religious significance of the bull in Mediterranean history.

The part of Provence which he admired most greatly was the Camargue, that area of the wild horses which has been so often recorded in painting and on film. He traveled about, claiming at least to have wrestled with bulls, to have thrown bulls, and finally, to have indulged in the most nerve-racking of all bullfighting games, the snatching of a bunch of ribbon tied between the horns of a bull, getting away before it manages to gore you. He asserts that he won prizes for this prowess. Campbell reminisces on these months of his life at some length in his autobiography *Light on a Dark Horse* (1951), and it is clear that it moved him very much and formed the basis of that attitude which was to remain with him for the rest of his years. Whenever he was in London, he was yearning to return to these rich, golden, sunny Mediterranean areas of southwest Europe. He saw in these areas the warmth and color and violence that were so familiar to him and so loved in his vivid earlier years of experience in South Africa.

VII *London*

When it was time for him to return to London, he made his first serious attempt to enter the world of the London literary scene. He grew closer to Wyndham Lewis whom he always strongly admired. He visited Edith Sitwell many times and he also met T. S. Eliot. He claims that in his very early days of poetry he admired Eliot so painfully that all of his first attempts to write verse were very obvious imitations of Eliot's style. None of these poems got into print. Campbell was most casual and cavalier with his poetry, and even *Adamastor*, his first and most significant collection, was apparently only put together by the assistance of a friend in South Africa, C. J. Sibett, who had access to the muddled manuscripts and those publications into which Campbell had distributed his early poems: "Whatever poems of mine I remembered I wrote down. . . . But I lost more than half of what I had written." (*L*, 225). We may take Campbell's word that his Eliot-type poems were written; luckily they do not survive and we do not have to consider such stuff that was the common early style of so many young poets. There is a great truth in Campbell's perceptive remark, "The influence of Eliot literally swallowed up many minor poets as a blue whale swallows mites of krill." (*L*, 243). Although Campbell himself very rapidly developed in a direction completely remote from Eliot, one can certainly see the dangerous power and predominance of Eliot's style upon many other poets of the 1930s as they sought an individual style. By coincidence it was Eliot—then an editor with Faber—who recommended the publication of *Adamastor*.

VIII *Marriage*

It was at this time in 1922 that Campbell got married. The event occurred with all the flamboyance and exhibitionism that we might well have expected from Campbell: "When I saw her I experienced for one of the few times in my life, the electric thrill of falling in love at first sight." (*L*, 243). The woman was Mary Garman whom Campbell met when he was helping a rather eccentric friend of his to move house by pushing a cart loaded with personal items around to the new room. Apparently the reaction of Mary to this extreme and ardent young man, who had gained the nickname "Zulu," was equally affirmative. Campbell assures us that the very next day they become engaged and on the second day he turned up with a special marriage license which cost him every bit of the savings he had, some mere three pounds, and they were married and settled down in her house.

In spite of this frenetic beginning their marriage was apparently a very successful one, and certainly Campbell's feelings for this beautiful woman did not wane or die. They are recorded again and again with very fervent passion in some of his more ardent and exotic poetry. He cannot have been the most easy man to get along with, yet somehow Mary managed. She seemed to have a strength and a fiery character that somewhat matched Campbell's own. He talks of her as being a challenge, of someone to be captured. Then, with another of those characteristic metaphors by which Campbell unintentionally gives away so much, he remarks, "None of my very best horses were ever too easy to break in; and on the human plane I like there to be some tension in the harmony so that it never grows stale." (*L*, 244). Even Campbell appears a little overwhelmed by this remark after having made it and avers quickly, "It would be blasphemy to talk about a divinely created soul in terms of horse-breaking, but . . . "; and then he goes on to remark cheerfully, "My wife had quite as much of a job to break me in, too." (*L*, 245).

Nothing in Campbell's life is, of course, allowed to go easily and, since he was so poor, everything was drama. He was still only, in fact, nineteen and he had some vague idea that he should go back to sea. He could make some money that way, and he could send his pay back home to his wife. Before shipping out he had to go up to meet his wife's family. He was apparently still dressed in his stoker's clothes, and a friend deeming his garb unsuitable took him around to a secondhand clothes shop where he bought a particularly hideous suit about a hundred years old "that must have belonged . . . to an Undertaker. It cost twelve shillings," (*L*, 248). He also got a frayed shirt thrown in. He must have been a daunting sight when his wife greeted him. She insisted that he fling out those hideous garments and put on his own battered but functional seaman's clothes. Her parents tried to prevent the marriage, but both parties were determined, although Campbell himself was under twenty-one and he took care that his own father did not even hear of the marriage until it was over. Some account of the extraordinary occurrences at the wedding breakfast are recorded by Wyndham Lewis in *Blasting and Bombardiering*, in a chapter he called "Augustus John and Jew Biceps."

The young couple settled down very happily in spite of the quarrels which arose out of Campbell's expected presumptions concerning the appropriate husband-wife relationship. He had what he calls "old-fashioned ideas about wifely obedience," and felt "any marriage in which a woman wears pants is an unseemly farce." (L, 248). One of his methods of dealing with his wife was to take her by the ankles and hold her out over the fourth floor window, threatening to drop her and, according to Campbell, "My wife was very proud of me after I had hung her out of the window and boasted of it to her girl friends." (L, 248). He was to remark, "It was five or six years before we broke each other in to our complete satisfaction and I wore the pants for good." (L, 253). His wife was naturally determined that he should not go back to sea, and indeed I cannot believe that Campbell himself can have taken this prospect very seriously. It neither allowed any development for his possible writing skills, nor did it suggest any way in which he could seek the spotlight of attention that his nature craved. He was prevailed upon to remain in England though he had no money, no job, and few prospects.

IX   First Publication

Somehow the young married couple made do. Campbell gained his income from some rather casual book reviewing. He even wrote "for the pink New Statesman, but without any shame." This rather haphazard income was increased by a small allowance which his reconciled father made to the young couple. With this minimal income he went to live in an incredibly wild, remote part of Wales. Rapidly two children came, complicating his domestic affairs. In his isolated cottage, not much more than a hovel, Campbell spent his time working on The Flaming Terrapin. There is indeed a very instructive contrast between the tropical, dazzling vision of the Terrapin and the situation which surrounded Campbell as he wrote of it: "[Our house] leaked every way, had only a mud floor, and the wind whistled through the walls." (L, 253).

But for two years while he was working on his first long poem, he describes not the harrassment of damp, cold isolation but "the continual intoxication of poetry." When he completed this poem, he sent it off to his friends who were thrilled with it and passed it on to Desmond McCarthy, the critic. It was Augustus John who submitted it for publication to Jonathan Cape who accepted it at once. By a curious coincidence one of their readers who examined the submitted manuscript in order to evaluate the possibility of its publication value was T. E. Lawrence, the great Lawrence of Arabia. He is not always the most balanced of literary critics, but perhaps he recognized something of his own nature in Campbell, the poet. If so, Campbell would have been flattered by such an affinity. His letter of recommendation to Cape in which he suggested that this poem should be published catches supremely well in a couple of sentences the nature of Campbell's achievement, both his power and weakness. Lawrence wrote: "Normally rhetoric so bombastic would have sickened me. But what originality, what energy, what freshness and enthusiasm, and what a riot of glorious imagery and colour! Magnificent, I call it!" (*L*, 255). He has exactly noted one of the unexpected things about Campbell's work. When he is successful, rhetoric which would indeed have appeared lush enough to be sickening and excessive, merely grandiose rather than heroic, is somehow acceptable within the context of Campbell's own flamboyant and ardent life and his own florid perception of his experience. His poetry cannot be dismissed as "excessive" by some external standard of appropriateness; its effect has to be perceived in the total impact those rich lines have upon the reader.

It is more difficult now to perceive the shock effect that such verse had upon the public in England. *The Flaming Terrapin* which saw print in 1924, immediately became something of a *cause célèbre*. Many praised, in the terms of Lawrence, its urgency, its passion, its colorful power; others saw it rather as merely a vulgar exhibition of energy. This division was so much the more marked because at this time the poetry of England was of a type of verse which was exactly opposed in style, form, language, and subject to the type of verse Campbell was then writing. The poets who exemplify this period of the twenties most characteristically are the so-called Georgians, a group of poets typified by J. C. Squire and therefore occasionally called the Squirarchy. It included poets like W. H. Davies—at their best, charming country lyric poets who wrote in gentle, smooth, moderate language of the delights of the more domesticated aspects of English country life. Campbell, of course, despised them and everything that they stood for. It is true that those who were not adequate poets did play a somewhat trivial game of being country gentlemen in tweeds, trudging with walking sticks to inns for glasses of ale, and that their verse unintentionally parodied the true pastoral scene. Campbell's most violent challenge came later with *The Georgiad*, a viciously sardonic attack on the group, but there were many experiences which were to come before he turned his attention to "a sort of psychic miasma which I slew in *The Georgiad.*"

For the moment Campbell was content to accept the praise that was offered for this remarkable poem, *The Flaming Terrapin.* From this volume he derived both the reputation and the money which allowed him for a moment to avoid the hack journalism with which he had tried to support his young wife during the first years of their marriage. At the age of twenty-three Campbell had become a literary sensation. Even though this poem will seem to us now merely a youthful excess, there is within it constant evidence of Campbell's power and urgency and ardor. Yet there is also a repetitiveness, a lack of direction, and a good deal of hyperbole. Campbell so often takes pride in flaunting his physical prowess, demonstrating his disdain of sentiment, that it is difficult for us to be sure what is true feeling, what is merely striking an attitude for effect. Even in his sensitive lyric poems there is a touch of the self-conscious in his emotions. Yet the intimate and true emotion of the exile flickers through lines which display technically all the characteristics which were subsequently to be developed and refined but are already very clearly apparent and abundant in this long poem.

X   *South Africa: The Return*

With the money Campbell gained from the successful publication of *The Flaming Terrapin* in 1924, he was able to undertake a visit to South Africa. For four years he attempted to establish a literary milieu in the country of his birth, the country which still moved his heart by the memoried warmth of his childhood. When this proved impossible and he finally left in 1928, it was the most decisive break of his life, for with the exception of an accidental visit which occurred in 1944, and his travel to accept an honorary doctorate, ten years later, he never again lived in the land of his birth.[3]

The consistent theme of this study will be the argument that separation from his native poetic inspiration, the poetic support which he had derived from the Africa he knew and loved so well, was one of the chief causes of the steady weakening of his literary capacity and poetic strength. It was the deprivation which led him to exaggeration rather than accuracy in his descriptions. However, the years he spent in South Africa after his return were personally and poetically abortive, and he is curiously brief about them in his autobiography, *Light on a Dark Horse.* It seems somewhat surprising though suggestive that he finds thirty-five pages appropriate to describe his first holiday discovery of Provence and a twelve-line paragraph sufficient enough to describe all the circumstances of his return to South Africa from his exile abroad and his four year failure to arrange a possible life for himself within the society of that divided and unhappy country. We have to seek for information about this period from his virulent satiric poem *The Wayzgoose*. This was the first of his poems of that tone that was to be one of the most basic and yet perhaps one of the most unsatisfactory of Campbell's poetic styles.

When he had returned to Durban, he had attempted to found a small literary journal, sharing editorship with William Plomer and Laurence van der Post. Plomer left South Africa at the same time as Campbell, and was attacked with the same angry resentment that Campbell received for his share in the attempt to intellectualize the literary world of South Africa. Their magazine was called *Voorslag*. This is an Afrikaans word whose translation allows one to guess readily who suggested the title: it means "whiplash," and it is quite obvious that with it Campbell intended to lash virulently the inadequate sensitivity, the prosaic dreariness of the South African society into which he had been born.

This "little review," one of the first that had been undertaken in South Africa, offended the South Africans for a common enough reason. It challenged the standard attitudes toward race and color which had always been the most touchy and sensitive emotions in that country. One unexpected aspect of the business is one's sense of surprise that a magazine run by Campbell should have gained itself antagonists by attacking the color bar. Campbell was in fact never particularly liberal himself in this racial way, as many anecdotes have shown. Perhaps this strand of the magazine owed more to Plomer than Campbell—it was Plomer's article that caused the major outrage. But the profession of liberal beliefs might be one more piece of evidence (and there are many others) that prove that Campbell delighted in antagonism, delighted in standing apart from the crowd. If South Africa was racist, then clearly Campbell would see it his duty to needle or "whiplash" its citizens on this subject. If in another situation, as in London, there was the almost excessive liberal support for the black underdog, then Campbell, in equally vigorous opposition, would appear racist in comparison and attack what he declared was the hypocrisy of the liberal's position in apologizing for his whiteness.

Campbell's poetic response to this South African experience

comes in *The Wayzgoose,* an actual event, which, as he describes it, sounds like a very unusual kind of literary gathering. In his notes to the poem he says, "This phenomenon occurs annually in South Africa. It appears to be a vast corroboree of journalists and, to judge from their own reports of it, it combines the functions of a bun fight, an *eisteddfod,* and an Olympic contest."[4] The wayzgoose of this poem, however, is not only attended by those who celebrate the function annually, but by all the swarms of would-be poets, novelists, philosophers, etc., in South Africa "who should be compelled to attend such functions *daily.*" The attack which Campbell generated in this satire was published in 1928 just as he returned to England for permanent exile abroad. The lines are sharp, witty, penetrating. Because there appeared, in a sense, to be less personal petulance and spleen and more general satire, this poem has survived a good deal better than *The Georgiad* and certainly far better than *Flowering Rifle.* This may reflect no more than the fact that we still at present react very strongly to the South African situation and that the personalities pilloried are generally unknown to us.

XI   *England: Again*

The couple with their two children were virtually forced to leave South Africa after the *Voorslag* fiasco. Almost penniless, they had to sail back to England in steerage class, and upon arrival were in such straits that they rented a tiny cottage and proceeded to try to subsist on fifteen pounds a month. They lived in such a miserable way ("comically sordid" are Campbell's own words for it) that they were tempted for the first time into the dubious fields of patronage. They accepted hospitality at one of the famous "Stately Homes of England" and lived on the charitable bounty of the owner. This was a bungalow in Kent at the home of Harold Nicolson and his wife Victoria Sackville West. Such patronage was so out of keeping with Campbell's ferocious independence that one is amazed he would attempt such a life and far more than surprised to find his subsequent reaction: "we were very stupid to relinquish our precarious independence in the tiny cottage for the professed hospitality." (*L,* 256). The stately home, according to him, "proved to be something between a psychiatry clinic and a posh brothel. (*L,* 256). At least this experience, though discomfiting in itself, provided the material for the sardonic "stately homes" sections of the acid pages of *The Georgiad,* and his unfortunate hostess herself supplies the title caricature, Georgiana. The lines of this poem, being "verbatim chapters of my life," were distilled from his observations in residence. The experience was neither continued nor repeated and the best that Campbell can say of it was that "it gave us an inoculation which has lasted us beneficially for the rest of our lives." (*L*, 256).

Things soon grew intolerable for the Campbells. It was not only the ugly circumstances of their day to day living, or the threatening alternative of poverty and squalor that dismayed them. It was the pernicious feuding, the running battle with the British intelligentsia. Half of them wanted to patronize pompously the gifted young poet; the remainder sought to put him in his place. The Campbells decided that, even if poverty were inescapable, it would be a great deal more acceptable in the sun—as far as possible removed from the continued grey and damp of England's bleak topography that contrasted so unhappily with the warmth and color on which both he and his poetry thrived. In 1928, they chose to take the bold step and set off for the Mediterranean.

XII *Provence Again*

The Campbells settled in Martigues, still with no money but with the relief of having escaped from London and its literary squabbles. Campbell began to work on a small farm and was soon exhibiting his physical prowess by jousting with the water team, a sport that he characteristically reminds us is classical, being "a survival of the naumachia of the Greeks in the Isthmian Games." (*L*, 263). He now seemed to be in his element; jousting, drinking, conversing; victorious and popular. Although he was living in a popular region for artists, he turned his back on the "tourist and painter-ridden side of Provence with its luxury hotels, hot baths, money and fat basking bottoms," (*L*, 268), which he accuses Somerset Maugham and other writers of preferring. There was bullfighting to go with the jousting, and he claims that there were regular victories and rich prizes that allowed him to live so well that he "bought expensive furs for my wife and had dandified suits made by tailors. (*L*, 283).

This was a time when Campbell, reacting against the London literary set, seemed to have felt particularly far from the world of letters. For more than a year he made no effort to write, sharing "Rimbaud's revulsion from the life of the letters." (*L*, 282). However, after some harsh exploits he also found the life of a bullfighter somewhat hazardous and "was forced to do a bit of honest work." He bought a soggy old boat and tried to make a living by fishing at night for roe-bearing mullet. His fishing expeditions brought him the discovery of some important wrecks in the area from classical days. Gradually, the discovery of Greek pot shards and partial statues became a significant source of revenue, for the items were all bought up by the mayor for deposit in the museum at Aix.

The beneficial climate of Provence—both personal and meteorological—gradually dispersed the revulsion at all aspects of literature derived from the regrettable period of London living. With the help of his Cape Town friend C. J. Sibbett he began to put together the collection that was to be called *Adamastor*. A great deal of his early poetry had simply been lost, but assiduous search by Sibbett through the South African magazines found some and Campbell himself rewrote remembered verses. Their joint activities finally had him ready to submit to a publisher his first real collection of poetry.

This he sent off to Faber and Faber, whose literary editor happened to be a young American named Thomas Stearns Eliot. It was accepted and during 1930 rapidly sold three editions. Unlike many first books of poetry, it even made some actual income for the young poet. He spent these royalties, rather typically, on a sardine net and some line for catching tunny!

Perhaps this activity and the continuing descriptions of bullfighting and bravery in the ring are a little less surprising than at first apparent. For it is out of such a life that Campbell chose to write. This much is clear from his occasional attempts to find literary leisure. When his several injuries required him to take an enforced rest, he was able to rent an attractive and quiet house with the idea of giving his full and uninterrupted time to writing to see if he could earn more money such as he had made from the *Adamastor* collection. The method did not work. The quiet and relaxation and long periods for concentrated poetry inhibited his writing rather than the reverse, for as he admits, poetry is "for me, the perspiration of *other activities*." (*L*, 311).

It was at this time that the young South African Afrikaans writer, Uys Krige, joined Campbell and his wife. He "was a good poet and a good boy, but as an incurable Calvinist he could never understand Spain or Provence." (*L*, 316). Krige stayed with them for many months, going on with them when they left France for Spain. During their stay in Provence, Campbell's own growing reputation as a poet brought him a series of visitors including the American, Hart Crane, whom Campbell found somewhat chauvinistic: "He read his wonderful poems like an angel and we were very fond of him, but . . . he had only one religion—the Almighty power of the USA—he believed in Whitman's vision of it altogether." (*L*, 312). Another visitor was Liam O'Flaherty, "a natural born genius: within his narrow limits, the best prose writer alive. . . . But I can only take him in small doses. . . ." (*L*, 312).

Under these circumstances of relative leisure and ease and new, amiable associations, Campbell began on a new book called *Marine Provence*, which was to be a similarly illustrated companion volume to the well-known *Taurine Provence*. Unfortunately, the commissioning publisher went bankrupt. For some reason it was never published, as Campbell appeared to make no real effort to find another suitable publisher. Its contents may have included some interesting anecdotes, for as he remarks, while laboring with *Light on a Dark Horse*, "I only wish I had had that book by me while writing this first volume of my memoirs so that I could refresh my memory from some of the chapters." (*L*, 314).

The abortive conclusion of this commission again threw Campbell into his not unusual, but still painful, restricted financial straits. This was a particular problem at this moment because for various minor reasons, Campbell began to feel himself less than welcome in Provence. He partially blames Hart Crane for this, feeling that his association with a man who "needed a keeper" was set against him by the locals, but there were also other problems. He decided to retreat to seek the new experiences available in Spain. He and his wife had spent several years in France, and he needed to begin to look for something fresh. In seeking immediate cash with which to effect the relocation, Campbell managed to get a commission to write his autobiography. This was the volume later to be entitled *Broken Record*. As Campbell candidly remarks, "It was certainly broken up enough to deserve the title." (*L*, 315). This disintegration is only to be expected from a book that he claims was written in a single surge of literary energy, day and night for ten days.

XIII *Spain*

A fifty pound loan supplied by his friend C. J. Sibbett allowed the family, along with Uys Krige, to decamp, and they were in Barcelona when the proofs were returned. Campbell was exhausted by all this hasty change, and since he was arbitrarily required by the publisher to add a further ten thousand words to the book, he slogged on through the fatigue: "I used to become overpowered by sleep every few minutes so my wife propped me against the chest of drawers while I finished." (L, 315). At least the immediate financial emergency was staved off.

Spain did not have very happy experiences for them at first. In 1933, Barcelona had few charms: the tensions which were going to foment the revolution were already most apparent, and Barcelona would undoubtedly have been particularly irritant to Campbell's philosophies, since it was one of the great strongholds for support of the socialist government. He examined the threatening daily events with characteristic prejudice in its exact literal meaning: he brought to the scene only the attitudes acquired elsewhere from which to establish his standpoint for evaluating the Spanish struggle. Not for Campbell any dispassionate middle ground, as he soon determined to "step into the front ranks of the Regular Army of Christ." (L, 317). His ideals were everywhere threatened, for the government's insidious propaganda was devoured on all sides. From this, Campbell was able to hypothesize the pernicious effects of education: "the curse of literacy can be far worse than any degree of illiteracy . . . for [it] at least saves a man from being taken in through his spectacles." (L, 317). A minor piece of luck allowed them to escape from the dangerous and squalid area of the Barrio Chino, "a worse hell than the reserved 'quarter' of Marseilles." Campbell won a prize in the state lottery which, if only a small amount, permitted him to rent an artichoke farm in the Ifac area near Altea. They stayed for a year in this rural place, where they were at least free of some of the more disconcerting and openly dangerous elements of the city—exemplified in Campbell's politically charged words as "those evil forces of socialism, the base self-seeking greed which is at the bottom of all modern reform." (L, 319). Campbell pretends to have driven these threatening international forces out of his own chosen village with the simple expedient of assaulting the foreign leader, Dr. Meyerstein, inevitably one with a Jewish name. He took him out into the village square "where I broke his glasses and watch, and throttled out his false teeth and broke them in pieces too." (L, 319).

At this point there was a sufficient sense of being established in Spain for Campbell to invite his mother from South Africa for a visit. By her simple and direct charm, she delighted all the neighbors, especially the children, even though she could not speak any Spanish. She too admired the innocent openness of the local peasant. Thus, Campbell began to feel more and more drawn to the Iberian peninsula, and it was here he was to spend a considerable part of his remaining years. He even chose to change his name, substituting Roig for the unhappy Anglo overtones of Roy, which, with Ignacio to begin, gave him a suitable Hispanicized name for any poster. The name was intended for bullfighting posters, but it also appeared on one exhibited by the revolutionary communist police, the dreaded Tcheka. As if the name change were not enough, the couple were newly baptized as Catholics and remarried in a service suitable for acceptance under the tenets of the Catholic creed. They had previously been man and wife under the convenient but minimal judicial ceremony that had been conducted in London, Campbell remarks with engaging cheeriness, "So we started life completely from scratch all over again—to our own delight." (*L*, 320).

At this time the Norwegian writer Helge Krog came to visit, and Campbell's account explains the mystery of how it is that a list of his works usually includes translations of Helge Krog's plays when Campbell certainly knew no Norwegian at all. The translation had actually been undertaken by a female relation but it was felt that Campbell's name would help the publication of the drama in England, as proved to be the case. For once, critical press attacks on his work seem to be totally unjustified, since he was hardly responsible for the "damnably bad translation."

In 1935, he made some money by getting involved with horse trading out of Toledo. Finally the family moved and began to live in that city in an attractive house opposite the cathedral. Toledo was to become one of the idealized cities of the civil war, and Campbell's dedication to its beauty and significance was apparent even before the extra intensity that derived from its role in the Spanish conflict and its importance to the Franco cause: "She is still the heart of Spain, the imperial capital of the Spains . . . the embodiment of the crusade for Christianity against communism." (*L*, 324). More success with horse dealing may be discovered from some boasting description. He was able to buy an excellent horse at a low price because of its reputation for savagery. It had actually killed its owner when he tried to break it in. Laconically, Campbell the horseman hero records that under his treatment "this gelding became a good quiet horse." Increasing efficiency in horse dealing brought the prosperity that allowed the Campbells to move to a fine house built right within the ramparts at the point of the old Visagra Gate of Toledo. It had in the past been the summer home of one of the cardinals.

It was here that the Campbells were living during that dangerously threatening period of 1936, during the last elections whose socialist-leaning results precipitated Franco's coup and thus the Spanish Civil War. Campbell had the chance to inspect firsthand the "warm blooded" anarchists who "out-babooned in atrocity anything I had ever read of before" and "the 'commies' who were less human." (*L*, 325). He reports being in the thick of several exciting events, one of them earning him a wound after a violent battle with an angry and jealous group. He was captured and beaten up; "a sanguinary mess they had made of my face." But because he refused to be daunted by threats and threw open a challenge to the officer, he was released: "No. I am not such a coward. The only satisfaction I ask is to fight it out with this cowardly corporal (who shoots peasants as if they were pheasants) either with knives, or revolvers, or if he is too cowardly, with bare fists." (*L*, 345). This fitted his determination, for "I did not wish to burden our embassy by caterwauling as Messrs. Koestler and Co. have done, though they received every courtesy and were *flown* to safety, whereas I had to fight my way out." (*L*, 345).

Who will ever be able to tell what shreds of truth rest in such tales? It is pointless even to ask others who might be able to indicate a more likely truth from personal experience. Often their own prejudices equally distort. Spain made all men liars in the support of some ultimate political truth they avowed. For example, it is recorded of Auden that he did nothing in Spain except play table tennis in a Madrid hotel—as unlikely as that Campbell heroically led troops into battle. Again in remarking on these tales one simply observes the importance of the myth to Campbell. The attitude that such stories indicate and the significant comment they make on his character give them importance regardless of their truth. In 1936, Campbell got out of the disputed area of Spain and returned to England staying briefly with his wife's relations. He returned in 1937 as a propagandist for the Nationalists and spent part of the war in Franco territory writing as a correspondent for the *London Tablet*. His insistence that he also fought for a while with the Carlist Requetes of Franco's forces is questionable. But within a year he had left Spain and settled with his family in southern Portugal. There he worked urgently on *Flowering Rifle* which was to be his defence of the Franco rebellion.

XIV   *Europe at War: The Army*

In 1939, when the war with Germany broke out, Campbell determined to join up. He had, in theory, completely changed sides from the political standpoint, since in Spain it was the armor and planes of Germany and Italy that had thrown the balance of power in favor of the antigovernment forces that Campbell supported. This change is less revolutionary than it may sound. First, there was a real loyalty to England in Campbell no matter the bitter petulance of his pronouncements. Second, he resented authoritarianism and reacted against it no matter from which direction its political source. He was an individualist in an age when such a role was considered at best quixotic if not downright dangerous. In this period of history the accepted options only granted a man the choice of which side obediently to serve.

He joined the King's African Rifles—a regiment based in the then Kenya Colony as a noncommissioned officer and in 1944 invalided out as a sergeant with a hip ailment. Most of his war years were in fact spent in Africa as a coast watcher; he also claimed to have fought in the North Africa campaigns around Tobruck. He was repatriated to South Africa after the war but stayed only briefly. The journey had been a simple military mistake in returning him to his place of origin rather than to the place of common residence.

XV   *London: Again*

Back in England Campbell published his last collection of poems in 1946, *Talking Bronco*, a title he took from a critical reference of a reviewer. After this he wrote very few further pieces of verse though a handful are to be found in the second volume of *Collected Poems*. For six years he lived in London, working as a producer for the British Broadcasting Company's famous intellectual Third Program and in 1949 he became for a time editor of the review *The Catacomb*. He had to reconcile himself to the fact that a wound precluded any more determined physical activities. But there were still occasions of impressive outrage when his temper was strung beyond control. His antagonism toward the liberal moralizing of Stephen Spender reached its climax when Spender was giving a talk in 1949 in the crypt of the Ethical Church in Bayswater to a meeting of the "Contemporary Music and Poetry Circle of the Progressive League." Campbell announced to his acquaintance Robert Armstrong that he intended "to drop in for a spot of mischief-making." He calculated his time of arrival to the moment when Spender was actually beginning to speak. He arrived with his most fierce and threatening manner, rendered the more obtrusive by contrast with the somewhat mild idealists who attend such occasions. Armstrong describes the scene beautifully:

Campbell entered in the doorway, hatless with a heavy fawn overcoat, no collar nor tie, but a dark jersey to his chin—looking for all the world like a tall, heavyweight, authoritative supervisor at Smithfield Meat Market. "Where is the bugger?" he demanded, "Bring him out, the bastard, where is he? Where is the dirty ——— hiding. . . . Come out and get your medicine."[5]

He then stepped up the stage and proceeded to direct a powerful if not very accurately controlled punch direct to Spender's nose. As Campbell pivoted on his cane and stormed out there were restraining hands and cries for the police. Spender behaved in a way as equally characteristic of him as the violence had been typical of Campbell. Giving evidence of the very gentle and compassionate nature he possessed, he cried out, "He is a great poet, he is a great poet. . . . We must try to understand . . . he is a great fighter for the things in which he believes."[6] That cry is the truth. Campbell would have preferred a counterblow and a scrap to such tolerance and sensitive awareness.

With some of the old enmities forgotten he was able to assume a more acknowledged rank among writers and undertook a Canadian and American lecture tour in 1953. As usual he was provocative and many anecdotes dwell upon his erratic behavior either in condemnation or admiration. The incidents were apparently not serious enough to prevent a second tour in 1955. Between these two trips he had the satisfying experience of a brief visit to South Africa where he had formally conferred upon him the degree of doctor of literature by the University of Natal at Durban. It must have given Campbell immense satisfaction to return as a literary hero to a city that had earlier dismissed him with such deliberate scorn.

XVI *Portugal*

The lure of the Iberian Peninsula seemed too strong to resist. Campbell avoided this time, however, the established dictatorship of General Franco in Spain and in 1952 bought himself a farm near Lisbon at Sintra. At this period of his life he occupied himself with translations of the plays of Lope de Vega and of the poetry of St.

John of the Cross and Fredrico Garcia Lorca. For five relatively contented years he lived in Portugal and undertook a series of prose works, most particularly *Portugal* (1956). He visited London occasionally, for the old feuds were less painfully tenacious. Perhaps it was now easier for people to set a perspective to accept Campbell for what he was; a provocative troubadour with a rich if inconsistent talent.

On one occasion in London he met his compatriot Alan Paton, now renowned as the author of *Cry the Beloved Country*. Paton recalls his luncheon with "this buccaneer . . . this red cherubic face under a Portuguese sombrero splashing solar colours over London on a rainy day." And he goes on to comment:

I witnessed a pyrotechnical display in the gloom of Sloane Square, so dazzling that the pale faces of the watercresses seemed to catch alight, if not with comprehension, then with admiration and envy that human beings could still explode and crackle in such a dreary world.[7]

Campbell died on April 23, 1957, in a car crash and his remains were buried in Portugal at San Pedro's Cemetery. It would be very easy to make significant symbolism out of this untimely death, as too many critics with a psychiatric bent have explained the inevitability of Hemingway's death. It would have seemed uncharacteristic if Campbell had died as it were with his boots off, in bed, comfortable, fattening, and prosperous. There is the intriguing fact that the despised technology supplied the jousting horseman with the mechanical instrument of violent destruction, as fate did similarly in eliminating T. E. Lawrence with a motor bike crash. Such speculations are beside the point. He died in action and with violence. In his death we can perhaps see him as a man with real dignity and nobility. The spites and feuds, the petulance and squabbles may be forgotten and the fine harmonies of the major lyrics, at least, can be read without undue consideration of all the irritating difficulties of literary politics within which they originally flourished. Take it for all and all, this was a man to be admired and a poet to be read. What writer could ask more for his final critical epitath?

XVII *Conclusion*

As always it must be Campbell who has the last word. In the introduction to his autobiography he talks of the intense motivation that led him to write *Light on a Dark Horse*. It was motivation that

went far deeper than the need to repudiate some of the ex-
travagances that remained to haunt him from the casually dashed-
off earlier autobiography *Broken Record*. His words are vintage
Campbell, both in the intensity of their sentiment and the equal ex-
hilaration of their language. He is talking of his new book. His lines
make rather a perfect statement of the motives which have determined both his entire life and all his poetry. The surge of nouns that
indicate how closely he touches upon the reality of his experience
by naming carry their own high conviction of truth. The sequence
makes a climax, and it is a vital fact that the culmination reaches
not places, scenes, or animals but men and women. Campbell loved
people far more than it has been fashionable to expect.

I have been literally forced to write [my memories] out in this book so as to
repay my debt both to Almighty God and to my parents, for letting me
loose in such a world, to plunder its miraculous literatures and languages,
and wines; to savour its sights, forms, colours, perfumes and sounds; to see
so many superb cities, oceans, lakes, forests, rivers, sierras, pampas, and
plains, with their beasts, birds, trees, crops, and flowers—and above all
their men and women, who are by far the most interesting of all. (*L*, 9).

CHAPTER 2

Early Poems

I *The Flaming Terrapin*

ALTHOUGH there had been earlier individual poems, Campbell's real poetic career beings with *The Flaming Terrapin* in 1924.[1] It was this poem that introduced the young writer to the shocked attention of the London literary intelligentsia. It is simply an incredible achievement for a young writer of only twenty-three, though even to make such a statement compounds the inaccuracy of the original reaction that saw the eccentricity rather than the art, that stressed the extravagant originality at the cost of recognizing what was consistent and traditional. This is a young man's poem, and yet to stress excessively the youth is to miss those qualities of the poem which are valid and mature, for such remark predetermines the characteristic standards of judgment which one might choose to apply to the work.

Unlike some of Campbell's fine shorter early poems—"Choosing a Mast" or "Mass at Dawn"—*The Flaming Terrapin* would perhaps hardly be retained in collections representative of major twentieth-century literature. Yet it does exemplify all the qualities of his work. In so doing it displays clearly those indissolubly interwined contradictions of originality and excess that make the paradox of Campbell's achievement. There is a brilliance—a glitter of color unmatched by perhaps any other poet in English, and yet that glitter starts, even in this one poem, to seem excessive; technicolor brash rather than sensitive. There is an energy that dazzles and yet leaves the intellectual muscles of the reader finally unresponsive, too exhausted by the continuous fire and drive of the poet's intentions. As one reads there is already the beginnings of an ennui, a sense that the energy is questionable, less perhaps in its direction than in its nondirection. At this stage we may not be concerned with debating or criticizing where the intellectual direction of Campbell's ardor

41

might be taking him, but we do wonder whether there is any direction, whether even he knows the poetic target that he is aiming to reach.

The poem exemplifies every skill that Campbell had and perhaps indicates the regrettable truth that he had them all from the beginning; that all the brilliance and fire and emotionalism of his verse was inherent in his youthful attempts and left little room for development and change. Perhaps more accurately, there could and should have been change that would have shown an increasing maturity measured by a tighter control of the lavish, too freely moving force; an intellectual depth to sustain the brilliance of the surface imagination. It is, finally, actually a condemnation to assert that all that one is eventually to find in Campbell is present in this poem written in his youth. That it exhibits immense and exciting skill and brilliance is the measure of the writer and the underlying reason for taking this man seriously as a poet. Yet—if one is not to distort by inappropriate comparison—one might well comment on how little the early poetry of Yeats or Eliot or even indeed Auden was to be the measure of their subsequent genius and achievement. Of course, the seeds of genius were there. But time created maturity which permitted them to achieve their final authoritative note. Between the early Yeats and those later desperately powerful poems like the Byzantium series, is a spread of creative achievement that requires the acknowledgment of a man's intellectual development toward greatness; a distinction between youth and maturity which may be as great as the division between, say, the first and ninth symphonies of Beethoven. In Campbell, for all his special skills and the excited interest with which we may often read his poetry, there was not to be, indeed could not be, such a poetic progression. In fact, one would have to argue that because there was to be no emotional and intellectual progression in the man there could not be that creative continuum of achievement that marks the artistic development of the truly great.

This seems a gloomy and restrictive note on which to begin, and yet it must be said, for without wanting to use a Yeats to belabor the less gifted writers of the age, we must have some sense of the perspective by which we judge the poetry of the period. It is perspective which is so consistently lost in relation to Campbell; as much lost in his own attitudes and life as it is in the reactions of the critics who have been so anxious to proffer their response to his invigorating and brilliant verse. It is this recognition of the total career that requires one to begin any analysis and discussion of *The Flaming Terrapin* in such a questioning and dubious way.

Yet, if there is, at one level, an accurate justice in the truth of the response that makes caution and qualification an appropriate basis to begin comment on this poem, such balance expressly avoids recognition of the effect of history. Forget for a moment the subsequent career of this brilliant and exasperating man. Take the imagination back to 1924 with all the calm understatement that marked English letters under such notables as the poet John Drinkwater or J. C. Squire. (Campbell in his high satiric vein could hardly have invented more telling and indicative names!) Consider the whole understated country-garden absurdity of contemporary letters. Somehow, even in 1923, some still seemed able to pretend that *The Wasteland* was a temporary aberration by one of those Americans full of his native behavior—uncouth and insensitive. Then take an even wilder and more violent colonial shore, Africa, and have a vehement young poet speaking like a Lochinvar out of the south in language which in its excessive and exciting savagery proclaimed a world inconceivable to the English literary tea parties. Then one has a picture that sets into appropriate context the impact of this poem; in retrospect it was exaggerated and extreme, and in 1924 it created an exciting and vivid hammer blow that announced a new comet. Perhaps if one wished to pursue the metaphor too far it contained the symbolic elements of the comet. Like a comet it was a sudden brilliant apparition, doomed by its nature to decline into inconsequent darkness. The shower of sparks and lights that announced its exciting birth would become burnt cinders after the meteoric and transient splendor of its flight.

Perhaps as one attempts to go back to this poem one grows too fanciful, but consider even now the contemporary impact of the opening lines:

> Maternal Earth stirs redly from beneath
> Her blue-sea blanket and her quilt of sky,
> A giant Anadyomene from the sheath
> And chrysalis of darkness. (*CP*, 59).

All the qualities are here; the obvious ones, words of color, violent verbs of movement, the classical association, the deliberate extension of the metaphor of quilt and sheath, stretched to include blanket, the natural concept that links chrysalis and the dark. There are the somewhat obvious rhythms of these iambic pentameters, the generally end-stopped lines, the exact rhymes. Yet there is something else that will not be explained away by the measurable obviousness of the structure. There is the sense of tension, of charged throbbing, that seems to exist in each of the lines. It threatens to break from control into a surge of burning and rhetorical verse, for in spite of the inevitable end of line caesura the voice is urgently whipped forward to the next in Campbell's progression. Line after line exemplifies these aspects which, we are later to discover, make the strong and individual verse of a Campbell and no one else. The repetitions breed up toward those carefully constructed thunderous explosions with which he asserts his power upon the spoken word. Not to put it too fancifully, there is a kind of orgasmic progression in such verse. Tension mounts and mounts, its intensity reaching continually more impassioned energy until it is dispersed in the hectic diffusion of the climax.

In its thematic structure Campbell deals in this poem with the imposition of the rule of man upon the world. Campbell called the work "a symbolic vision of the salvation of civilization," an interpretation that would certainly fit his declared and implicit attitude that with determination and strength man is capable of controlling the beasts—both real and political—of his environment. *The Flaming Terrapin* itself is a symbol of power and energy. It tows a newly launched Noah's Ark on a voyage of discovery. The Ark represents the world created by man and the Ark is brought to the point where it can attend and witness a whole series of apocalyptic events. These incidents threaten the ideal civilization that is possible, if the benign and rational ideology of the terrapin sustained the world. By his inheritance man is able to determine the triumph of the terrapin's will. Threatening attitudes personified attack the potential of man. These are Corruption, Anarchy, Mediocrity—dangers that were to challenge Campbell in both his life and his poetry.

Campbell begins with the vision that truth against which he measured all things in his philosophy:

> I see him as a mighty Terrapin,
> Rafting whole islands on his stormy back, . . .
> Thoughtless and fearless, governing the clean
> System of active things. . . . (*CP*, 60).

Temporarily I will ignore comment on the diction except to observe the supremely Campbell skill of that inspired and unexpected participle "rafting" sounding like Milton in its initial line stress position. Significant for the moment is the philosophy, a little Hemingwayesque perhaps, of that "clean system of active things," for it was rapidly to be established that the nonactive were to be despised for their inept apathy. In spite of its generalized pronouncements, one of the curious and interesting aspects of this poem is the way it consistently exposes the most intimate aspects of Campbell's own innermost private nature. There are unexpected moments of introspection among the urgent bravado of many sections. Such lines indicate a far more sensitive and self-observant soul than is regularly acknowledged. The following lines in particular make one wonder at their personal truth, and if true, of the impress their expressed attitude might have had upon Campbell's poetry with its unrestrained expression:

> How often have I lost this fervent mood,
> And gone down dingy thoroughfares to brood
> On evils like my own from day to day;
> "Life is a dusty corridor," I say,
> "Shut at both ends." But far across the plain,
> Old ocean growls and tosses his grey mane. . . . (*CP*, 60).

There were occasions in London certainly when he was to brood on those imagined and actual slights to which he was subjected. The fervent mood that is the impetus and drive of all his poetry is sometimes absent. In these places Campbell's verse limps heavily indeed. Its restoration can only be achieved by that "plain" and "ocean," the non-English scene that counters a "but" against London's "dingy thoroughfares."

More significant still are the famous lines:

> Far be the bookish Muses! Let them find
> Poets more spruce, and with pale fingers wind
> The bays in garlands for their northern kind.
> My task demands a virgin muse to string
> A lyre of savage thunder as I sing. (*CP*, 77).

This is at once a personal credo and a poetic manifesto. It identified the young poet forever in spirit with that awesome, superhuman region "where old Zambesi shakes his hoary locks." It indicates a challenge that he intended to take up with every line of his verse, a deliberate reidentification of the origin of his inspiration. A "lyre of savage thunder" was Campbell's instrument, and when he played upon it at the peak of his skill it was a formidable and impassioned instrument indeed.

This poem is studded with lines like gems; colorful, dazzling, ravishing the eye. If the overall response to this poem is, as it finally must be, that it is excessive, baroque, rococo, it takes a real poet with a poet's eye and sensibility to create such images as are found so regularly here. Note the light and color of "to shake the golden bonfire of her hair" or of "the faint flamingoes burn among the reeds," or "by day the sky put on a peacock dress" or "to drain the moonlight smouldering from her hair," or again more extendedly the lines:

> When the dawn
> Across the Ocean's polished floors of gloom,
> Sweeps her faint shadow with a golden broom. (*CP*, 80).

and similarly the extended vision of:

> The lilies of Africa rustled and beat
> Their giddy white flames with the whistle of sleet.
> As they quilted the land with snow. (*CP*, 86).

Emotionally, these are quite simply gorgeous. Technically, one can determine two specific qualities here: the unusual and yet utterly appropriate verbs that catch the eye and then illumine the senses with their visual and verbal accuracy: "burn," "smouldering," "quilted." (Similarly note the apparent verb pun in "career" in the phrase "the whinnying stallions of the wind career. . . .") Second, there is the consistent use of color words that make an optical and sensual impact on the reader. Each of these images is essentially visual in form; yet Campbell is adept too at developing more intellectual associations out of what at first appears merely sensual imagery. The metaphors are given more impact because their first presentation always includes, along with the intellectual association, a prior primary sensory impact and overtone. There is the unforgettable image of the Devil, "set in Hell, dejected and alone, / Rasping starved teeth against an old dry bone," a comment that sets the reader's own teeth on edge with the sense of the abrasion. Then there is the Bunynesque portrait of "Contentment, like an eating slow disease," or the evocative phrase "the livid mambas of deceit."

It is these things more than the overall theme of the poem that indicate the potential quality of the poet who was writing in 1924. If the virtues were already obvious, so too were the vices. It is one of the curiosities of Campbell's career that they remained the same throughout his life. He is, as it were, even at this early stage, already established for all his success and failure. It is clear that the poem goes on too long both in totality and in individual sections. Many metaphors establish their impact in a single incisive line and are then repeatedly developed, swollen, until the point seems excessive and belabored. When this occurs the effect of the poetry is lost, because the apparent intention appears to be less to convey meaning through metaphor, but to create and extend metaphors. Each may have its own lively and separately formed existence, but their gilded lines cannot be justified by the fine poetic utility. It is remarkable, for example, that although the lines are regularly end-stopped, they are most often stopped with a comma or a colon; occasionally simply by the necessary caesura of speech, but very rarely with a period. The average sentences stretch across ten or even twenty lines. It is a style which in some ways matches Campbell's thought. It becomes the evidence of determination to pile intensity upon intensity and thus create the culminating impact of a generated ecstasy of effect. But unless the ardor is very strong, or the reader particularly fresh, the reaction might be diagrammed as increasing parabolas of tension. The lines drive hard toward their end reaching upward toward powerful effect. Then yet another breath is required for another line and then another similar rise and fall of the voice occurs across the pentameter structure. This sequential rise and fall of the voice introduces a note of repetition and monotony, even among the most urgent lines of this work.

Besides some initial stylistic doubts which are to be confirmed in later work, there are also some moments where questions of taste could be raised. An obvious example is the description of the mating of the earth and the sun. This is a common enough general metaphor of fecundity and growth, but it is usually necessarily an abstraction. When Campbell approaches it with great passion, his ardor makes the scene only too literal. We are forced to visualize the event, and the imagined copulation is then either ludicrous or merely distasteful. Consider the lines:

> Fleeced like a god in rosy curls of fire
> With massive limbs, stiffened by fierce desire,
> He leaps, and as she yields her golden thigh,
> Gigantic copulations shake the sky! (*CP*, 82).

Or, later, with a similar misjudgment of appropriate tone:

> How the Earth meets the Sun; through nerve and limb
> Trembling she feels his fiery manhood swim:
> Huge spasms rend her, as in red desire
> He leaps and fills her gushing womb with fire. . . . (*CP*, 88).

Philosophically the argument of this poem also anticipates many of Campbell's later attitudes. It is important to see the stress on the African background, not only in the source for much of the imagery, but in the violence and power it is asserted to indicate. It is Africa that generates the vehemence of both language and deed. The significance of energy is lauded until it virtually becomes the measure of human achievement. The attitudes which were to culminate in Campbell's hatred of the shirkers on the dole and the slackers in the welfare state are implicit here in nonpolitical form in his assertion of the creative power of man's individual energy. He reveals also his obviously deeply ingrained sense of the hierarchy of human qualities and values that judge men by their heroic and successful response to the challenge of their environment. All these ideas intermingle later to give Campbell his sense of defiant individualism; his peculiarly open heroics, his naive quasi-Fascist beliefs. They are the source of his extraordinary enthusiasm and energy for a life that is colorful; they urge him to seek achievement impossible for those "charlies" and "wowsers" who "shuffle in the streets;" defiantly ignoble.

This culminating world view is not precisely enunciated at this stage. Aspects of such thoughts are caught on the wing, as it were, detected in passing comments discovered in several of the lines. The sense of an elite measured by strength of individual will, is inherent in such lines as: "Now up from the intense creative Earth / Spring her strong sons: the thunder of their mirth." (*CP*, 59). Then there is the elation induced by individual prowess in: "This sudden strength that catches up men's souls / And rears them up like giants in the sky. (*CP*, 60). Always there is that central vision of man as a creature who seeks the extreme of his existence. In so doing man is not necessarily acting as a challenge to God, not exhibiting the physical hubris of strength, so much as rejoicing in his God-given strength—praising Him, if you will, by showing the vigorous potential of His noblest creation: "And Man, triumphant, feels their strength and speed / Thrill through his frame as music through a reed." (*CP*, 91). The physical response of man, stirred by the wind that passes, reminds one of those later descriptions of movement in the animal poems—the kaleidoscope of those zebras. Even if there could be accusation of pride, there is a belief that it is somehow justifiable; the relationship appears like that between a father and a clever if brash child. The boy is merely showing off; flexing his muscles at issues that are minor and lowly in the great cosmic scheme of things. There is delight and pride in his ambition and self-assertion; and indulgence at the overconfidence. God rejoices at the bravado and prowess of his finest creation:

> There as amid the growing shades he stood
> Facing alone the sky's vast solitude,
> That space, which gods and demons fear to scan,
> Smiled on the proud irreverence of Man. (*CP*, 92).

The capitalization of "Man" is indicative of the mood.

This tone is exactly equaled in the last lines of the poem where, with a declamatory finale a little like the sunset conclusion of a movie, he asserts his confidence in the arrogant, strangely harmonious strength of man: "Pass, world: I am the dreamer that remains, / The Man, clear cut against the last horizon!" (*CP*, 93). The role of dreamer is conventional enough as the mood of a poet, and yet it obviously does not have the conventional associations here. In Campbell's sense, being a dreamer has to include his own determination that the poet is also the active and committed man, reveling in his strength and the opportunities it can gouge out for him, for:

> Though times shall change and stormy ages roll,
> I am that ancient hunter of the plains
> That raked the shaggy flitches of the Bison. (*CP*, 93).

The colloquial rasp of "shaggy flitches" and that inspired verb "raked" sets accurate language to battle against the threatened hymnlike crudity of the falsely organ sonorousness of "Though times shall change."

Perhaps the quality of this poem as a whole can best be seen in any of the several "set pieces" which exemplify all of Campbell's brilliant skill and the dangerous excess to which his lines invariably veer. One of the allegorical figures is "Anarchy," which rushes by in a frenzied speed typical of Campbell's heady pace in both life and verse.

> Anarchy, jolted in a rattling car,
> Crested the turrets of the storm, and plied
> His crackling whip with forked lash to scar
> Red weals across the gloom: with frantic stride
> His gusty stallions clenched their bits and tore
> His whirling spokes along the pitchy rack:
> Their gaping nostrils drizzled foam and gore,
> And where they passed the gurly sea grew black. (*CP*, 73).

Here Campbell too has "clenched the bit and tore" but it is enterprising and powerful verse, exciting even as it falters toward loss of control.

This poem is such a fitting beginning for Campbell's subsequent career that it epitomizes all that will be reiterated in critical commentary on the later poems. *The Flaming Terrapin* had an explosive effect on English poetry in 1924; exciting some, dismaying and shocking others; generating eager enthusiasm and snobbish disapproval. Campbell was simultaneously an exciting new voice that would redeem the etiolated blandness of contemporary poetry and also a wild young colonial savage incapable of realizing the essential virtues of restraint and subtlety that should mark English poetry. The responses were obvious; sides were drawn and were not to change much during the next quarter century of his lively career. Indeed there is no middle ground of debate appropriate here—the antitheses are too open and too strong. Assumptions of what poetry is and can do are conceived at an early stage of education.

Campbell either enthralls or appalls. He continued doing both these things during his lifetime, both in his personal connections as much as in his published verse. The sonnets and lyrics in his first important collection of short length poems diminished, if only to a minor extent, the totality of impact that the long work *The Flaming Terrapin* provided in jolting the faded sensibilities of the London intelligentsia. There were many shorter poems of dash and fire as will be demonstrated, yet they were accompanied by poems responding to moods of calmness and contemplation which balanced the more exotic and violent notes. In *The Flaming Terrapin* there are few moments of calm where the reader can catch his breath; and even in these oases, the calm is afflicted by the ready awareness that the poet too is merely hesitating, waiting to generate his next surging meteoric burst of exhibitionist fancy. That is the source of its impressive creative grandeur and also its threatened demolition.

One can argue that it is in *Adamastor* that the best of Campbell's early poetry is to be found: *Adamastor*, with its profound and superb lyrics of the quality and spiritual commitment of "Mass at Dawn" and the wry wit of "To a Pet Cobra." But that is part of a further judgment. In estimating the significant weaknesses in *The Flaming Terrapin* (and it has obvious and open flaws) one might ask two important things. First, what is the cause and nature of the failures? The answer, inevitably, is that they are failures of excess, not of overmoderation. Parts of this poem rather aim too far, too high, in eagerness and determination to scale alpine reaches. In a young poet this should not be seen as simply a weakness, for moderation and restraint are only the virtues of middle age, not to be wished upon youth. They dully restrain the excitement and challenge that present the young with a vision of apparently limitless possibility. Second, one might set oneself within an historical context through an analogy with our present age. Suppose this book were published this month, fifty years afterward. Would it even now have lost its passionate ability to move? Would it not still bring fire and drive to the poetry of our time? We too make virtue of understatement and calm, looking in our poetry for that detachment of irony that is going to make simultaneously the comment and distancing of human feeling. It is an expectation that negates, for all its suggestive obliquities, the possibilities of direct statement and open and ready feeling. Against that expectation a new young Campbell would equally flame like a meteor against the grey skies of caution. In our time too, many would mock and sneer, as many would be excited to admiration. That this divided response would undoubtedly occur is the degree to which he speaks, not so much to the intellect as to the feeling, exposing the appeal of color and passionate excess in a drab understated world.

   The Flaming Terrapin itself is not much read, and it could hardly become more popular. One could scarcely recommend it as a poem that because of its own individual importance demands rereading and reappreciation in our particular decade. But the fact that this poem may not in itself be revived into far wider readership does not in any way invalidate the importance that it had in 1924. It was seen, then, less perhaps as a poem than as an idea and a principle; a judgment that would be equally true of it at present. If this assessment appears to indicate little of the continuous and consistent quality in the work, it might, in scholarly levels of literary analysis, still be a true evaluation of its limitations. *The Flaming Terrapin* is not, I am almost ashamed to write, a very good poem. But what fire and fervor and spirit and love it exemplified! Whatever excess one might detect in the cold pontification of a reading in the study, what splendid and superhuman excess! Could we not use such deliberate exciting extremism now—and from that admission see how strongly it still speaks, reminding us of areas of experience as devastating to contemplate as it was when it exploded like a bomb among the country gardens of English poetry in 1924?

II   *The Wayzgoose*

The Wayzgoose (1928)[2] is an extraordinarily lively piece of satire and perhaps remains Campbell's most effective longer poem in this vein. The Spanish Civil War seems too painful and serious a subject for the banal mockery provided by the crude and simplistic politics of *Flowering Rifle*. The Georgian poets have achieved virtual oblivion so that one wonders that they could ever have seemed sufficiently significant for the extended excoriation of *The Georgiad*. *The Wayzgoose*, however, retains a lively and witty effect. Part of its superior effect derives from the fact that its general target is still clearly alive in regions far from South Africa, so that the satire remains cutting, avoiding the sterility of distant battles and dimly remembered lost causes.

Still, an assertion of continuing contemporary relevance would not be the entire explanation of the superiority of this poem over Campbell's other long satires. There is greater skill in his handling of the purely technical elements. In being less tediously long than his other similar works it avoids their diffuseness and repetition. Above all it has the best justification for satire, attacking general follies and foibles, not mere opposition to Campbell and his views. Although there are a number of local references which require the elucidation of footnotes, the theme has a much wider application than South Africa. It ridicules the cultural pretensions of many new nations as they seek pompously to find their significant cultural nationhood while they also simultaneously take aggressive pride in the traditionless youth of the political consensus which they represent.

The Wayzgoose is a kind of annual literary convention in South Africa.[3] Campbell was particularly scathing about its utility; in the notes to his poem he describes the occasion in the following sardonic way:

The Wayzgoose: This phenomenon occurs annually in South Africa. It appears to be a vast corroboree of journalists, and to judge from their own reports of it, it combines the functions of a bun-fight, an Eisteddfod and an Olympic contest. The Wayzgoose of this poem, however, is not only attended by those who celebrate the function *annually*, but by all the swarms of would-be poets, novelists, philosophers, etc., in South Africa who should be compelled to attend such functions *daily*. (*CP*, 293).

Many of us who have attended a number of similar occasions will share Campbell's devastating scorn.

The opening lines are as good as any in this poem and perhaps can best demonstrate the type of satire which Campbell could so successfully construct. In them he invents the memorable epithet for South Africa, "Banana Land." The opening couplets run like this:

> Attend my fable if your ears be clean,
> In fair Banana Land we lay our scene—
> South Africa, renowned both far and wide
> For politics and little else beside:
> Where, having torn the land with shot and shell,
> Our sturdy pioneers as farmers dwell,
> And, 'twixt the hours of strenuous sleep, relax
> To sheer the fleeces, or to fleece the blacks:
> Where every year a fruitful increase bears
> Of pumpkins, cattle, sheep, and millionaires—
> A clime so prosperous both to men and kine
> That which were which a sage could scarce define. . . . (*CP*, 243)

The first page offers a good example of the type of extended metaphor of which Campbell was to become very fond. He talks about the country, "The 'garden colony' they call our land, / And surely for a garden it was planned. . . ." (*CP*, 243). And then, over the course of the next forty lines or so he rather excessively develops this garden metaphor, making a whole series of satiric analogies out of it:

> What apter phrase with such a place could cope
> Where vegetation has so fine a scope,
> Where *weeds* in such variety are found
> And all the rarest *parasites* abound. . . . (*CP*, 243).

And so the concept of the metaphor, continues:

> Beetroots should sit in editorial chairs,
> Or any cabbage win the critics' praise. . . .

> A hundred mushroom poets every day;
> Where Brussels scientists should hourly sprout. . . .

> Behold our Vegetable Athens rise
> Where all the *acres* in the Land are *wise*! (*CP*, 244).

This is a reasonable joke, yet it is pursued, as usual with Campbell, a good deal too far. In a similar way, his handling of the actual eating at the Wayzgoose is equally excessive in its extent. Some fifty lines here concern the wrapping of food in literary notes. The assertion that the final end of journalism is something in which food is wrapped for a picnic is a minimal joke at best: "Bred on the bland senilities of '*Punch*' / How can you serve us save to wrap our lunch? " (*CP*, 248).

What Campbell does most successfully is to indicate the fundamental dullness of colonial culture. He sets against this the potential and caliber of William Plomer, whose story for the *Voorslag* had been declared obscene. Since Campbell was not a modest man himself, he begins his championing of Plomer by announcing his own importance: "My words, O Durban, round the World are blown / Where I, alone, of all your sons am known. . . . " (*CP*, 251-2). But his praise for Plomer is genuine, sincere, and entirely deserved. Plomer, although he has to some extent repudiated specifically South African elements of his writing, is still one of the most underrated of his country's writers. Like Campbell, Plomer is here presented as a vital force who, by his writing, scourges those dull half-wits of Durban. His reaction is described in Campbell's terms—Plomer unlike Campbell was hardly the kind of man who would solve his intellectual disputes with fisticuffs. "Plomer came too, unable to resist, / To bash fat heads together with his fist." (*CP*, 256). Campbell does admire the man, although their temperaments were so different. His words have an honest generosity within their exaggeration of rhetoric:

> Plomer, t'was you who, though a boy in age,
> Awoke a sleepy continent to rage,

> Who dared alone to thrash a craven race
> And hold a mirror to its dirty face.
> Praised in all countries where the Muse is known
> But hunted like a felon from your own,
> Whom shall I sacrifice, what blood infuse
> On the neglected altar of your muse? (*CP*, 254).

Again he reiterates his own superiority, his strength, as he remarks:

> My Pegasus, who loves in warlike raid,
> O'er Durban thundering with his golden hoofs,
> To drop great bombs of laughter on your roofs. . . . (*CP*, 255).

These two men are certainly the most significant writers of South Africa until we reach the contemporary efflorescence in the stories of Nadine Gordimer. Campbell links them through the mutual blame they have occasioned: "Let Plomer's art as smutty filth be banned— / And own us prophets in our native land!" (*CP*, 257). One remembers the appropriate conventional phrase of those prophets "without honor in their own land." Campbell bitterly reacting to this lack of recognition constantly repeats his accusation of the insensitivity and dullness of this literary group. As they gather he remarks:

> Some came in hope and others came in fear,
> Diverse in shape the multitude appear,
> But all, with one indomitable will,
> Loyal to Dullness—and to Dullness still. (*CP*, 256).

This word "Dullness" reminds one, as it is quite certainly intended to do, of Dryden's *MacFlecknoe*. There is a similarity in the personification of Dullness:

> And when their rites to Great God Grub were paid
> To Dullness next the mighty concourse made
> Libations of ambrosial lemonade. . . . (*CP*, 264).

The poem goes on to describe a comic competition to decide who could produce the dullest single piece of writing. It is won by somebody reading a collection of names and addresses out of a directory as his work of art:

> The Muse, unseen, upraised her magic wand—
> "Anointed Dullness, faithful still to you,
> And to Colonial Culture staunchly true." (*CP*, 264).

The analogy with Dryden is continuously clear. Campbell makes it quite deliberate with his couplet: "Was this the boomerang that Dryden threw / To crumple Flecknoe as I crumple you?" (*CP*, 251).

The reference to Dryden's work also permits Campbell to generalize briefly about the nature of satire and what he expects this tone to inspire in his verse. The only trouble is, that although he is entirely just in his interpretations of the significance of wit in the effect of satire, he does not personally always live up to his impressive theories. "How much, alas, on hateful wit depends," he remarks. He is absolutely right to point out the dullness and stupidity of those who write satire without wit so that it becomes simply abuse. Unfortunately, the exactness and judgment with which he *describes* what is necessary in satire derives from his appreciation and reading of Dryden and Pope; it is not always what he actually creates in his verse. In his own lines, abuse too often remains the corrupt residue of satire without humor. The vitriolic and shrill note of anger which he exhibited when he wrote his longer satiric poem *The Georgiad* later in England, alas, does not display the wit which, as he points out in *The Wayzgoose*, is the basis of satire in the Dryden manner:

> Yet without wit your anger has no point,
> And when you strive to blister, you anoint;
> You flatter to insult, you praise to shame,
> And soar to panegyric when you blame.
> Yea, without wit, you merely soothe and lull,
> Both tamely fierce and passionately dull! (*CP*, 248).

If there has to be more severe criticisms of later work, many sections of this early poem do achieve a sharp wittiness. There is the attack upon the South African girl, rough, gauche, virginal, "the prototype of all colonial girls": "For like a V upturned, stork-like and thin, / Her long straight legs forked downward from her chin. . . . (*CP*, 263). But the effectiveness of such satire, unless it is in the brilliant satiric portrait style of a Dryden, makes its impact, partially at least, in our ability to recall the things that produced it. For if satire makes its impact by exaggeration, it is essential that we are familiar with the norm. Only by displaying deviance from the appropriate standard can satire foster its healthy redeeming comedy. Aberration is indicated only by reference to commonly held cultural assumptions of the truly desirable.

It is undoubtedly the political satire which began this poem which appears most relevant to the present day reader. The attack he makes on the lazy indifference of the Durban workers has perhaps even more force now than when the poem was written, since the satire has been compounded by another forty years of racial antagonism. Beyond the racial aspect, the succeeding lines are also significantly indicative of Campbell's attitude to labor, that opinion which later will cause him to choose the right-wing fascism of Franco rather than the trade union strength of the left-wing communists in Spain. His concern here is not in fact with the color bar as such, but an attitude of lazy apathy which he despised wherever he encountered it. One theme draws his varied satires together, his attack upon the indolent, the bored, and the indifferent in society who disgrace their human potential for excitement and action. Work is his creed: "Work, that can turn a draper to a Man / And give a human accident a plan." (*CP*, 253). His scorn for apathetic weakness spreads wider than racial prejudice. In these following lines it is the white South African who is condemned; the character most given to talk of the incompetent indolence of Africans:

> Stand up and look a black man in the face!
> Is it the sign of a "superior race"
> To whine to have "the nigger kept in place"?
> Where is his place save in his strength and sense,
> And will he stand aside for impotence,
> Does Evolution wait for those who lag
> Or curtsy to a cheap colonial Flag?
> Is this "White Labour"—lolling on this stool,
> Fed by a black with every needful tool,
> The white man sits and uses but his hands,
> The black man does the thinking while he stands:
> Five years in long apprenticeship were passed
> Ere, fit to loaf, the white emerged at last,
> And yet in kicks and blows the black must pay
> Unless he learns the business in a day. (*CP*, 253).

The topic of this poem is argued again in another satiric poem called "A Veld Eclogue: The Pioneers." This was written in 1928 but not published until 1930 in *Adamastor*, Campbell's first collection of lyric poems and the source of most of his major work.

There is a side to *The Wayzgoose* more positive than these comments may have indicated. It is a truism to remark that all satire is based upon positive rather than negative beliefs in that it has to be posited upon the optimistic assumption of the remedial nature of man. Campbell takes two positive stands; one appropriate to his sense of manhood; the other to his role as a poet. His first declaration is the more obvious. It asserts the dignity of all men measured by their actions and integrity. This is obvious in the quotation above. The second assertion rests upon the significance of the English heritage politically but more crucially in literature:

> Show first that English blood you love to brag
> And prove the spirit—if you claim the Flag.
> Is yours the giant race in times of yore
> That bred a Dryden, or a Marvell bore? (*CP*, 250).

And later, "Is it so English . . . to whine your impotence in feeble prose?" And more degrading still, "And is it to be English—to be dull?" Such patriotism may seem extraordinary to an American reader, but residual loyalty to England as "home" remains an urgent emotion in the hearts of expatriate, English-speaking South Africans even if they have lived several generations outside of Britain. Nowhere is this attitude more fervent than in Natal, Roy Campbell's birthplace and the location for this *Wayzgoose*. There may be some absurdity in the extreme of this attitude, but in Campbell's lines the feeling earnests an urgent integrity that was always the legitimate counterpoise of his exaggeration.

CHAPTER 3

The Making of a Poet: Adamastor

I T is the collection entitled *Adamastor*,[1] published in London
in 1930, that is Campbell's most significant achievement. It is in
fact the one volume upon which must rest any justification he may
have for being considered a major poet. The poems themselves are a
collection of brief pieces, many of which had been published
separately in magazines for several years before this. The most
effective and impressive lyrics had seen print, in particular, in *The
New Statesman* and *The Nation,* the magazines which later merged
into the well-known influential left-wing journal, *New Statesman
and Nation.* These poems were printed between 1926 and 1930, and
then were incorporated with other material into *Adamastor.* Only
the verses for which it is possible to trace actual magazine publication can be exactly dated from the material we have at the moment.

Apart from the South African publication the earliest poem
printed seems to have been "The Serf," which was published in
England in *The Nation* in November, 1926. "The Zulu Girl"
appeared in the same magazine later in that month. It is thus obvious that although the collection was published after he returned
to England, several of the *Adamastor* poems were written while he
was still in Africa. Others, although concerning specifically African
experience, were apparently written after he left his country. "Veld
Eclogue: The Pioneers" was not published until March, 1930. This
makes it one of the last previously printed pieces to be incorporated
into the *Adamastor* volume, yet the experience was presumably a
product of his Durban visit, several years before.

I *Lyric Poems*

It is in *Adamastor* that we discover Campbell's most famous,
often anthologized African poems, "The Serf," "The Zulu Girl,"
and "The Zebras." These three poems describe the African scene

with an accuracy that equals love. It is impossible to be so intensely aware of these African places and animals and not demonstrate that one is bound to that continent in some close emotional reaction. This remains true even for poems which perhaps have apparent evidence of South African racial attitudes implicit in them. A contemporary Nigerian poet, John Pepper Clark, suggested that a poem such as "The Zulu Girl" has nothing to do with Africa, since although it is full, as he puts it, "of breast-feeding babies in the sun," it is an outsider's poem, it is a white man's exterior vision of Africa. There is a deliberate flaunting exaggeration in such a remark, yet there also is some truth. Obviously Campbell does not share that Zulu identification with the African scene and the African emotion any more than Joseph Conrad could in writing his Congo stories. Yet self-inclusion is not the only manner of perceiving the scenes of this continent. Identification is not the only source of poetic compassion. In Campbell's exactness there is an accuracy we share and a lyricism we can admire.

A   *"The Zulu Girl"*

"The Zulu Girl" (*CP*, 30), describes simply the common enough scene of an African mother feeding her child. It is possible, I think, that we may feel a faint qualm of moral disapproval in the image in this poem that compares child to puppy, evocative as it may be. But this requires only passing comment. Our primary awareness here is of a most exact and precise record of this Zulu landscape, the area which Campbell knew so well as a boy. The scene is constructed for us with careful sensuality. The use of color words, the purple blood, the darkness of shadow, evoke the scene supported by sounds. The "sharp electric clicks" produce an onomatopoeic effect that reinforces the visual observation. There is also an accuracy in that grunting feeding, a record of that moment when a child, hungry for the breast, is no more human than any other greedy life-seeking animal.

Beyond this setting of scene Campbell carries us into another area which shows his understanding and his sympathetic recognition. He knows this "curbed ferocity." The "solemn dignity" makes clear that however much the system maintains serfdom for the Zulus and the Zulu girl, there has been no spiritual defeat, and there is a sharp note of warning in the last lines. In this poem Campbell has moved beyond the point of description which has so often been asserted to be his major forte. He exhibits an intellectual awareness and, if not identification, at least a recognition. It is this profound knowledge of a situation in which he lives which can stand against the possible accusation that there are tourist photograph aspects in his African poetry. The success of this poem in moving beyond such merely colorful description is strengthened by the technical skill with which he handles these lines. In particular, one notices the rhythmic reinforcement between the topic and the stressed patterns of the lines. The broken, bouncing consonantal syllables of "Tugs like a puppy, grunting as he feeds," audibly indicate that seeking, nudging of the child. There is a controlled transition to those "deep languuours ripple / Like a broad river sighing through its reeds," where not only the obvious device of the repeated sibilants indicate the moving water, but the extremely slow phrases suggest more exactly the movement of those slow-running, languid African rivers.

B "The Serf"

Very similar in tone and very commonly coupled with "The Zulu Girl" in anthologies is his sonnet "The Serf." (*CP*, 30). Here again we have a description of an African scene which could bog down into the merely picturesque like a color slide, extended into a potent feeling for the African. Again Campbell shows his awareness of the veneer by which this South African society maintains its existence.

The first four lines set the scene with great evocation, particularly for those who have ever witnessed the plough cutting into the brilliant red earth of Africa. This crimson furrow, exposed by the sharp blade of the plough, is seen as a blood-stained gash. The inevitable drought has so desiccated the earth that little puffs of dust appear with each step, as the African ploughs his dry and infertile patch. The blood suggestion of the red earth provokes Campbell into a continuing development of this extending metaphor. He comprehends that this serf labor which the African is compelled to do is a repudiation of the old brave warrior life which the Zulus once lived as the great military people of southern Africa. There can be a special identification here because, black or white, Campbell comprehends this loss of soldier prowess, the elimination of individual bravery, for such feeling motivated much of his later life. Campbell avers that there is a dual wound; the wound in the earth is the symbolic replication of the heart's wound in the man, linked by the blood color of the soil.

This sonnet carries us to an even more openly historical, if not overtly political, statement. The very choice of the word "serf" links this African, not to his own specifically African heritage, but rather to a memory of a stage of European development toward individual freedom. We know the medieval historical record of change and growth, of serfs gradually struggling against a landowning oligarchy toward something approaching independence. Campbell, by his very title, implies that this same historical process is going on now in South Africa. It is not a resistance that will provoke immediate revolution; there is that "patience" of the serfs. But the mood is also "surly" and, although patience may appear "timeless," it is, in fact, moving through time and will change. The very proximity of such men to the earth is something so constant that the palaces, thrones, and towers that grow up are transient by comparison and will inevitably be destroyed.

C "The Zebras"

The foregoing poems, which have been primarily praised for their lyric descriptive qualities, can be shown to carry us forward into quite a different area. This discovery is equally true when Campbell goes on to descriptions of African animals which he admired and enjoyed so much. In perhaps the most famous of all Campbell's poems, "The Zebras," (CP, 40), the description is fairly direct, but there are a number of later poems like "To a Pet Cobra," in which there is a carry-over into a much greater sense of poetic and imaginative identification. "The Zebras" is certainly perhaps the most colorful and effective poem of Africa that Campbell achieved. It is another sonnet and gives evidence both of the love with which he reacted to the African scene and African animals, and also supplies us, in microcosm, with evidence of the techniques which he regularly employed in order to describe that emotion.

What is significant here is a classic example of the techniques which Campbell employs throughout his collection. Most potent is the way in which his brilliant use of color is reinforced by his deliberately chosen verbs of action and of movement. To describe these zebras who wander in their striped herds across the African high veldt, he not only uses the evocative color adjectives "gold," "scarlet," "fire," and "rosy," but also chooses his verbs to give a sense of participating action. It is not enough that the scene is pictorial; in a sense, it becomes cinematographic, a moving picture. When he describes the striped effect of the zebras, he uses the term "zithering" to impose the idea of the rapidly moving strings of that harplike instrument. The sunlight is not seen simply as a static golden glow but flashes with the movement of these animals. Their coats are barred in a design similar to the contrasted lines of sun and shadow, in the landscape. But zebra stripes form "electric" tremors, and suggest vibration. It is movement that constitutes the effect of these lines. The sight of the wind slipping across the elephant grass "Like wind along the gold strings of a lyre" is an image of transient movement.

Action within the poem is continued even farther and more extravagantly when we have the description of the actual beasts in their ardent mating maneuvers where "the stallion wheels his flight." The zebra's movement is seen as exploiting the freedom, the unrestrained movement of a bird. The zebra's beauty is not only an "engine" with its symbol of action, but it also is "volted." From the dictionary one learns that "volt" is a French-derived verb describing the gait of a horse, yet it is unusual enough that on first response is likely to find a connection between the continuation of the electric idea of power volts, and also perhaps a hint of the jumping which would be associated with a different spelling, "vaulted." The deliberate ambiguity extends the imagination triply. The action and color are precisely brought together in the last line where the copulation, representing its most complete of unions, is splendidly and eagerly performed among the lilies of the scene. The handling of the verbs to create this degree of movement is appropriate. This is because where the scene has its own physical violence, Campbell's somewhat violent language is not excessive, does not set up a discordant discrepancy in our minds between what is appropriate in the scene and what is exact in the language. When he describes the color of Africa, we know the exotic hues of Africa are themselves as brilliant as Campbell writes. It is when he later chooses to apply these terms to England that they become bombastic metaphors that only surprise rather than delight.

D *"The Albatross"*

The same devices are very apparent in another successful poem, "The Albatross." Here, a very specific personal identification is made, a more direct one than that response of affection or emotional connection he claims to feel with the "Pet Cobra," for example, or the dog in "African Moonrise." In "The Albatross" the

identity is asserted from the very beginning by openly announcing
the albatross as the *persona*. The "I" form makes the bird the
speaker of the poem. This poem is one in which Campbell's use of
powerful verbs and action words can be argued to reach its
legitimate climax. When, later, he does attempt to pass beyond this
tolerable limit, his energetic language becomes suspect. Here in a
last, almost frenzied, excitement, he achieves the boundless movement of the albatross' flight with perfect verbal exactness. The location of the albatross in the air, supreme above humble man's creation, gives Campbell the sort of identity that appeals to him, and he
describes it in swinging, mobile phrases.

> The ranges moved like long two-handed saws
> Notching the scarlet west with jagged line:
>
> Swerved like a thin blue scythe, and smoothly reaping
> Their mushroom minarets and toadstool towers,
> My speed had set the steel horizon sweeping
> And razed the Indies like a field of flowers:
>
> Feathered with palm and eyed with broad lagoons,
> Fanned open to the dimly-burning sky,
> A peacock-train of fierce mesmeric moons,
> The coast of Africa had rustled by. (*CP*, 33).

These are typical of Campbell at his confident best. There are the
action verbs of the cutting, slicing movement, and here too are the
colors—scarlet, blue, peacock. The concept includes Campbell's
omnipresent sense of superiority. It can be perceived in the implicit
sneer of "mushroom minarets" and "toadstool towers." They are
not only literally foreshortened in their appearance from the
altitude of the bird's celestial viewpoint, but somehow from this
vantage point they are also dwarfed in significance. On earth they
seem evidence of man's prowess and grandeur; the bird's eye
belittles them to miniscule fragility. Such apt diction creates the
closeness between description and scene that makes, after all, any
effective image. A similar comparison is found when the curved
edge of this large, handsome bird's wing is likened to the ap-
proximate shape of the scythe's blade, and then that image is extended by being developed from shape into idea. The curved wing
reaps or cuts down the pretensions of men who remain earthbound
with their shrunken "mushroom" monuments. This metaphor takes

on a further dimension when the scythe shape and color is transferred to the steel of the horizon. Campbell's lines become more vivid, more fierce when he describes the playing of the porpoises:

> Striped with the fiery colours of the sky,
> Tigered with war-paint, ramping as they rolled,
> The green waves charged the sunrise letting fly
> Their porpoises like boomerangs of gold. (*CP*, 34).

Here again there are the colors—the green, the gold, the fire. The very exact description of the striped lines of the sun, the streaks of shining across darkened skies, gives Campbell the tiger image which is exciting although it may appear an active one for the particular situation. Yet action is exactly appropriate for the porpoises, those "boomerangs of gold." On inspection, we find this simile satisfactory because there is such clear color, movement, and shape identity between thing and word. The metaphor is not, as it were, thrown in to give an effect of poetic action. We move from the exactness of words to the development of the description. The bent boomerang shape is appropriate as the curved fish leap from the water and drop as they play, returning to their original place like the homing of the weapon.

When he goes on in this dawn description to describe the birds in the sky, he also uses similarly noisy verbs. Perhaps here we may begin to doubt the appropriateness and the effectiveness of such diction:

> Exploding from white cotton-pods of cloud
> I saw the tufted gulls before me blow,
> The black cape-hens beneath me, and the proud
> White gannet in his catapult[2] of snow. (*CP*, 34).

The "cotton pods" idea of small puffy clouds is a very obvious visual analogy, but one notices that these birds are very violently moving, inappropriately perhaps for their smooth flight. They "explode" from these clouds, and the white gannet's movement is likened to the catapult maneuver; it is shot forward. One begins to wonder at this point whether the verbs have not been chosen in order to suggest an action which is more vibrant in Campbell's mind than in the scene itself. This doubt is deepened when in the following verse we have the phosphorescent whales which are like bursting rockets. This noisy association is continued again with suspect exaggeration in the description of the spray as the ocean hammers against the coral reefs.

> Far coral islands rose in faint relief
> Each with its fringe of palms and shut lagoon,
> Where with a running fuse of spray, the reef
> Set off the golden crackers of the moon. (*CP*, 34).

We know the sudden noisy surge of the waves dashed against such a reef, but at the same time, we wonder at the simile. In spite of the possibility that the moonlight spray might look like gold flecks, in spite of the undoubted fact that waves do make a banging noise on the rocks, one begins to find perhaps the image of firecrackers a little intrusive for the scene. One might have a similar feeling that one is moving beyond the borderline of acceptability in other lines of this poem where the bird, now dying, reminisces about its past youth.

> I had been dashed in the gold spray of dawns,
> And hit with silver by the stars' faint light,
> The red moon charged at me with lowered horns,
> Buffalo-shouldered by the gloom of night! (*CP*, 36).

There are such a series of violent activities attributed to the completely neutral elements, the passive shining lights, that one realizes the ungentleness of the action is within Campbell's vision, not within the scene. How can one be hit by fragile starlight? This tone continues. Perhaps two other stanzas are worth recording as further clear demonstrations of this type of effect in Campbell.

> Clashing the surf-white fringe that round it runs
> Its giant mesh of fire-shot silk, unfurled
> And braided with a chain of flashing suns,
> Fleece the craggy shoulders of the world. . . .

Two stanzas later:

> Night surges up the black reef of the world,
> Shaking the skies in ponderous collapse,
> I hear the long horizons, deeply hurled
> Rush cataracting down through starless gaps. (*CP*, 36).

All we should say here after having indicated this stylistic trick is that it became something of a habit with Campbell later. Perhaps if we did not recognize it as a tendency we would say no more than that the feeling which is created by these lines appears to be Campbell's own sense of energetic action transposed to the life of the bird. Since this identification has already been noted in the use of the "I" form, we should not be surprised. The urgent life-loving nature of Campbell, never a man to hide his love and admiration for the physical things, is his emotional basis for what often seems mere frenzy. As the albatross *persona* in this poem becomes aware of its impeding death it stirs Campbell's own sense of the pain as vitality is lost, his horror of the prospect of the physical abdication of death.

> I saw how vile a thing it is to die
> Save when careering on their sunward course,
> The strong heart cracks, the shivered senses fly,
> Stunned by their own expenditure of force. (*CP*, 35).

It is dangerous and yet tempting to read disproportionate amounts of autobiographical insight into occasional lines which do not after all always deliberately refer to the poet himself; but that "stunned by their own expenditure of force" must surely make a curious reflection on the last ten years of Campbell's life. It could become a kind of partial apology for the lack of poetic output that was missed during those years of his life in Portugal.

E *"To a Pet Cobra"*

A very similar identification with an animal can be discovered in Campbell's poem, "To a Pet Cobra," except that here the reflection touches on an entirely different aspect of Campbell's personality. With "The Albatross" he was celebrating that part of himself which delighted in action, in heroism, in the bold heroic death. In the Cobra poem he is pandering to his sense of rejection of isolation from men, his occasional cold hatred of human beings. The poet begins the description of the snake which Campbell has allowed to crawl across his arm:

> I love on my arm, capricious flirt,
> To feel the chilly and incisive kiss
> Of your live tongue that forks its swift caress. (*CP*, 31).

But soon he is moralizing on the identification and posing a little too:

> Our lonely lives in every chance agreeing
> It is no common friendship that you bring,
> It was the desert starved us into being,
> The hate of men that sharpened us to sting:
> Sired by starvation, suckled by neglect,
> Hate was the surly tutor of our youth:
> I too can hiss the hair of men erect
> Because my lips are venomous with truth. (*CP*, 31).

Even if we take it that the starvation and neglect that Campbell is talking about is the absent admiration he feels that his reputation should deserve from his countrymen, it remains nevertheless somewhat excessive, especially when he moves to the point of symbolic murder, in the quatrain:

> I love to think how men of my dull nation
> Might spurn your sleep with inadvertent heel
> To kindle up the live retaliation
> And caper to the slash of sudden steel. (*CP*, 32).

It is only too clear that Campbell is commanding his satire to take on the sharpness and murderous edge of the Cobra bite.

In the penultimate verse Campbell goes beyond identifying with the snake. The poem becomes overtly personal as he makes a declaration which cannot apply to the Cobra at all. The snake has been reduced to being only the trigger for a much more individual poetic mood. From this stanza we get a very clear impression of the attitude of Campbell at this point in his life. So much anger, so much sense of isolation, so much determination to violently succeed, and so much arrogant sense of his own perfection rage within him:

> There is no sea so wide, no waste so sterile
> But holds a rapture for the sons of strife:
> There shines upon the topmost peak of peril
> A throne for spirits that abound in life:
> There is no joy like theirs who fight alone,
> Whom lust or gluttony have never tied,
> Who in their purity have built a throne,
> And in their solitude a tower of pride. (*CP*, 32).

That "tower of pride" in solitude is to be the place where Campbell condemns himself to live through much of his writing life, and one might well remember that pride is not a virtue as it appears to Campbell but one of the seven deadly sins.

F   "The Snake"

This angry pride is not an isolated mood; it is repeated in a number of other *Adamastor* poems. One is called "The Snake." It is not accidental that Campbell chooses to associate himself with this dangerous and hated reptile. In the opening stanzas, which are illuminating about this part of Campbell's disposition, he describes the snake as growing out of the arid desert and therefore more remarkable than something which comes from the easier areas of more fertile land. Is there a suggestion that a poet from Africa is more remarkable than a poet fertilized by the encouraging literary environment of Europe? He likens himself to the snake, but of course a superior snake, a snake which has the capacity now to speak truth:

> A glory, such as from scant seed
> The thirsty rocks sufficed to breed
> Out of the rainless glare,
> Was born in me of such a need
> And of a like despair,
> But fairer than the aloe sprang
> And hilted with a sharper fang. (*CP*, 55).

Here is Campbell with the sharper fang, the fang honed by despair that will continue to bite through all his verse, not to be dispersed with a single individual snap.

Why does he see himself as the biting snake? What are the characteristics of his nature which he feels are represented in this way? He suggests that he has a heart fierce and is capable of love if not antagonized.

> The heart whom shame or anger sears
> Beyond the cheap relief of tears
> Its secret never opes,
> Save to the loveliest of fears,
> The most divine of hopes,
> And only when such seeds may find
> A tough resistance to the rind—(*CP*, 55-6).

Fears and hopes he knows, but they are only inspired by resistance and a tough resistance at that. It was the tough resistance of life in London that provoked his biting angry wit as it had indeed provoked precisely similar reaction when he had felt equivalent resistance to his activities in South Africa three years before the publication of this collection. He goes on to talk of the rock which gives water when it is smitten by the prophet and then again makes this a personal analogy.

> But it was a sorer dint
> Flashing from a harder flint
>
> That, smitten by its angry god,
> My heart recoiling to the rod
> Rilled forth its stream of pride,
> A serpent from the rifted clod
> On rolling wheels to ride,
> Who reared, as if their birth were one,
> To gaze, an equal, on the sun. (*CP*, 56).

Here is Campbell's assertion of virtue, even divinity, that exaggerates his remarkable sense of authority.

G   *"African Moonrise"*

Adamastor is divided into lyric poems and satiric poems, and most of the latter are brief sardonic epigrams. One, however, seems to straddle the division of the two sections by combining moods. If on the one hand it has the ironic tone of satire, it does at the same time continue Campbell's lyric mood that examines the African scene in order to discover a personal relationship, an image of his own character within the creatures of its land. "African Moonrise" is in that sense like his snake poems. Campbell is looking out onto the scene of the high veldt at night when there is a brilliant moon.

> But wide I flung the shutters on their hinges
> And watched the moon as from the gilded mire
> Where the black river trails its reedy fringes,
> She fished her shadow with a line of fire. (*CP*, 191).

He explains why he is driven to watch the scene in curiously eighteenth-century language: "Insomnia, the Muse of angry men, / To other themes had chid my faithless quill." This is an extraordinarily dated sort of phrase to use when contrasted with the realism of the opening lines: "The wind with foetid muzzle sniffed its feast." (*CP*, 190).

With all this tone of preliminary irony to inspire him, the poet begins a moonlight vigil, and in this way the very diction becomes part of the irony by the frustration of expectation. He looks out on a night scene which he describes in these lines:

> Against her light the dusty palms were charred:
> The frogs, her faithless troubadours, were still,
> Alone, it seemed, I kept my trusty guard
> Over the stone-grey silence of the hill. (*CP*, 191).

To my taste the exact color word "charred" with the idea of dry, unreflecting black that the beams of the moon give to a tree seen up against the skyline's matte-light finish, is a valuable enough insight that I am willing to overlook the arch tone that comes with the frogs being poeticized into "faithless troubadours," a tone which is to some extent continued in the term "trusty guard."

If the tone of the opening stanzas must be treated with some circumspection, the last three are dramatic and successful. The poet suddenly hears a wretched mongrel dog howling, screaming its whining cry at the moon:

> Till a starved mongrel tugging at his chain
> With fearful jerks, hairless, and wide of eye,
> From where he crouched, a thrilling spear of pain,
> Hurled forth his Alleluia to the sky.

> Fierce tremors volted through his bony notches
> And shook the skirling bag-pipe of his hide—
> Beauty has still one faithful heart who watches,
> One last Endymion left to hymn her pride! (*CP*, 191).

Again there is an unpleasant archness of tone in the mutt being called the "Endymion" with its association of the Grecian moon worship; and the spirit of the one "faithful heart who watches," though linked by the same intention of a deprecatory mock-heroic style, grates a little. But this is not, I think, the essential point here. Rather one recognizes the way that Campbell has realized this dog. The bagpipe is a witty and effective image, describing how the body is compressed by the urgency of the howl that the dog lets out, and it has both a shape association and a sound effect as it recalls the leather bagpipe's squeal. Then that "thrilling spear of pain" combines the pain of the dog who lets it out with that caused to the listener who has his ears assaulted by it. But the cry becomes something more than the squealing of a dog. This "Alleluia" becomes significant, suggestive. This quivering, tremoring dog, howling, baying the moon, obviously becomes a very clear symbol to Campbell who directly identifies himself with it in this last stanza of the poem.

> Sing on, lone voice! make all the desert ring,
> My listening spirit kindles and adores. . .
> Such were my voice, had I the heart to sing,
> But mine should be a fiercer howl than yours! (*CP*, 191).

This identification is doubly suggestive, because it was precisely that "fiercer howl" that he would attempt to develop in London, a London that would find a fierce howling vulgar and exhibitionist rather than dramatic. When taken out of its African context it was to become suspect and perhaps meaningless, just as the howling of this dog is not inherently important but somehow given significance by the brilliance of its setting under the African moon.

II   *Satirical Poems*

A   *"The Pioneers"*

The largest and most developed satire occurs in "The Pioneers" which is inexplicably found in the "lyric" section of the collection.[3] In this poem Campbell assaults the whole idiotic colonial ethic. The title is charged with developed sarcasm, mocking the laziness of the whites in this land where only blacks work.

> Rough was the labor of those hardy swains,
> Sometimes they lay and waited for the rains,
> Sometimes with busy twigs they switched the flies
> Or paused to damn a passing nigger's eyes. . . . (*CP*, 22).

His couple, Johnny and Piet, representing the English and Afrikaans-Dutch element of South Africa are parodied figures, modern degenerations of the old settler pioneers. Campbell satirizes them in these words:

> They were true-bred children of the veld
> It could as easily be seen as smelt,
> For clumsier horsemen never sat astride,
> Worse shots about their hunting never lied—(*CP*, 23).

He goes beyond this to an open attack, not on individuals, but on an attitude which pursues the anxious writers of new countries. Somehow, because they feel a kind of humiliated inadequacy against the long history and extensive social tradition of the European countries, they seek to find an alternative experience which Europe does not share, an experience which is not only equal but in fact actually superior to the cultural heritage deriving from the spirit of the old established European lands. They assert the intense impatience of these new countries with their wide open spaces and free beauty. It would not be difficult to find such an attitude in American writing of the nineteenth century. In Australian, Canadian, and above all, South African literature it is found in the twentieth century. These absurd pretensions are undoubtedly as foolish as the reverse assumption of the arrogant European that civilization stops outside their continent. But whatever the correct apportionment of blame, in a rightful and entirely satiric attack Campbell describes the reaction of these writers who so ludicrously seek to find some mystic association in their heritage:

> But 'nameless somethings' and 'unbound spaces'
> Are still the heritage of 'younger races'—
> At least our novelists will have it so,
> And, reader, who are we to tell them 'No!'
> We, who have never heard the 'call,' or felt
> The witching what d'ye-callum of the veld? (*CP*, 24).

So he ridicules the exaggerations:

> And there are far more furlongs to the mile
> In Africa than Europe—though, no doubt
> None but colonials have found this out.
> For though our Drakensberg's most lofty scalps
> Would scarce reach the waist-line of the Alps,
> Though Winterberg, beside the Pyrenees,
> Would scarcely reach on tip-toe to their knees,
> Nobody can deny that our hills rise
> Far more majestically—for their size! (*CP*, 25).

And he goes on to catch superbly a sort of illusive false philosophizing which defends this logically fallacious position:

> I mean there's something grander, yes,
> About the veld, than I can well express,
> Something more vast—perhaps I don't mean that—
> Something more round, and square, and steep, and flat—
> No, well, perhaps it's not quite that I mean
> But something, rather, half-way in between,
> Something more 'nameless'—That's the very word!
> Something that can't be felt, or seen, or heard,
> Or even thought—a kind of mental mist
> That doesn't either matter or exist
> But without which it would go very hard
> With many a local novelist and bard—
> Being the only trick they've ever done,
> To bring in local colour where there's none. . . . (*CP*, 25).

One thing that might be noticed about these lines, in addition to their amusing satiric force, is the way in which at this point Campbell has broken from the falsely heavy iambic couplet effect which makes so much of his satiric writing very tedious in its too regular rhythmic stress. These lines have in fact fairly regular iambic feet. They are certainly in couplets, but somehow the whole colloquial tone, the conversational ease achieved by the hesitation, the dashes, the repetitions and paraphrases have all broken his poetry from the overrigorous commitment to uniformity which is to render so many of his long series of iambic couplets so tedious.

B *"Epigrams"*

There are several other poems in the satiric section of the *Adamastor* collection; with the exception of "The Pioneers," the quality of the satiric poems sometimes seems in direct proportion to their brevity. Where Campbell can bring himself to stop at the point where his satire is epigrammatic, he can often sting and wittily reprimand. There is the bitter and direct attack on Field Marshall J. C. Smuts, then prime minister of South Africa, which is perhaps less known because the situation needs a certain amount of footnoting. Nobody has come closer to penetrating the hypocrisy which controls the administration of this unhappy land. It is called "Holism" and is simply four lines:

> Love of Nature burning in his heart,
> Our new Saint Francis offers us his book—
> The saint who feeds the birds at Bondleswaart
> And fattened up the vultures at Bull Hoek. (*CP*, 197).

Holism and Evolution (1926) was the title of a rather naive book of philosophizing which had been published by General Smuts. The event that provoked this retort and the situation behind it was that Smuts had felt called upon to destroy two African villages for refusal to pay, of all things, the dog tax. The vultures, as they do in Africa, attempted to clean up the carnage his police had caused. The very bitter analogy between the method used by St. Francis to feed birds and that employed by General Smuts is the basis for this viciously brilliant epigrammatic assault by Campbell.

It was not only politicians who had to bear his acid tongue; there were also the minor literary figures of Campbell's land. One poem, "The Land Grabber," records his scornful response to a South African poet who was impassioned enough to offer his heart for "a handful of South African soil"—a most romantic exchange. Campbell refers to it more sardonically: "The bargain is fair and the bard is no robber, / A handful of dirt for a heartful of slobber." (*CP*, 199).

Not content with the poets, he can make ridicule of "Some South African Novelists" in what is perhaps his most famous epigram:

> You praise the firm restraint with which they write—
> I'm with you there of course:
> They use the snaffle and the curb all right,
> But where's the bloody horse? (*CP*, 198).

This is one of those occasions where it is interesting how Campbell gives himself away as he attacks someone else. We all know the dullness, the mediocrity which Campbell so justly despises, where technique and an immaculate style do nothing to conceal the poverty of the imagination or the lack of drive in the novelist's spirit. But Campbell, in his poetry, is riding a horse that itself could only too obviously use that snaffle and curb to advantage. By effective use, they could to some extent restrain the racehorse of his excess, for Campbell's technique is never quite certainly victorious over imagination. Dryden suggested the necessity for clogs upon a too free ranging imagination. The snaffle and the curb Campbell despised in others would have made useful clogs upon Campbell's stylistic horse.

Much more openly is Campbell exposed in another quatrain entitled "Home Thoughts in Bloomsbury," with its very obvious mocking of the European nostalgia of Browning in Italy. It is a very revealing little poem:

> Of all the clever people round me here
> I most delight in Me—
> Mine is the only voice I care to hear,
> And mine the only face I like to see. (*CP*, 196).

It is very obvious that in this reaction he is showing off. It is anticipated that he would repudiate Bloomsbury, which was, at this time at least, Campbell's shorthand for the whole cultish literary salons of London. He would repudiate the clique and its posture in his individualized arrogance. If these lines had been true, his situation in London would undoubtedly have been a much happier one. He would have been able to be sufficiently assured in his superiority to ignore the whole effete literary set which arrogantly despised him. In fact, they provoked his shallow venom because he was not able to have that confidence that would permit him simply to ignore them. Rather, he had to challenge them, fight them on their own shabby ground, defeat them or kill them off. Campbell had too much courage, or obstinancy, to fall in with the American dictum of "if you can't lick 'em, join 'em." Rather, he attempted desperately and continuously to try to lick them.

C   *"Poets in Africa"*

Resentful anger similar to that just witnessed was to be the basis of Campbell's next long (and tedious) satiric poem, *The Georgiad*. But there is another poem in the satiric section of *Adamastor* which is also revealing of a very significant aspect of his poetic sensibility. It is called, very directly, "Poets in Africa," and its theme is the ironic contemplation of the material out of which the poetry of Africa is created. Londoners assume Africa is a savage and violent region and that therefore its poetry can only be a vicious portrayal of the lure of the jungle, of the harsh desert life in which Africans exist. They smugly contrast this with the attitude to nature and the nature poetry which is permitted by the gentle restrained light of an English nature scene. He describes it thus:

> The fauna of this mental waste,
> They cheer our lonely way
> And round our doleful footsteps haste
> To skip, to gambol, and to play;
> The kite of Mercy sails above
> With reeking claws and cry that clangs,
> The old grey wolf of Brother-Love
> Slinks in our track with yellow fangs. (*CP*, 193).

To Campbell, this is not a hardship, nor is it destructive to the development of poetry. His interpretation of the poetic state creates quite a different attitude.

> We had no time for make-believe
> So early each began
> To wear his liver on his sleeve
> To snarl, and be an angry man:
> Far in the desert we have been
> Where Nature still to poets kind,
> Admits no vegetable green
> To soften the determined mind. (*CP*, 192).

And so from the African scene the poet, in Campbell's estimation at least, derives nothing but advantage; you can remain angry, your mind hardened. A color, for instance, "must disinfect the sight":

> We have been stung
> By the tarantulas of truth. . . .
> No snivelling sentiment shall pander
> To our flirtations with the moon. (*CP*, 192).

There are other suggestions of this nature culminating in the stanza where the very savagery and violence of Africa is in itself perceived as a deliberate poetic inspiration:

> And it is sweet at times to hear,
> Out of the turf we trod,
> Hysterical with pain and fear,
> The blood of Abel screech to God,
> Hurled shivering up through vaults immense
> Where, whirling round the empty sky,
> Green fossils of Omnipotence
> The bones of his Creator fly. (*CP*, 193).

The whole philosophy is brought together in the specific lines of the next stanza, where it seems the theme of the poem is present in microcosm:

> True sons of Africa are we,
> Though bastardized with culture,
> Indigenous, and wild, and free
> As wolf, as pioneer and vulture—(*CP*, 193).

That verb "bastardized" is very carefully chosen and exquisitely apt for Campbell's work. It was precisely the reaction to the false culture he derived from England which was to prevent his being this "true son of Africa." He was indigenous, but he was transplanted and wrote from England, from Spain in exile without the sense of the wild and the free spirit which he might conceivably have maintained in his African homeland. The sad aspect is that however accurately he can define the intellectual situation with his word "bastardized," we find that he was incapable of putting this recognition into practice in his poetic life. In fact, he deliberately attempted to "bastardize" himself by associating with the London literary society, indulging in pointless thin battles with people who were advanced and extended even by being the subjects of his scorn. Their spite could have been rendered meaningless by the superior writing Campbell might have produced had he not been sidetracked into this kind of petulant battle.

D   "*Georgian Spring*"

One brief poem foreshadows much more. Called "Georgian Spring," it makes a brief and quite amusing attack on the Georgian poets. It was an attack that was amply sufficient, wittily vindictive, and rendered totally unnecessary the grossly extended version of the same theme which was published later in 1931 as *The Georgiad*. Lines such as these are an exact takeoff of the Georgian mode of modern pastoral poetry, and add a generous ration of laughter too. There is none of the shrill anger that marks later poetry. Here the joke can be appreciated surely even by the poets themselves.

> As for the streams, why any carp or tench
> Could tell you that they "sparkle on their way,"
> Now for the millionth time the "country wench"
> Has lost her reputation "in the hay"
> But still the air is full of happy voices,

> All bloody: but no matter, let them sing!
> For who would frown when all the world rejoices
> And who would contradict in the spring,
> The English Muse her annual theme rehearses
> To tell us birds are singing in the sky?
> Only the poet slams the door and curses,
> And all the little sparrows wonder why! (*CP*, 181).

Perhaps the key line in this section is "happy voices / All bloody: but no matter, let them sing!" There is an indulgent generosity in the face of folly and inadequacy that Campbell only rarely managed to maintain later.

The above comments will be enough to suggest the dual nature of this first *Adamastor* collection. It includes the most effectively colorful of Campbell's poems about Africa, the most briefly witty of his satiric epigrams. For the rest there are two aspects that are worth consideration. One is the number of times in which Campbell makes a comment about a scene, occasionally about beauty itself, which seems to be highly suggestive and relevant to his particular poetic style. He describes, for instance, the scene in a poem "Autumn," the falling of the leaves as the trees bare themselves for winter:

> I love to see, when leaves depart,
> The clear anatomy arrive,
> Winter, the paragon of art,
> That kills all forms of life and feeling
> Save what is pure and will survive. (*CP*, 52).

This is a somewhat spurious reaction for Campbell. It almost gets us to the deliberate, calculated simplicity of Hemingway's declarations concerning style. The urge for the perfection of simplicity that will survive is a somewhat ironic concept in a poet who so rarely manages to achieve that purity; so often, in fact, verges rather toward vulgarity. Against his admiration for the ruthless purity of winter, Campbell is always flamboyant high summer! The type of poem which is the best reflection of his desire to achieve this pure, stark style is "Mass at Dawn," considered below.

E   *"The Festivals of Flight"*

In the vein of the poetic comment we have considerable further information upon Campbell's status of poet; about the nature of his inspiration. "The Festivals of Flight," for example, contains just this type of reference to his own reaction. The opening stanzas set this sequence off so well:

> Too sensitively nerved to bear
> Domestication, O my friends
> On the perpetual change of air
> Whose sole stability depends,
>
> By what phenomenal emotion,
> Alas, is each of us obsessed
> The travel, flight, and ceaseless motion
> Must keep us in a state of rest?
>
> Called by the new gymnastic Muse
> In barbarous academies,
> The rifle and the running noose
> Conferred upon us by their degrees,
>
> To play our more precarious parts
> Trapezed above the rolling decks
> Or in the high equestrian arts
> To graduate the broken necks. (CP, 37).

The pose here is very clear. He can never be a domesticated animal. For him there is always the necessity of change, of movement, the obsession with motion, the "gymnastic Muse" learned in barbarous academies, the necessity of the rifle as the origin of his education in Zululand. All these things become assertions of a deliberate reversal of the normal poet in a tone of irony. Here he deliberately utilizes metaphors which offer an entirely different aspect of poetic activity from the ones most obviously associated with what he would scathingly call the armchair poet.

> Or like a poet woo the moon,
> Riding a arm-chair for my steed,
> And with a flashing pen harpoon
> Terrific metaphors of speed— (CP, 38)

More immediately concerned with the stylistic tricks, he will write:

> Deranger of the intellects
> Of those who flee before a curse,

> Fixative of blurred effects,
> And laxative of minor verse! (*CP*, 38).

His own vision is quite a different one, a lonely one, and a separate one, a vision which can conclude: "Far from the famed memorial arch / Towards a lonely grave I come." (*CP*, 39). The loneliness is an essential part of Campbell, although it is a loneliness which is brandished with pride. It is something that sets awkwardly upon a man capable of so much human feeling.

F *"The Making of a Poet"*

It is this loneliness, this separation, which is again the substance of the attitude that forms the basis of his poem "The Making of a Poet." Here he likens himself to a bull, a device which was to delight and flatter him on many other occasions. He takes a stand on the identity with the bull's proud isolation, using a device which also appears in a less significant poem, "Estocade," though in this case, curiously enough, the situation is reversed and he has become the tormentor of the bull, the tricky toreador. Even so, the attitude and the description of his reaction is similar to "the Making of a Poet" because the last stanza runs:

> For though to frenzy still be stirred
> The unwieldly lecher of the herd,
> Still to its brain
> I am all wings and airy lightness
> And make a comet of my whiteness
> In that black sky of pain. (*CP*, 51).

The words "wings," "lightness," and "comet," bring a vision of himself surging, escaping from this sense of being hindered by the opinions and feeling he cannot control.

"The Making of a Poet" constructs a much more definite, exact analogy between his attitude and the "restive steer," as he puts it. Here Campbell has very obviously determined to expose himself, and the revelation the title provides proves to be less the man than his facade as public persona. In this poem there is self-justification rather than self-awareness; his feeling in being less accurate must be less honest. The poem has three stanzas, but only the first is truly significant; it makes its point before he continues the bull analogy unnecessarily far into areas which are hardly specific in relation to his particular attitude. The first stanza is one of the most indicative and illuminating that Campbell was to give us at this stage of his writing:

> In every herd there is some restive steer
> Who leaps the cows and heads each hot stampede,
> Till the old bulls unite in jealous fear
> To hunt him from the pastures where they feed. (*CP*, 27).

There is again, of course, a good deal of posing. Campbell as the great lover, the valiant leader, is finally driven off by old bulls, who deny opportunities to youth. They hunt him off from their pastures, presumably hunting him off from Durban, the town in South Africa where he lived, and finally ganging up again to drive him away from England to Provence and Spain where he at last felt himself appropriately appreciated. But for all that, this is a pose, and its psychological importance is not diminished by this knowledge. A pose that is so deliberate is in itself highly indicative. Attitudes do not have to be true to be revealing of a person's nature and character. It does not have to be proved that the people in Durban really ganged up against Campbell and Plomer and the *Voorslag* magazine to drive him away from his homeland. The fact that Campbell repeatedly considered himself a person antagonistically assaulted by others, isolated by his superiority to their mediocrity, remained an attitude that he would take with him to England. There in a similar reaction he began his sharp, sometimes hysteric attacks upon the Georgian poets and later the Oxford group of 1930 liberal left-wing writers.

G "*Horses of the Camargue*"

There are two other poems in the collection where this image, this vision of the isolated poet, is also made very clear. The first is cloaked in a somewhat more distant symbolism and the second concealed in a retelling of the story of one of Byron's poems. The first of this type is "Horses of the Camargue."

It has already been mentioned what a tremendous impact and excitement it was for Campbell when he left England for his first brief visit to Provence and the Mediterranean which so captured him then and bound him to it in later years. This poem is some reflection of the intensity of that experience. Across this area of the Camargue are wild horses which are renowned in painting. In *Light on a Dark Horse*, his autobiography, Campbell takes a great deal of space to describe his enthusiastic admiration for these beasts. In a not too subtle way it is clear that their distinction is found in their independence, their heroism, their isolation; and such qualities not only appeal to him, but appeal because he feels a close personal identification. He describes them and then records how impressed he was with their strength.

> With white tails smoking free
> Long streaming manes, and arching necks, they show
> Their kinship to their thunderbolts of snow.
> Still out of hardship bred,
> Spirits of power and beauty and delight
> Have ever on such frugal pastures fed
> And loved to course with tempests through the night. (*CP*, 48).

Hardship, a sense of power and beauty, frugality leading to delight—it is almost as if Campbell is describing the idealistic life which he claims to have led as a child and which seems to return in his mind constantly as a kind of vision of the perfection that might by physically achieved.

H "*Mazeppa*"

In a similar, but perhaps more remote way, the retelling of the Byronic epic "Mazeppa"[4] culminates in the same attitude and mood. The early stanzas are perhaps remarkable for the violence which Campbell unleashes when he permits himself to describe a scene which is already naturally savage. The boy is tied viciously to the wild horse and driven out into the desert. His cracking sinews and racking joints, the pain he suffers as the horse moves under him, are precisely relished. When the boy survives this and goes on to become the heroic horseman leader, the terms that Campbell uses reflect the attitude he so often repeats, the vision of the single man of strength, the sense of authority and power that can only come through independence and action. He describes how the young man will soon become the great prince who will hurl his Cossacks rumbling through the world. But then he goes on to philosophize, to generalize in this way:

> And so it is whenever some new god,
> Boastful, and young, and avid of renown,
> Would make his presence known upon the earth—

> Choosing some wretch from those of mortal birth,
> He takes his body like a helpless clod
> And on the croup of genius straps down. (*CP*, 21).

And this idea culminates in the last stanza:

> Out of his pain, perhaps, some god-like thing
> Is born. A god has touched him, though with whips:
> We only know that, hooted from our walls,
> He hurtles on his way, he reels, he falls,
> And staggers up to find himself a king
> With truth a silver trumpet at his lips. (*CP*, 22).

We cannot suggest that Campbell is going as far as to make a deliberate personal self-identity here, but certainly this idea of something ordinary, something broken, awakening to the final point of a godlike vision with "truth a silver trumpet at his lips," cannot be too far from Campbell's concept of his poetry as a weapon, his poetry of clarion calls. He talks too often of poetry as truth for us to miss the similarity between his more general statement and conclusion of this ferocious but significant poem. But the sense of individuality which carries with it its own independent heroism also carries with it a less agreeable assertion; an assertion of a man not as a harmonious social being seeking to assist others to live in generosity and social order, but a man who is isolated, not only in his strength but in his arrogance, a figure who recognizes only his own prowess. In this mood when he looks at others, he sees not equally struggling individuals, but people lacking his power and caliber. He starts seeing them as mediocre masses, as people without the spirit and distinction of soul, the "Charlies," the "wowsers," in Campbell's later words. One begins to see Campbell adopt an attitude which, I suspect, can only really be called intellectual fascism; a self-arrogance which depreciates others rather than elevates them by joining in sympathy.

I *"A Song for the People"*

Elitist sentiment in strong terms is seen clearly in a poem which comes out more openly for this dangerous and shameless point of view than perhaps Campbell intends. It is called "A Song for the People," but in his interpretation "the people" are not creatures of nobility, not potentially human souls, but the wretched, the meek.

One notices the rather false rhetoric of the opening lines of this poem:

> I sing the people; shall the Muse deny
> The weak, the blind, the humble and the lame
> Who have no purpose save to multiply,
> Who have no will save all to be the same:
> I sing the people as I watch, untamed,
> Its aimless pomps and generations roll—
> A monster whom the drunken gods have maimed
> And set upon a road that has no goal. (*CP*, 28).

At first one gets the effect of concern in the lines, "shall the Muse deny / The weak," asks the rhetorical question as though Campbell, in his "Song for the People," were going to be the poetic spokesman, the voice of these wretched and humble and inarticulate. But there is a very dangerous sneer involved in phrases like "no purpose save to multiply." This is made much more explicit in the later lines; "the people" seen in the sense of a mob become monsters, and the next verse continues by describing with disgust the ugliness of the human body:

> Huge buttock-faces slashed with flabby lips,
> Gouged into eyes, and tortured into ears.
> A shapeless mass to any rhythm worked— (*CP*, 28).

Campbell goes on to separate himself almost entirely from this "mass." He sets himself up not solely as the defender of poetry, asserting the superiority of the poetic sensibility and sensitivity against indifferent mediocrity—a position which would no doubt be acceptable; rather, he speaks in a way that despises the very humanity of people, seeing them as not capable of the nobility of human response which he feels that he displays so clearly:

> Do they too have their loves, and with these clods
> Of bodies do they dare in their abodes
> To parody our dalliance, or the gods',
> By coupling in the chilly sport of toads?
> Do they too feel and hate—under our wheels
> Could they be crushed the deeper in the slime
> When forth we ride elate with bloody heels,
> Or jingle in the silver spurs of rhyme? (*CP*, 28).

The tone reminds me for a moment of the Horse King of Gulliver's fourth journey. The tone is not exactly the same, for there is not the humorous irony that marks Horse King's questions about the pretensions of people that so humiliates Gulliver. In Campbell's verse there is far more sense that the human actions are despicable rather than absurd. There is less charity. His vision of the despicable bourgeoisie continues with the following absurd declension:

> When from the lonely beacons that we tend
> We gaze far down across the nameless flats,
> Where the dark road of progress without end
> Is cobbled with a line of bowler hats. (*CP*, 29).

Thus Campbell sets his sardonic tone upon progress and all the pretensions of the middle-class businessman, and he becomes even more open in his dislike as he begins the next stanza with these lines:

> Searching the lampless horror of that fen,
> We think of those whose pens or swords have made
> Steep ladders of the broken bones of men
> To climb above its everlasting shade:
> Of men whose scorn has turned them into gods,
> Christs, tyrants, martyrs, who in blood or fire
> Drove their clean furrows through these broken clods
> Yet raise no harvest from such barren mire. (*CP*, 29).

One of the most disturbing things about these lines is the curious way in which Campbell appears to make no moral distinction between the appeals and challenges which are made to this amorphous mass, this mob which he despises and fears. You can be Christs or tyrants; the effect seems to be the same, and in a sad sort of way, one has to admit the blood and fire is certainly the same whether done for tyrannical or Christian purposes. Campbell argues that none of these can possibly inspire the "broken clods." It is interesting, of course, that the mire and mud somehow allow the clods to take on a double meaning, not only of the very hunks of earth, but also the subsidiary meaning of the dull, the stupid, the moronic. Now the poet has become a person recognized by the god—and respected.

> And the great Master of radiant spheres
> Turns from the sleeping multitudes in scorn

> To where he sees our lonely flames and hears,
> And when before him sang the sons of morn. . . . (*CP*, 29).

There is a justifiable and appropriate pride in the affirmation that gods delight in poets' songs. Campbell seems to require that such prestige be increased by an equivalent belittling of the less gifted. The gods "scorn" the masses, "the sleeping multitudes." Such elitism is a constant element in both his life and his poetry.

J *"Mass at Dawn"*

It would be unfair to conclude an examination of *Adamastor* on this note of depressing arrogance. This volume is Campbell's masterwork, and the poems reflect the colors, the intensity which at his best shows the soul of which this man is capable. One should also consider a brief example of an entirely effective poem. It is one of those which achieves its success after one has expectations that it is going to be a failure. I would explain this by arguing that the scene of the poem is at one level just a bit too much. The feeling is a little perfect, a little strained. The effects are so self-consciously understated that one waits for the effect of this poem to disintegrate, for the thing to dispel its effect in self-consciousness; in theatriccality. Then, somehow it does not; somehow Campbell's poem does not seem mannered, but exact; does not seem a pose, but a truth. Where he can achieve this balance, where he can convince us that his extra intensity of feeling is a just and true quality, then we may share it with immense conviction that this is the essence of poetry. At such times we find his poetry superbly successful and powerful, and wish to indulge ourselves equally in the most literal intensity of his physical well-being, his sensitivity through the senses.

Too often, we have heard the theme of this poem: the idea that when food and drink is devoured in simple harmony with the body at peace, the act takes on a kind of reverence. It was something beautifully caught by Ingmar Bergman in his film *Wild Strawberries*. The eating of food under these circumstances becomes a ritual that approaches transubstantiation. This is the point Campbell makes here—makes not by a crude emphasis of religious blessing upon action but in a tenderness of total physical delight:

> I dropped my sail and dried my dripping seines
> Where the white quay is checkered by cool planes
> In whose great branches, always out of sight,
> The nightingales are singing day and night.

> The wall was grey beneath the moon's grey beam,
> My boat in her new paint shone like a bride,
> And silver in my basket shone the bream:
> My arms were tired and I was heavy-eyed,
> But when with food and drink, at morning light,
> The children met me at the water-side,
> Never was wine so red or bread so white. (*CP*, 47).

It is in that last line that Campbell's deliberate simplicity achieves poetry, not in its actual diction but only through the intensity of the context which has been established for it, in the manner of King Lear's famous series of "Nevers." This is the mark of major poetry, which does not have to be complex, does not have to be overpoetic in order to make its imaginative impact upon the reader. The apparent ease of its achievement is a mark of impressive skill.

K   *Conclusion*

There are many other poems than those discussed which could equally exemplify Campbell's poetic qualities. The ones which I have critically examined show that through the years in which he had been writing *Adamastor*, between 1924, when the first of these poems was written, and 1930, when the collection was put together, Campbell was developing a lyric gift that was unmatched in the contemporary English tongue. I do not think this is too excessive a statement. No one else had achieved this vivid, virile note, this authoritative power, coupled with the sensitivity to sensory experience. Everything appeared to suggest that this man was going to be a new force in English poetry, an invaluable antidote to the prettiness and etiolated intellectualism which had so filled the style of poetry at this particular period. On the one hand, T. S. Eliot had made his own revolution by asserting that the nonpoetic could be the substance of poetry, that the damp souls of housemaids were as appropriate a subject for poetry as the women breast-high amid ripening corn, and that the scenes of slum evenings in the "Preludes" were as suggestive and impressive as the views of the Lake District had been to the earlier Romantics. Campbell came with his own revolution which, as it turned out, appeared to be an antagonistic one, but could well have been coupled with Eliot in introducing a change in English poetry. Campbell was asserting the possibility of sensual vehemence, of intensity for a poet, but not deriving this from the shallow and falsely poetic excess that had cluttered the remnants of Victorian verse. Campbell was trumpeting that it was possible to create a new and modern poetry which did not have the dry, prosaic, deliberately conversational flatness which was the calculated basis of Eliot or Pound's style.

The significant point is that at this time Campbell could have brought to English poetry a new vision. It is not for nothing that most revolutionary British poetry of the twentieth century is entirely the product of foreigners, often themselves living in exile. The major names are Yeats from Ireland, the Americans T. S. Eliot and Ezra Pound living in London and Italy. It is this non-Englishness which permits change because it allows their vision the detachment of internationalism. They were not trained in and therefore restricted by the excessive power of the great tradition of English poetic forms and styles. Such new, clear, intense voices from younger countries could make their vital revolution simply by speaking their own international voice, the voice of their own lands. They affected a revolution in English poetry almost unintentionally by being themselves rather than attempting to conquer any particular fortresses of English literary styles.

Here was a direction for Campbell to take. It was in one sense the road that Eliot had chosen. This is not to pretend that Campbell was even at this stage in his poetic career as potentially significant as Eliot. It is equally true that nothing that Campbell ever wrote could equal the power of "Gerontion" or the social impact of *The Waste Land*. Nevertheless, theirs was an identity; in Campbell too there was a new voice. If he could have been true to the intellectual ideal, the clarity of his African vision, then his success as a poet would have been assured, and through this success his influence and prowess would have been recognized and admitted. Unfortunately, many dominion poets from new lands come to the mother country, in the same way as people from parochial and minor areas of this nation go to the great metropolitan center, New York. Such travelers bring with them this same sense of the inferiority of their own environment, the sense that somehow they must adjust so that they can become part of the literary scene, or react in a grieved display of petulent bravado. In doing either, they deliberately and willingly forego the authentic freshness of vision which they should maintain and should cherish as the antidote against being swamped by the pressures of the conventionality of the literary fashion of the time. Campbell himself, in fact, did not allow himself to be swamped or changed directly by the disparagement which, to his anger and humiliation, he met with from the leading literary figures in the English Georgian movement, but his reaction drove him to write poetry of shrill satiric excess. It allowed him to dissipate his talents, quarreling and feuding with the minor literary figures which he should have had the good sense to ignore as being unworthy of his concern or interest. It also led him to take more and more virulent stands, both in his political and intellectual beliefs, and more specifically, in the poetry which he wrote, straining to gain the effects which would more than ever shock and dismay the poets whom he despised.

In a way this is doubly sad because it occurs in such an early volume; but one might insist that his first collection represents possibly the poetic climax of his career. After this, although there are many successful individual poems and poems which reflect the qualities which he achieves at his best in this volume, they are often isolated examples among a matrix of excess, of absurd satire, of ugly anger. The vision which he had as he recapitulated the Africa of his youth, the Africa of his intense feeling was lost, as was the skill which he brought to his poetry and which so illuminated and inspired these powerful emotional effects.

Campbell's potential was lost by being exchanged for another determination, a belief that the London literary scene could be conquered within its own odious, narrow terms. Its terms were those which he had the good sense completely to despise and reject. But the unconscionable arrogance, the certainty of these people was sufficient to drive him into rebellious assault upon their assured citadel. In doing so, he lost his integrity, lost his vision of himself as a poet, and became only a shrill, angry man, humiliated, defiant and, as a poet, irretrievably lost.

L   *"Rounding the Cape"*

Biographically speaking, the most revealing poem in *Adamastor* concerns Campbell's desire to leave his country permanently. It is not possible to date the poem precisely and match it against the exact moment of autobiographical personal experience. It is found in the "Early Poems" section of this collection and reference to the god Adamastor presages the title of the work. Even if written belatedly in England, I feel very sure that "Rounding the Cape" has in it at least that suffusion of mood which he must have experienced as he left for Europe. At first he describes the scene:

> The low sun whitens on the flying squalls,
> Against the cliffs the long grey surge is rolled
> Where Adamastor from his marble halls
> Threatens the sons of Lusus as of old. (*CP*, 27).

The last two stanzas of this poem make a much more personal intepretation, and one is driven to seek an autobiographical note of explication:

> Farewell, terrific shade! though I go free
> Still of the powers of darkness art thou Lord:
> I watch the phantom sinking in the sea
> Of all that I have hated or adored.

> The prow glides smoothly on through seas quiescent:
> But where the last point sinks into the deep,
> The land lies dark beneath the rising crescent,
> And Night the Negro, murmurs in his sleep. (*CP*, 27).

It is not necessary here, perhaps, to point out the political prescience of that image of "the Negro murmurs in his sleep." We have seen the effect of this in the development of independent Africa in the last ten years. I am more concerned to note that emotion he feels, this warmth toward his country. He can satirize it. He often has ridiculed it. Yet that ambivalent emotion "all that I have hated or adored" is declared while he is looking back at the Cape, the southern and last tip of South Africa. His concern and agitation at this is asserted, even "though I go free." In a sense there is freedom in escaping. For Campbell it was not political freedom but certainly the potential for literary and intellectual freedom, freedom which has driven so many dominion writers to leave their restricting countries and seek the extensive opportunities of Europe. He knows this advantage, yet there is an agony in his farewell.

M *"Tristan da Cunha"*

No less intense and personal, but more developed in its psychological analogy is another poem he wrote on this voyage as he sailed by the volcanic island "Tristan da Cunha." That the concept of this derives from an earlier poem by Johannes Kuhlemann does not seem to reduce the intimacy of the conception. This volcanic island looms up, unexpectedly, in the South Atlantic. In passing this strange, lone, sentinel island, which seems to be unconnected with any body of earth's geology, Campbell soon begins to perceive an identity with it. It is as though he sees its lone, sad aloofness as an equivalent to his own sense of separation from the human race. This sense of separation is to become the more obvious when the literary affinity which he might have hoped to achieve in London was also denied him. Then he had to face the sense of double rejection both from his own country and from England to which he traveled to escape. The opening two stanzas describe this volcano accurately but with some neutrality of feeling:

> Snore in the foam; the night is vast and blind;
> The blanket of mist about your shoulders,
> Sleep your old sleep of rock, snore in the wind. (*CP*, 40).

By the third stanza he is already making his personal identification: "Why should you haunt me thus but that I know / My surly heart is in your own displayed?" (*CP*, 41). The analogy continues, the comparison becoming more intimate, more emotional:

> My pride has sunk, like your grey fissured crags,
> By its own strength o'ertoppled and betrayed:
> I, too, have burned the wind with fiery flags
> Who now am but a roost for empty words. (*CP*, 41).

One of the things that one feels very strongly in this poem is a sympathy for Campbell, and that is quite a rare reaction. We are getting a much more humane reflection of the man behind the boastful, arrogant, and rather foolish facade of the bullfighter, warrior, and embattled writer. Now we can feel sympathy, even compassion. This makes the opening lines of the next stanza even more revealing and extraordinarily prescient, although Campbell could not have recognized where the idea of these lines was to lead his life.

> Did you not, when your strength became your pyre
> Deposed and tumbled from your flaming tower,
> Awake in gloom from whence you sank in fire? (*CP*, 41).

Later, Campbell, in the most obvious of poetic senses, had the same experience. His strength became his pyre. His capacity, his very development as a poet became the quality which effectively destroyed his potential. He continues this most remarkable and revealing lyric:

> Exiled, like you, and severed from my race
> By the cold ocean of my own disdain,
> Do I not freeze in such a wintery space,
> Do I not travel through a storm as vast
> And rise at times, victorious from the main,
> To fly the sunrise at my shattered mast? (*CP*, 42).

The sense of exile is clear and strong, and in a sudden moment of almost excruciating honesty he sees the basis for his separation, not in the actions of other people, not in what is done to him, but in his own nature, his own disdain. When he must summarize, in a sense digest, this painful experience, he concludes:

> We shall not meet again; over the wave
> Our ways divide, and yours is straight and endless,
> But mine is short and crooked to the grave:
> Yet what of these dark crowds amid whose flow
> I battle like a rock, aloof and friendless,
> Are not their generations vague and endless
> The waves, the strides, the feet on which I go? (*CP*, 43).

This farewell continues to be the farewell to Africa, the recognition that he will not return. His aloofness and friendlessness will later totally cost him the capacity to develop his poetry in the lyric style which this poem represents.

It is, in the final analysis, this collection by which Campbell's reputation must stand or fall. The sad critical argument of this book is that his poetic career is a declension from the virtues, the poetic skills of his early work, as he was never again to achieve, on any consistent basis, poetry of the level which he was able to write as a young man of thirty. There are occasional flashes of brilliance, sometimes a mere line, sometimes brief poems which serve to remind us of the old skill, the old poetic strength. Sadly, such flashes also serve to show the weakness of the dross in which those occasional poetic gems are set. One tentatively advances the thesis that the type of life he chose to live, the type of beliefs which he brought to his later years, were factors which pressed upon his intellectual attitude and his humane concern in such a way that they precluded the production of significant poetry.

The stimulation which the violence and color of Africa lent to his verse may have been the source of his genius. When these were withdrawn, there was no equivalent to take their place in European life. The passion and fire he later pretended to have found in Spain were nothing but a dim reflection of the true tropic fervor which he found in the Natal of his African youth. This speculation must wait. One can rather point to the effectiveness, the skill, the beauty, the tenderness which marks so many of the deservedly famous poems in this collection, the type of poem which has caused people like G. S. Fraser to remark, "Mr. Campbell's place amongst a dozen or so important poets of our time is assured. Is there another lyrical poet of our time who combines, just as he does, vigor, directness, technical control, and the most vivid scenes of natural beauty? The answer to that rhetorical question is undoubtedly 'no' ". [5] The qualification one would have to add is, alas, that only a portion of Roy Campbell's work itself, in fact, combines those qualities in a way that is an effective poetic synthesis. So often there is vigor without control, a directness without intellectual balance, and the vivid sense of natural beauty flares to mere colorfulness.

CHAPTER 4

Campbell versus Bloomsbury:
The Georgiad

T HE 1930 publication of *Adamastor*, when Campbell returned to England, had marked him clearly as a poet of promise and distinction, even if the direction of that distinction was regarded with some suspicion by the poets who had most significant reputation in England during the 1930s. Edith Sitwell might be mentioned as one of those who had the perception and the generosity to admire and support the work of Roy Campbell, even at this stage. This was certainly not the first time that Dame Edith had been prepared to aid the work of a controversial young writer. From her early enthusiasm for Wilfred Owen to her later support for Dylan Thomas she had often shown a generosity, even if partisan, toward many young writers. With the *Adamastor* collection, which had brought together all his best work to date, Campbell could reasonably have hoped that he would now be accepted in the literary hierarchy of London society.

It is difficult to know why such a man would wish to be involved in this dreary, back-scratching game of patronizing popularity between writers and critics. Perhaps simply because of his colonial origin he tended to be fascinated by the arrogant confidence and judgment of this group. Equally clearly, such a group would be horrified by much of what Campbell was writing. Such people would show very little sympathy for, and interest in, a young poet who so rudely resisted their attempts to patronize him, who dismissed their opinions with an offhandedness that must have appeared to them to be merely surly, who showed neither consideration nor moderation in his mockery of their most ingrained attitudes.

The climax of this feud came with the publication of *The Georgiad* in 1931.[1] It was the result of a developing antagonism that had about it many of the features that had initiated the publication of *The Wayzgoose* in 1928. Campbell, again feeling himself unreasonably put upon and antagonized, decided to settle all the scores that he held against these people by writing a poem of lusty and sharp satire which was deliberately contrived to hack apart those who refused to recognize his literary quality. *The Georgiad* is an unfortunately long poem, and as indicated earlier, "Georgian Spring," in a single page, manages to make most of the points which he now chose to spread across an entire poetic volume of more than fifteen hundred lines. The length was made the more tediously obvious by the utilization of that difficult and inflexible poetic form, the rhyming couplet borrowed from Dryden and Pope, both more subtle and sophisticated versifiers than Campbell.

The title, *The Georgiad*, makes it very clear that we are supposed to see a similarity between Campbell's *Georgiad* and that other denunciation of trivial society, *The Dunciad* of Pope. Unfortunately, the title, the intention, the existence of rhyming couplets are all that we can find in common, for Campbell had not sufficient capacity to generalize about his victims. Paradoxically, good satire not only immortalizes the individual satirized, but it only retains interest to the extent in which the individual people take on universalized characteristics. The most effective satiric challenge is made against the qualities of all folly. Whatever variety of human idiocy is characteristic of the person concerned, receives its proper but generalized pillorying.

For the enjoyment of satire we do not necessarily have to know a great deal about the background of the period. Considerable biographical information about the life of Thomas Shadwell, for example, is not an essential preliminary to an appreciation of the type of criticism that Dryden makes in his *McFlecknoe*. But in Campbell's case the characters are all too private, and we feel we ought to know the persons to appreciate the personalities. We may still be able to recognize a number of the characters, particularly the more significant writers, but those are, almost by definition, the most unjustly treated. The nonentities who are recorded in this poem have so completely lost any pretension to serious consideration as writers that the satiric barbs which stab them no longer have any effect. You cannot demolish the reputation of a writer who is already completely forgotten. What remains the point of prodding the dead in this way? Of course they are not good writers. Of course no one takes them seriously. Why then did Campbell? This is not a question permitted only by the luxury of our hindsight, aided by the reevaluation of literary history. They can never have been mistaken for significant writers. Against such lightweight opposition Campbell's spleen and antagonism is seen for the absurd and exaggerated thing that it is. He does not have to be driven to such antagonism against these trivial scribblers. To do so reflects limited qualities as much in Campbell as in these men.

There are, inevitably, in such a poem, a number of couplets of sharp wit. The barbs sometimes stick and occasionally, if we know anything at all of the background of this period, we can get a chuckle from the way in which these bloodless litterateurs are so properly parodied and rejected by this young, sharp voice from South Africa. As Campbell chose to see it, here was another group of flatulent arties behaving as the South African literary poseurs had done in Durban. They prevented him from enjoying the opportunities of the literary life of England. His attack was immediate and sharp:

> But of all other cults that here are found,
> The cult of "Youth" most firmly holds its ground—
> "Young poets" as they call them in "The Nation"
> Or "writers of the younger generation"—
> Spry youths, some under ninety, I could swear,
> For two had teeth and one a tuft of hair
> And all a die-hard look of grim despair:
> Real Peter Pans, who never age in mind,
> But at the age of ninety wake to find
> They've left ripe age and manhood far behind. (*CP*, 214).

There is an historic justice in these lines, because certainly the poets of this period did very little to encourage the new clear voices of the young English writers to be heard. The irony, as far as Campbell was concerned, was consumated when a new school of poets, the next generation of Auden and Spender, did become published and articulate. They at once became, at least in his biased estimation, a hierarchy as selective, as narrow, as restrictive and exclusive as the Georgian one had been.

Campbell's personal battle against the Georgian school was quadruply worthless since it no longer had even its original limited literary strength and resilience. Eliot's *The Waste Land* could be interpreted as a death blow to the entire Georgian movement and this

poem, after all, had been published in 1923. Now, ten years later,
Campbell chooses to go on making these trivial parodies of the
already trivial Georgian style of the type one might call the minimal
pastoral. Characteristic are little sections such as this:

> Now hawthorn blooms above the daisied slope
> Where lovelorn poets after milkmaids grope,
> Or troop whore-hunting down the country lanes
> With flashing spectacles and empty brains,
> To hang their trousers on the flowering spray
> And sport with lousy gypsies in the hay.
> Here Bulbo comes his amorous hours to pass
> Tickled by spiders on a tump of grass:
> And sure, what blushing milkmaid would despise
> Humpty's great belly and protruding eyes,
> Who in his verses plainly has revealed
> That when he ogles every maid must yield!
> If they should fail to win the joys they sing
> Or get a cuff to make their eardrums ring,
> It makes no difference, they forgive the crime
> And finish off the merry feat in rhyme—
> Editors are the safest go-betweens—
> All maids are willing in the magazines. . . . (*CP*, 205-6).

This is an amiable enough joke, and the circumstance of these
highly urbanized people deliberately seeking a not-too-wild pastoral
residence in which they can play the country squire in the old
eighteenth-century way deserves what in England is now called a
"send-up." There are even occasional couplets which achieve a certain epigrammatic force. For example: "Now Spring, sweet laxative
of Georgian strains, / Quickens the ink in literary veins." (*CP*, 207).
The monotony and duplication of this conventional bucolic and
rural subject matter is patently obvious in this whole school of verse
and is rightly ridiculed. Campbell continues to lambaste this unfortunate Georgian bunch, and sometimes with genuine humor he im-
pales them upon his wit. They were not, after all, a very difficult
target to catch; the movement verged on self-parody from the
beginning:

> Seek some old farm (the image of your mind)
> Where in some farmer's ledger you may find
> Fodder to please the ruminative mind,
> Which, thrice-digested, into cud refined,

> May clatter down in cantos from behind:
> There, safe-sequestered in some rusty glen,
> Write with your spade, and garden with your pen,
> Shovel your couplets to their long repose
> And type your turnips down the field in rows. (*CP*, 229).

It did not suffice Campbell merely to attack in this generalized way. He is equally anxious to bandy personalities, challenging those whom he feels have not sufficiently recognized his quality. As suggested earlier, the problem is that many of these now are only names that can be brought to memory through the aid of a crutch from the footnotes. Several are introduced only by first names which need research to acquire any association for us today. There is, for example, the mysterious Raymond who, we are told, "plays the gramophone so nicely." One famous pair, Robert Graves and Laura Riding, are attacked jointly and rather unfairly in his poem because of their mutual literary endeavors, an attack the more unreasonable in that they were scarcely of the Georgian set. These lines begin the poem:

> Since Georgians are my theme why should I choose
> Any but the most broadly smiling muse?
> Inspire me, Fun, and set my fancy gliding,
> I'll be your Graves and you my Laura Riding,
>
> . . . .
> Let us commune together, soul with soul,
> And of our two half-wits compound a whole;
> Swap brains with me "for better or for worse."
>
> Till neither knows which writes the other's verse:
>
> . . . .
> There's nothing for it but to burst all fetters
> And from a joint Hermaphrodite-of-letters. (*CP*, 201).

"Fun" seems an inappropriately mild term for an attack such as this, but at least we recognize these people. In ridiculing the affection of the Georgians for dogs: "Of all the bow-wows, poodles, tykes and curs / That Georgian poets ever hymned in verse," (*CP*, 210), Campbell gets into the subject of Horatio Bottomley, recapturing for future years the unfortunate occasion when his much-loved dog turned and bit him:

> First Bottomley (Horatio) was seen,
> With pet on leash, to pace the shaven green,
> And oft in verse addressed the faithful "Toby"
> That bit his poor old muse on hydrophobie. (*CP*, 211).

And there is the leader of this group, J. C. Squire: "Next him Jack Squire through his own tear-drops sploshes / In his great flat trochaical galoshes." (*CP*, 211). Then there are Nicholson and Bennett and Lewis and Roberts, writers and critics who once held impregnable positions in English letters with a confidence which insulted Campbell's sense of the appropriate:

> How Nicholson who in his weekly crack
> Will slap the meanest scribbler on the back,
> Who praises every Gertie, Bess, or Nelly
> That ever farrowed novels from her belly,
> At the mere thought of Lewis goes quite blue
> And to cackle turns his weekly coo—
> And so with all the weekly-scrawling crew. (*CP*, 233-4).

He seems particularly antagonistic to the women writers. Even critics who praise him receive a lashing if they equally praise women writers as well.

> Amongst the pillars of my reputation
> Who've propped my fame, without my invitation,
> As they do that of every Nellie, Gertie
> Or Daisy that was ever six-and-thirty,
> Or ever left her own unlettered stews
> To skivvy in the kitchen of the Muse. (*CP*, 227).

If this had any particular impact at the time, it certainly has very little left, and it is rather tedious stuff. Much more effective, and occasionally very amusing, is his description of the general mood of the literary scene in the early 1930s. As with the South African satiric poetry, these sections remain vigorous because they are less tied to merely transient personalities. We care about the scene in South Africa enough to realize that the satire of *The Wayzgoose* is pointed and essentially relevant in modern times. We are utterly indifferent to whoever Gertie, Nellie, and Daisy may be, but we do know the literary luncheons they attend with their scathing, critical attacks on modern writers. Campbell's savaging, as usual, perhaps goes on a little long, but nobody has managed to capture quite so sardonically and yet still with wit, these literary meals offered by rich devotees to the fashionable writer:

> The Stately Homes of England ope their doors
> To piping Nancy-boys and crashing Bores,
> Where for week-ends the scavengers of letters
> Convene to chew the fat about their betters—
> Over the soup, Shakespeare is put in place,
> Wordsworth is mangled with the sole and plaice,
> And Milton's glory that once shone so clear
> Now with the gravy seems to disappear,
> Here Shelly with the orange peel is torn
> And Byron's gored by a tame cuckhold's horn. . . . (*CP*, 207).

Sterile destructive criticism of greatness was certainly ready for laceration. After such description we all fervently share his attack upon the literary dinner:

> O Dinners! take my curse upon you all,
> But literary dinners most of all,
> Where I have suffered, choked with evening dress
> And ogled by some frowsy poetess. . . .
>
> . . . .
> But cursed be poetesses, thin or fat,
> Who give these dinners of eternal chat,
> Where knife and fork dissect the latest plays
> And criticism serves for mayonnaise. . . .
>
> . . . .
> Where the last novel, in a salver set,
> Is masticated, a la vinaigrette,
> By hungry cannibals till naught remains
> Of the poor calf that wrote it, or his brains,
> All his fine feelings and his tender fancies
> Ruthlessly ravened by his fellow-nancies,
> The fruit of all his labour sucked to strips
> And nothing left of it, but peel and pips—
> Cain had more Christian mercy on his brother
> Than literary nancies on each other. (*CP*, 231-2).

Here again, the recognition generated by our own experience confirms the basis for Campbell's satire, and therefore reinforces it in a personal way. It gives the sense that the sharpened edge is appropriate, necessary, and above all, continuously contemporary.

For anyone interested in Campbell's development as a poet and a man, concern may be sparked by the revealing nature of some of the unhappier lines. There is the silly assertion of schoolboy violence when he tells the Nicholsons and Arnold Bennetts:

> For thus, your tails before my boot to stick—
> It's hardly worth the pleasure of a kick,
> It makes me hesitate, and spoils my fun,
> Who love to take my victims on the run. . . . (*CP*, 217).

The whole idea of a kick in the bottom as literary act makes a pretty childish piece of satire, reducing satire to the pratfall. More revealing boasting comes when he defines his own concept of a poet. This model is obviously based on himself and his own achievement both in verse and in life: he sets himself apart from and above these feeble and, in his view, effeminate people. In lines such as these he separates and elevates himself:

> I'll own my fault—what I love is rare:
> The shapely limbs, the tossing flame of hair,
> The eyes whose flame a winged sylph reveals
> Riding to battle on their crystal wheels;
>
> . . . .
>
> The glance of friendship, keen, and staunch, and true,
> Signalled above the heads of such as you. (*CP*, 218).

In contrast to these literary "Nellies," Campbell chooses to seek a romanticized sex. He describes such women with typical verbal flamboyance: "The faces, forms of women, ever new / That milk the lily, bleed the rose of hue. . . ." (*CP*, 218). More than beauty makes such Campbell women worthy; they can admiringly distinguish the soldierly courage of Campbell from the impotent spite of the "Nancy boys" of literary England.

> Women! but for the flicker of whose smile
> Ten times the woes they bring us were worthwhile:
> Who mock at horn - rimmed spectacles, and pass
> The soulful poet for a soulful Ass:
> But for the gay, the generous and the brave,
> Will float with Aphrodite from the wave

> Or raise another Helen from the grave:
> Women who love the outward signs of power,
> Wit, valor, strength, and Danae's golden shower. . . . (*CP*, 219).

"Wit, valor, strength"—those are qualities which Campbell desires. Campbell almost did achieve these virtues had not later in life his wit degenerated into rudeness, his valor become bravado, and his strength declined into exhibitionism.

There is a genuine passion as he indicates his rejection of the concept of a utopian society which was so prevalent at the time; the concept of a social harmony created by human engineering. Naively enough the vision created by Aldous Huxley in *Brave New World* was occasionally taken seriously, not seen as the devastating satire which was intended. He talks of Shaw and Russell and their socialist dreams:

> They hatch Utopia from their dusty brains
> Which are but Hells, where endless boredom reigns—
> Middle-class Hells, built on a cheap, clean plan,
> Edens of abnegation, dread to scan,
> Founded upon a universal ban:
> For banned from thence is all that fires or thrills,
> Pain, vengeance, danger, or the clash of wills—
> So vastly greater is their fear of strife
> And hate of danger than love of life. . . . (*CP*, 223).

In such attacks with all their inspired justice, the character of Campbell becomes apparent again. There is an impassioned love of life which motivates him. Only occasionally is it falsely ardent, though often it seems misdirected. Nobody can deny Campbell his eagerness, that sensual appetite which approaches a greed for all experience. Although Campbell, as the outsider, could see better than any, the folly, the dullness implied by the narrowness of judgment and restrictive caution that these poets represented, it is often his own nature which is exposed to us more than those he attacks. One of the lines of this poem could be taken as a most fundamental assertion about the nature of Campbell's life; it is a remark thrown away inside parentheses:

> And in two lands my fellowship I'll share—
> (Since I belong neither here nor there)
> Spain[2] for the brave, and England for the fair! (*CP*, 219).

"I belong neither here nor there" is a further comment on the in-
cipient sense of exile, that lack of geographic attachment which was
continuously to undermine Campbell's poetry by taking away the
certainties and confidence that a close national link can give to a
writer. Campbell had deliberately and sharply cut himself away
from his own national connection. Occasionally, he openly admits
the deprivation; often there is simply an implicit sense of loss. In
this casually colloquial line, there is an indication in a very direct
way of his recognition that he can never belong.

It is this sense of rootlessness which reinforces his attitude of
detachment from English poets. Sometimes the distinction which
he makes between himself and these writers is a very genuine and
honorable one. One knows that the violence of Campbell's reaction
is regularly excessive, yet it is never in any way hypocritical. His
relationship with people is neither evasive nor dishonest. There is
never in Campbell the "sanctimonious smile" and "greasy piety"
he finds in others. There is an open honesty, a sort of honor. His
declaration of self-confident prowess makes one willing to respect
the man for his directness. Yet soon after such a warm appraisal, the
reader is sometimes affronted by an especially virulent feeling of
irritation at another malicious personal attack. There is one very
revealing section in which Campbell escapes from satiric petulance
and goes on to create an honest assertion of his own life-loving
nature. The lines that follow this are simply ugly and vicious. It
seems so exasperatingly characteristic of Campbell that he can go
from an honorable declaration through cheap attack to a credo of
his own life-loving nature that commands both our belief and respect within a few lines. Throughout this poem he can be cheaply
mean about others, but about himself he exhibits an exhilarating integrity:

> Meanwhile let love and laughter wing my soul
> And what is there to laugh at save the droll?
> And when I hate, my hate shall bare a spike
> Clear in intention, though it fails to strike—
> Not like your own that dribbles, week by week,
> Like a luke warm bilge out of a running leak,
> Scented with lavender and stale cologne
> Less by its true effluvium should be known
> The stagnant depth of envy that you swim in,
> Who hate like gigolos and fight like women;
> There's time enough to live, to laugh, to fight,

> Until incapable of more delight,
> When beauty drives me doddering from the door
> To cut my love in pieces for the poor. . . . (*CP*, 220).

"Until incapable of more delight"—this becomes a prescient comment upon Campbell's later years. In this respect I have increasingly felt that there is a kind of life-identity between Campbell and Hemingway, however different in their styles, beliefs, and attitudes. As Campbell aged he found like Hemingway that he was incapable of "more delight," and his car crash, in its own way, was as definitive a statement of life-conclusion as Hemingway's suicide.

At the end of this poem, the reader has become tired by the repetitive nature of these attacks. Each of the extracts quoted could have been replaced by a number of others, giving exactly the same information or effect. Campbell begins to wonder himself whether he is really using his poetic capacity to good purpose, remarking:

> And if you should regret the precious time
> You've spent to read (as I to write) this rhyme,
> Deploring that a poet thus should sink
> To daubing simpletons with Stephen's ink,
> Who, long before this fantasy was written,
> Were blue with it as any ancient Briton. . . . (*CP*, 239).

"If," indeed, for we may very properly and appropriately ask him just that question. He offers this explanation:

> Such foibles served to pass his idler hours
> Without diminishing his lyric powers
> And in no way detracting from his fame
> And prowess in love's bronco-busting game,
> Where many a lively filly he bestrode
> And to the winning-post of glory rode. (*CP*, 240).

Unfortunately this as a statement is totally untrue. It is mere bravado. It is one thing to have foibles to pass idle hours, like crossword puzzles, but in Campbell's case this has not been achieved "without diminishing his lyric powers." The point is, that to develop his poetry, to find his true lyric voice, what Campbell needed to do above all was to rid himself of the vindictive spleen that drove his verse to bitter and barren excess. Instead, poems like *The Georgiad* amply confirm his attitude, allow it to feed on itself so that

it becomes evidence of the way in which Campbell's whole nature is
being swamped with this shallow and sometimes brutal satire. He
cannot, at the same time, as he lives in this narrowly critical world,
produce a continuation of verse of the caliber of "Mass at Dawn."
Such a poem requires, quite obviously, a harmony of soul, a feeling
of contentment and attachment to his environment. One of the
troubles, to use a word which has become a modern cliché, is that
Campbell was so alienated from the English society that he could
not draw upon it for poetic sustenance. In Africa he was part of the
scene. He was completely in harmony with the experience of that
landscape. There he could express his congruence with the continent in verses which appeared to flow freely from the very lyric
heart of the man. Such verses could not develop in England. There
he was a man fighting social battles in a way that disrupted his
whole nature as a man and a poet; exaggerating one aspect at the
expense of all others. In self-defense, he decided to take another trip
into exile: an exile in Spain. There, although separated from the
language he knew, he gained a remote reminder of the African
scene from the exoticism of the Iberian peninsula. Before he
departed he was determined to scourge those who had failed to ac-
cord him appropriate recognition. Hence the sardonic lines which
stud the pages of *The Georgiad*.

CHAPTER 5

Lyrics and Bullfighting

I   Taurine Provence

IN 1932, Roy Campbell published a very slender seventy-nine-page book called *Taurine Provence*[1] which was to be an explanatory study of bullfighting in France and Spain. The *corrida* had greatly caught his imagination on his first visit to Provence. The original idea was presumably to expound upon the complicated mystique and technique of bullfighting. Such explications of the sport are not rare; if *Taurine Provence* were another attempt by an enthusiast to explain and defend bullfighting to the disapproving Anglo-Saxons, it would be of little further concern to us, and indeed this volume has been largely forgotten. Yet the work is of considerable importance in any attempt to understand Campbell's philosophies. Because of his impassioned, almost mystical devotion to bullfighting, the book becomes the occasion for a remarkable and revealing series of observations, part psychological, part political, telling us less about bulls than about its author. It is suddenly clear that this work, consciously or not, has become the manifesto of Campbell's entire range of beliefs, some of which now strike us as extraordinarily naive, others as utterly deplorable. Yet, in this prose work, among the inaccuracies and absurdities there is that engaging energy, that unflinching directness, that cannot be argued away just because some of the ideas proffered seem to us untenable or despicable. Our reactions are similar to our response to the poetry. Once again, there is evidence of an urgent human being organizing this material in a way that cannot be discredited entirely merely by challenging its assumption at the level of intellectual debate and factual validity.

Granted our present concern, we can perhaps dismiss from this study of the book those actual sections which do deal with the bullfighting of Southern France. Campbell is apparently a knowledgeable devotee and is well able to bandy the extensive technical vocabulary of the sport. A single sample will be all that is required to indicate the kind of specialized knowledge and detailed discussion which Campbell enjoys exposing:

The *vuelta, capotaza,* and *recorte* are easy and rough movements, the former two of which sweep the bull away and the latter causes him to turn in his own length which is not good for him; both passes are permissible: or the end of a series of *veronicas* which are all close-in, one swirls the cloak far out so as to get the bull away. (*TP*, 71).

The basic theme of this book rests elsewhere in its pages. Campbell's argument is a dual one, or rather this double attitude merely reflects the alternate sides of the single coin. There is the praise for the entire bullfighting culture, raising it above sport to spiritual endeavor. To support this pseudotheology, he dwells at length upon the divine significance of the god, Mithras. The other side of this discussion is the attack on those who do not share this elevated, quasi-religious interpretation of the bull cult. This argument ranges from condemnation of the hypocrisy of fox-hunting English colonels to scornful dismissal of businessmen who fail to see the world as culminating in this archetypal and symbolic challenge to manhood. In this simple dichotomy it is obvious we have the core of much of Campbell's own attitude toward life. He claims an extensive experience as a bullfighter, though it is likely that these assertions are highly exaggerated. Be that as it may, the idea of the dramatic act of individual heroism, of manhood consistently challenged by a deliberately chosen violent event, is very commonly found in all aspects of Campbell's life and thinking. The rejection he makes of those who cannot share his admiration for the prowess displayed in the bullring very rapidly extends to wider attitudes of condemnation. People with such attitudes are then identified more generally with those who cannot recognize the similar prowess demonstrated by Campbell in other aspects of his life, as a man, and, above all, as a poet.

Taurine Provence, therefore, begins with an attack on the people that we might expect Campbell to deplore. It is, expectedly, a broad, vehement, and somewhat one-dimensional assault. His attack on the humanitarian basis for disapproval of the sport is obviously just: "It always surprises me to hear English people decrying the bullfight as being cruel, when they hunt defenseless foxes with packs of dogs." (*TP*, 14). And again: "Any pot-bellied draper who has made a fortune, can arm himself with a rifle and go out and 'bag' his elephant, lion, tiger, rhino, then he returns as a hero." (*TP*, 15). So far, at least, the challenge is rational. From this acceptable condemnation he takes a rather characteristic long jump to the generality of his disgust: "the most vulgar and degrading spirit which is active in modern life is that bastard of decadent protestant-ism which expresses itself vicariously sometimes as humani-tarianism, as socialism, as fabianism, as 'sportsmanship,' or as vegetarianism." (*TP*, 18). One notes how Campbell's imagination rapidly expands, moving from the specific to the widest of generalities to cover a rather gross collection of variables. It is not long before he is indulging extensively in his too regular fervent and totally unsubstantiated rhetoric:

Look at any of our democratic prophets of today. They have mean little peeping eyes and sly expressions. It is they who in the name of humanity, liberty, love, and evolution, set youth at war with age, black against white, rich against poor, class against class, female against male, in order to de-stroy the individual, to destroy sex, to break up the family, thereby cheap-ening labour, imposing a set formula on the human face and lineaments, and finally, selling them to Big Business. (*TP*, 19).

The jump from the banning of the bullfight to the breakup of the family and the cheapening of labor will seem to most of us as a rather extended gulf. Big Business with capital *B*s is inevitably the arch plotter against all of Campbell's beliefs. He can go on to be specific, as when he attacks Bernard Shaw, for he argues, "Has not Shaw blasphemed in turn against the glorious human attributes of courage and sexual love, deifying cowardice. . . . the only signs of human nature that appear in Shaw's humanitarian Utopia, are pun-ished by death or humiliation." (*TP*, 20).

When not being so specific, Campbell can generalize about his famous "Charlie," "a kind of man who wears woollen under-pants, carries horrible little black umbrellas, is afraid of germs and objects to almost everything in life, especially to anything that surpasses him in valour or skill." (*TP*, 20). In frigid England, to object to the comforts of warm underclothes may seem a cruel blow. It none-theless constitutes an obvious parody of the ordinary humble, honest, and perhaps humdrum man whom Campbell despised with all his being. It is mediocrity that he deplores above all. Apparently, according to Campbell, he shares this attitude with the best of the bulls, for he claims, "at the sight of a tourist or a bad painter, the mistral, the guardian bull of the true Provence, will lash its sides, paw the ground, and with a single snort of its nostrils . . . send him coughing and grumbling back to the Riviera." (*TP*, 32).

An activity that generates this degree of ardor must clearly be considered as more than a sport. Campbell develops it into a theology and raises its movements to the very apex of ritual. Bullfighting, according to Campbell, is "a choreography as complicated as that which governs the ballet, [which] imposes a test on every nerve. The drama of the bull-ring is the drama of human life—the attempt of the intellect to dominate the brute instincts and to impose its harmony on them." (*TP*, 13). But even this evidence of skill is not enough: bullfighting is also made out to be a religion: "Tauromachy is both the most Ancient and the most *living* of all Aryan religions; and it numbers more passionate believers and more devoted priests (devoted even in the face of death) than any other religion to this day." (*TP*, 15).

The worship of Mithras, Campbell claims, was one of the few significant forces to oppose Christianity as a dominant religion of the Roman Empire. Besides being a sport and a religion, bullfighting is also seen to be an art: "Bullfighting is the only sport which is at the same time a great art. . . . it is the only sport which has inspired great painters and poets." (*TP*, 14). Brazil is significant evidence of this since, as opposed to other South American republics which have bullfighting, "only Brazil is not a Taurine country, it is nearly all forest and is peopled by pedestrians, traders, smousers, and shopkeepers: and it is the only Southern American republic that has not produced a galaxy of shining poets, but is merely a paradise for bug hunters and every kind of scavenger." (*TP*, 56). The link which must seem so remote to a reader, to Campbell is very obvious. As he observes, "the very symbol of poetry is the horse. Pegasus, and the god Apollo was a breeder of sacred oxen." (*TP*, 56). Similarly, the link between poetry and sport may seem somewhat questionable to many of us, but to Campbell it is very simple and direct:

Athletes, the poets of action, are inspired equally, as poets are, by an inward necessity to surpass, and to perform feats of excellence and skill: and like poets, the greater that necessity is, the more they will undertake. A poet of limited ambition, like Tennyson, remains in the precincts of the croquet lawn: but a great poet like Shakespeare will wrestle with the phantoms of terror, fear, jealousy, hatred, madness and death, imposing the laws of his own victorious imagination upon them. (*TP*, 12).

Then continuing this argument and bringing it more specifically to the geography considered in his book, Campbell remarks, "Nothing could prove better the splendid alliance that exists between the intellectual and the physical athletes of Provence than the fact that the anniversaries of their poets are celebrated by bullfights." (*TP*, 36). In a final point of self-assertiveness, he announces, "It is necessary to all poets that they should know the algebra of the thews and the trigonometry of the nerves: and I am sure I have learned them honestly." (*TP*, 36).

The age-old question of the order of the chicken and the egg may intrude at this point. Can one assume that this exciting new experience among the dry heat of Provence and the sparse plains of the Camargue caught the imagination of the young colonial Campbell so suddenly that his disposition was forever fixed? Or does one rather need to argue that a man inevitably recognizes things he is predisposed to admire; that Campbell was always predestined from his African birth to seek this particular kind of physical violence as the metier of his poetry and his life? The debate may appear pointless in attempting to ascribe the psychological priorities, but the fact remains that here in 1932 Campbell is indicating both the mood and the belief that was to sustain such a significant part of his subsequent literary life; reinforcing, in a new geography, those earlier attitudes implicit in his first African poems.

Probably in any context other than an examination of the nature of Campbell as a man and as a poet, this slender book with its attractive black and white drawings would be of minor consequence. It would hardly stand as the equal of the many more elaborate discussions of the enthusiasm that has been engendered by the discovery of the enticing thrills of the bullfight. But as an open prose declaration of what is so regularly implicit in a number of Campbell's poems, *Taurine Provence* becomes an important source of psychological information. Its assertion must necessarily be considered in the light of Campbell's subsequent career. Because of the revelation it makes of Campbell's most deeply held beliefs, it becomes something more than the slender enthusiastic travelogue that it might at first appear. It becomes a kind of credo, nonetheless valuable for the demonstrable fact that its ideas may be shown to embrace a range from the imaginatively profound to the totally absurd.

II   Flowering Reeds

In 1933, two years after the *Georgiad*, Campbell published a second collection of his shorter lyric poetry called *Flowering Reeds*.[2] This was a slender gathering of poems, many of which, as those in the *Adamastor* collection, had seen publication in *The New Statesman* and *The Nation* during 1932 and early 1933. It very likely includes some residual pieces omitted from the first collection as well as fresh verse from the previous two or three years; again accurate dating is difficult. It is not a very exciting group of poems, for it appears that the inspiration of Africa which gave point and direction to the verse which Campbell wrote in *Adamastor* can no longer be tapped. The form is all there—the outer shape, the use of dazzling coloration, the themes of a particularly exotic and technicolor nature; but somehow the justification is no longer present within the subjects. The poems are still highly pictorial in their form, but it appears as if there is little more vital purpose than the exhibition of the poet's capacity to write lines of brilliant evocation. They lack the conviction which is the source of true poetic life. They do not carry forward, as does, for example, "The Zulu Girl," beyond the pictorial description into valid poetic statement. The existence of these poems remains caught at the purely visual level. However brilliant the visual is, one somehow feels that there is little statement being made.

A *"The Shell"*

Perhaps this criticism can be demonstrated by quoting "The Shell," one of the earlier poems in this collection, as an example.

> The azure films upon her eyes
> Are folded like the wings of terns;
> But still the wavering tide returns,
> And in her hair an ocean sighs:
> Still in her flesh the Anger glows
> And in her breathing seems to hiss
> The phantom of the fiercest kiss
> With which we slew its crimson rose—

As in a flushed barbaric shell
Whose lips of coral, sharked with pearls,
Of the remembered surges tell,
A ghostly siren swells the roar
And sings of some deserted shore
Within whose caves the ocean swirls. (*CP*, 98).

This poem has an obvious conventionality of the sonnet form in spite of the rarer extra color with which Campbell pigments his lines. Possibly this impression of conventionality derives from the overregularity of its iambic lines. The use of only the most obvious primary and weak stresses induces a heavy monotony, unless, as too rarely happens in Campbell's lines, the effect of variety is created by the calculated use of secondary and tertiary emphases. Such subtle devices do not seem to come very easily to Campbell.

To the heavy effect of too regular a stress pattern we must also add the repetitive effect of the strong rhymes which often conclude the regularly end-stopped lines. Indeed, such stress falls upon the terminal words throughout Campbell's rhyme scheme that it creates an insistent effect of end-stopping even if it is syntactically possible to run-on the lines. Even when the punctuation does not insist upon a voice stop at the end of the line, the rhyming form requires that a pause be held. Such metrical and rhythmical obviousness makes these poems appear to be so highly conventionalized in form that any originality that there might be in their topics cannot survive the commonplace structure in which they are locked. The common Campbell devices are here in "The Shell": the color words "crimson," "rose," "azure." There are the unexpected verbs like "sharked," the noisy words such as "sigh" and "hiss," and the violent words of movement such as "surges," "swells," and "swirls." These devices were used most effectively in "The Albatross," discussed earlier. Here, however, there is something rather static about the exercise; all the activity is in the words themselves. The awkward mixture of the remembered Boticelli Venus, so gently passive, and these vigorous, lustful sirens, seems unresolved.

B *"The Flame" and "Wings"*

The question, as always with Campbell, is whether he can hold the reader, allow him to retain some sense of poetic conviction, in verse that threatens to disintegrate into a rhetoric so fierce as to verge on the hysterical. In this regard, there is to my ear a significant distinction between two somewhat similar poems, "The

Flame" and "Wings." "Wings" seems demonstrably superior in the
final analysis, partly no doubt because the personal element gives a
note of human truth to the event. It could also be demonstrated
that for all its apparent unrestrained urgency even the structure is
more effective. This would be significant in the light of earlier
remarks concerning "The Shell," for it would sustain the issue that
it is the *form* in which Campbell chooses to contain his vehement
imagination that is ultimately the deciding factor in the success or
failure of his individual poems. When the formal structure disintegrates, no flares of unexpected imaginative lines nor vital assertion of ardor and belief can sustain that conviction in the reader by
which the poetic response is uniquely established.

These poems, "The Flame" and "Wings," are comparable in that
both concern a love relationship and both make extended metaphors out of a woman's dark hair.

> In the blue darkness of your hair,
> Smouldering on from birth to death,
> My love is like the burnish there
> That I can kindle with a breath. (*CP*, 99).

The structure of this poem is a series of rather uninspired similes;
"My love is like" and, in case that one will not do, "Or like the
flame," "Like a great star," and the terminal comparison, "As I
have seen." The repetition of "like" makes for a rather weary construction. It is disturbing and revealing to note how, when reading
aloud, the voice inevitably droops toward the end of each line.

In contrast, "Wings" has sufficient ardor that it carries the reader
with the poet through its urgent authoritative lines. More significantly, the poetic images are created out of the greater compression
of the metaphor rather than the diffusive form of the simile. These
images also bear inspection, since they exist at several levels, and
thus create the emotional and intellectual density which makes for
effective poetry. Although "Wings" does employ many of the
devices which become mannerisms in Campbell's suspect poetry,
"Wings" is a richly textured and moving poem:

> When gathering vapours climb in storm
> The steep sierras of delight,
> Wings of your hair I love to form
> And on its perfume soar from sight.

> For in those great black plumes unfurled
> The darkest condor of my thought
> May stretch his aching sinews taut
> And fling his shadow on the world.
> When sick of self my moods rebel,
> The demon from his secret hell,
> The eagle from his cage of brass,
> They have been lent such scented wings,
> Over the wreck of earthly things
> In silence with the sun to pass. (*CP*, 101).

From Campbell's opening lines there is conviction. "The steep sierras of delight," for example, imaginatively links the visual excitement of mountain peaks and incorporates the sense of individual challenge and enticement that they bring to men. This, in all its mixed emotional and intellectual associations, is then linked with the concept of the challenge and beauty of loving. In a similar way, the "condor" image draws upon the free power of the flight of that great bird to indicate its soaring authority so far above the earth. How appropriate this is for Campbell's thought, and how typical is his emphasis on the "taut sinews," on the physical tension and prowess. Again, how accurate is the arrogant note in which he insists that the bird "fling" his shadow on the world beneath it, as Campbell scorned those he felt too pedestrian to raise themselves to the rarified air of his own poetic flight. It is unexpectedly revealing that he should admit to that devil inside him, the demon self that was to bring him to such aggressive, violent relationships. The poem ends on a harmonious and controlled note, after the vehement verbs "soar," "unfurled," "stretch," and "fling" have urged their power. This draws the fervor of the poem into a point of reconciliation that suggests, as so many lines of Campbell's do not, that the poet is utilizing the vehemence for conscious purposes which he can demonstratively control by forcing his fierce lines back into the balanced structure. The last line, with its emphatic monosyllables which defy rapid reading, acts as a significant, superbly controlled harmonious culmination, both poetic and intellectual, to the urgency he has earlier declared.

C "Canaan"

Other poems in *Flowering Reeds* are less successful. "Canaan" is very characteristically Campbell, but it is Campbell when his writing has become typical to the point of becoming a stereotype of his work. Three stanzas will indicate most obviously what these characteristics have come to be. The first demonstrates the deliberate use of ingenious verbs. Often this is successful; and indeed verbs can mark impressive poetry far more than supernumerary adjectives or adverbs:

> For never was she half so fair
> Whose colours bleed the red rose white
> And milk the lilies of their light. . . . (*CP*, 96).

"Bleed" and "milk" are effective in their novelty. Another feature, of course, is the colors, the constant utilization of color words, as in a later stanza:

> The azure triumphs on the height:
> Life is sustained with golden arms:
> The fire-red cock with loud alarms
> Arising, drums his golden wings. (*CP*, 97).

In these lines, "fire-red cock" might be deemed appropriate, but the "golden arms of life" seems rather a cliché, and "triumphs of azure" can only suggest something like "reaching for the sky." The third device is the use of the numerous action words. Even in circumstances where the activity would normally be considered a quiet or a mild one, Campbell insists upon vigorous activity:

> O flying hair and limbs of fire
> Through whose frail forms, that fade and pass,
> Tornadoing as flame through grass,
> Eternal beauty flares alone,
> To build herself a blazing throne. (*CP*, 97).

"Tornadoing," though not a very graceful word, is typical of the kind of verb Campbell often defiantly sought to give arbitrary energy and force to an emotional attitude.

D "*Vespers on the Nile*"

Two longer poems in this collection have been anthologized. "Vespers on the Nile" describes Campbell's reactions as he considers the painful slavery that was imposed in order to build the pyramids. The opening stanza is certainly the best, with an intensely accurate description of the Nile ibis recorded in just that sensitive accuracy with which Campbell could so often catch the natural characteristic of animals:

> When to their roost the sacred ibis file,
> Mosquito-thin against the fading West,
> And palm-trees, fishing in the crimson Nile
> Dangle their windless effigies of rest. . . . (*CP*, 102).

That description of the birds so silhouetted against the sky that they appear two-dimensional, without depth, looking "mosquito-thin," is an intensely effective visual phrase, and the reflection of the palm trees as "fishing" is also striking. However, after that opening stanza, the tone disintegrates, and Campbell's lack of taste, his curious vulgarity of tone become depressingly apparent. "Frogs," for example, become "the wingless warblers of the bogs," which has an absurd air of contrivance, unintentionally comic. Then with "bogs" at the end of a line, and resisting either "frogs" or "logs" as too obvious a rhyme, he has jackals singing "their first selenologues." This seems not only arch and artificial, but discloses a poet driven by the awkwardness of his insistence upon rhymes. The task of assonance he has set himself drives him to the selection of words which have little poetic inevitability except that they create the necessary terminal sound.

This stanza is followed by several verses which contrast the cruelty of the Pharoah's foremen and the pretentiousness of the urge for immortality upon which the decision to create the pyramids was based. He concludes with a stanza in which he attempts to make this building enterprise a general symbolic statement; to demonstrate the ironic folly of all human pretension. The attempts at such grandiosity are doomed to the failure of being meaningless gestures. Unfortunately, Campbell achieves this assertion with quite staggering bathos. There is no evidence that he intends his own poetic bathos to add an ironic counterpoint to the factual absurdity of the Pharaonic quest for eternal survival and glory:

> Where royal suns descending left no stains,
> Where forms of power and beauty change and pass,
> One epic to eternity remains—
> The hee-haw-hallelujahs of the Ass. (*CP*, 103).

Besides any intellectual qualification one might have about the last line, it is demonstrably unpronounceable.

E   *"Choosing a Mast"*

The best-known poem in this collection is a long discussion called "Choosing a Mast" that takes some of its imagery from Valéry's work "Au Platane." In this poem Campbell celebrates his decision to make a mast for his boat, with lines such as:

> I chose her for her eagerness of flight
> Where she stood tiptoe on a rocky height
> Lifted by her own perfume to the sun. . . . (*CP*, 104).

It is pointless to go through this poem in order that we may again demonstrate the characteristic qualities of Campbell's poetry at this period. Lines like "We ride the snorting fillies of the sea" exhibit at the same time the most characteristic and the most questionable elements of his verse.

Most interesting to those of us who are concerned to follow Campbell's development are some of the implicit comments he makes about his own position and destiny. When he talks of the timber selection he remarks, "I chose her for the glory of the Muse," a line which makes very obvious his assumption that there is identity between his poetic personality and his life as a bold and experienced sailor. When he declaims,

> Lover of song, I chose this mountain pine
> Not only for the straightness of her spine
> But for her songs: for there she loved to sing . . ." (*CP*, 104)

the lines constitute a further example of the way in which Campbell finds in so many things the evidence of the particular poetic imagery by which he conducted his own life and created his own universe. In another stanza he remarks "And for the soldier's fare on which she fed: / Her wine the azure, and the snow her bread. . . ." (*CP*, 104). Here we are back into Campbell as the soldier, but the emphasis stresses the Spartan role of the simple man, that "bread and wine" concept by which Campbell so physically chose to link himself with the peasants of Iberia and Europe.

Spain and the loved Provence which he mentions with such affection were at this time symbols of peace and assurance. His next collection *Mithraic Emblems* is dated 1936. In this year the Spanish Civil War broke out, catching the Campbell family while they were living in Spain. His poetic style, as his emotional, and by implication, his political attitudes, had already been forged by this period. There was little new to be expected from the next collection, and yet it contains some intense and effective poetry. The intensity of the event and his inevitable response for once balanced each other, his art equaling the emotion Campbell brought to it.

III   Broken Record

In many cases one might take an autobiography as simply supplying the biographical details of a man's life. As such its interest would be primarily for the information it supplies. To some extent this is true of *Light on a Dark Horse* (1951). Although there are most undeniable elements of bombast, exaggeration, and probably pure invention, it is still the basic source of our understanding of the events of Campbell's wandering life. *Broken Record* (1934)[3], however, is quite another matter. Like *Taurine Provence* it is apparent that the book is not what it pretends to be. *Taurine Provence* begins with a discussion of the techniques of bullfighting and rapidly becomes an occasion for airing a whole range of political and social beliefs. In a similar way, *Broken Record*, although ostensibly based upon some thoughts from Campbell's early years, is equally seen as an occasion for debate concerning his credo, for it describes the early formation of all his ideas and prejudices in a way both open and vehement. It therefore becomes a document that requires further study, as did the bullfighting work, for it illuminates the nature of the man who created the poetry and establishes that extraordinary character which was to present such extreme challenge to others.

Broken Record was written at great speed in 1934. Campbell says he did it all in only three weeks. He also claims that it was much against his wish that he turned to such prose writing, but that he had considerable need for cash at the time, since he had no other income than his writing and was having to support his family as best he could. He subtitles the book "reminiscences," but the volume could be more accurately called "speculations," for it has an introspective discursive nature. Much of it seems only tenuously connected with the actual events of his life. Incidents seem the merest

initial peg on which to hang his sometimes shrewd, more often outrageous, remarks upon life and the world.

One wonders, and with Campbell it is an eternal speculation, just
how seriously one has to take much of the discussion. Sometimes
while one is reading one is simply driven to near apoplexy by the
comments. Surely no one can begin to believe a quarter of this un-
principled and unspeakable nonsense. It is remarkable how this exasperated feeling has persisted across the last thirty years:
Campbell's lines still have that power to move and shock. For this
present study I have been using a library copy of this work in which
students have penned urgent marginal comments inspired by insen-
sate wrath or vehement agreement. "Damn right" as an approving
response to Campbell's more Fascistic pronouncements is answered
in another penciled hand with an ironic *Seig Heil*. This in turn is
treated to a third scribbled reaction "Is this annotator a 'consymp'
or something?."

I suspect that Campbell would enjoy the way the battle continues
to be joined in these other ages and other climes! But the reaction
probably reveals his intention. In the colloquial idiom he is "a
stirrer and a mixer," delighting in provocation, deliberately affect-
ing the extreme position while knowing all the time that extremes
are absurd. It is for this reason that he is able to contradict himself
without any sense that great certainties have been challenged. The
vehemence in a sense becomes a substantial part of the statement,
as it was so obviously part of Campbell. Since the actual details of
the events of Campbell's life have been largely described in the
opening section, I shall concentrate upon the evidence of political
thinking and psychological attitudes exposed by *Broken Record*. It
is only this approach that justifies a separate study of this volume.

Campbell begins with the assertion, found also in George Orwell,
that "Humanity can be divided into two classes; the Quixotes and
the Sanchos." He proudly affirms, "I belong emphatically to the
former." (*BR*, 10). For him the Sanchos are the apathetic, lazy,
cheerful, accepting, ordinary men, the "Charlies," so one can imagine why he would feel this so strongly. Both the tone and the
authority of this assertion can be anticipated as can equally the excess of feeling that generates this reaction: "To live one must
always be intoxicated with love, with poetry, with hate, with laughter, with wine—it doesn't matter which." (*BR*, 10). More
significantly for this whole book, he openly and engagingly
remarks:

I am so passionate a spectator of action that I have often found myself taking part in things which do not come in the way of most other poets, and a series of disjointed romantic adventures have been the result, some of which project into my imagination, but for that I can make no excuse, as my memory and my imagination work as one. (*BR*, 11).

We have been warned. Yet, of course, at one level this does not matter. All autobiography is virtually a story based upon the selection and interpretation of the events of life; perhaps only biography can begin to set up truth as an expressed aim. The selective and explanatory process in a person's own perception of himself is inescapable, perhaps even desirable. The revelation of a man, after all, comes from what he considers to be the truth, as much as what the outsider chooses to claim are the scientific and measurable facts of his life. Autobiography is man without the psychological explications that question all motives.

Campbell begins by telling of his grandfather William and the distinction of his doctor father. There is obvious strong admiration and affection even to the point of insisting on an intellectual closeness which seems unlikely. The fact, for example, that in 1906 his father published *The Blister*, "the first political satire published in Natal," is made occasion for hailing the work as "the predecessor of my *Wayzgoose*." (*BR*, 18). In describing his childhood in Durban, another aspect of his vision that was to influence strongly his subsequent career was his observation of color. Again and again one has to remark, in commentary on his poems, on the impressive sense of visual color, the impact of dazzling polychromatic words upon the reader's eye. This obviously derives from Africa, where the virulence and variety of color in plants and vegetation is in such exotic contrast to the mild understated green freshness of an English scene. Campbell recalls how this reaction was generated by his surroundings when he was young: "If Natal has one glory, it is in its great flowering trees that burn throughout the year, each one springing out of the ashes of the other." (*BR*, 79). It is this awareness of the flowers of his environment that apparently, though to the reader most obviously, inspired the brilliance of color of his lines:

If there is anything that makes me rejoice, it is the colour scarlet. I am writing with a red pen, on white paper and find it very pleasant. In all my poems there is plenty of red ink and my wife is nearly always in scarlet. My

vision was partly trained by these magnificent explosions of colour and the
long avenues of flamboyants. Africa is, I suppose, the most skillful engineer
of physical beauty. (*BR*, 79 - 80).

Soon one learns the complexities and conflicts within the man.
There is a direct truth in his remark, "If I feel myself enclosed in
any system, I break through it, but not unless. I am no reformer."
(*BR*, 21). But this has to be balanced against the apparently
paradoxical philosophy that "Military discipline is the only sort I
like or understand." This thought is continued in the more surprising remark: "A military life in peace-time is admirable for a
poet; it has all the leisure for meditation and true comradeship of
the monastic life without celibacy." (*BR*, 22). It is an intriguing interpretation and one that seems to meet Campbell's needs at least.

There is the story of his cargo ship voyage to England on the S.S.
Inkonka, and the charming anecdote of his donkey ride arrival in
state into London on his way to visit his family in Scotland. Of Oxford there is the admiration of Thomas Earp and the meeting with
several now well-known names: "Each has acquired some sort of
fame or notoriety since then." When he goes to visit Paris the prejudices, always close to the surface, drift up and are declaimed. "In
Paris even at that time there were negroes by the dozen, and their
paralytic shuffle and imbecile hypochondria was already getting a
hold on the whites of Western Europe. Montparnasse made me
sick." (*BR*, 41).

It is at this point that he articulates at its fullest extent his famous
hatred of Charlie Chaplin. It is a curiously improbable vehemence
at one level, and yet it would have been readily possible to anticipate Campbell's reaction. It is not only Chaplin's Jewishness
which charged Campbell's general anti-Semitism, but also the way
that Chaplin represented the whole concept of the "little man."
Campbell preferred to think in terms of big men of heroic stature,
who are precisely the goad and butt of Chaplin's debunking humor.
In spite of all this explanation, Campbell's consistent scorn of the
"Charlies" still seems inappropriately posited on the actual films
displaying Chaplin's unique genius.

That tragic symbol of the Decline of the West, Charlie, as he is so lovingly
called, had sneaked into the most august and sacred places and stood pick-
ing his nose in the middle of the Parthenon of Western culture. Anything
that savoured of conscious power, privilege, authority, was violently spat
upon and derided: the qualities that were within everybody's reach; nai-

veté, skittishness, naughtiness, and affection were exalted, as faith, enthusiasm, and reverence were debased. (*BR*, 43).

From this of course it is a relatively short step to admiration of the Fascist creeds that keeps such dangerous derision in its place. "Futurism"—a term he invents—"has triumphed in life."

We see it working in Fascism and Hitlerism ornamentally and efficiently. It affected two complete revolutions without bloodshed, untidiness, or dirt. Compared with workers' revolutions and their bloodshot frenzy, these two bourgeois revolutions indicate the infinite superiority of the bourgeois over workmen, from the point of view of humanity. . . . (*BR*, 43).

At the present time, when fascism seems reduced to an abstract term to be hurled at extreme members of the Republican party, it is Campbell's comments upon race that seem the most objectionable to the contemporary ear, though in a measured context they would be no more eccentric and unreasonable than his remarks concerning politics—or Rugby football: "The abolition of the slave trade, of course, aggravated trouble, and put an end to a perfectly natural relationship between the races. . . . One might as well abolish parenthood because some parents are cruel." (*BR*, 57). Other themes constant in Campbell's thought and writing are also present. There is the question of hunting; the vital relationship between animal and man, between hunter and hunted:

The administration of death to a beautiful animal is a sacred sort of rite. Only a few people should be allowed to hunt, and the priesthood of killers should be chosen from the most highly civilized and cultured people. . . . Nobody with a pot-belly or knock-knees should be allowed a licence to hunt. . . . The hunt is a highly intellectual and spiritual performance. . . . There can be only one law about hunting. Unless a part of the beauty one destroys passes into the spirit of the destroyer in adding to his skill, style, and delicacy, it is a mere waste of life. . . . There is a very strong bond in nature between the slayer and his victims. (*BR*, 69 - 70).

One other curious feature of Campbell's views which is advanced quite often is a dislike of dogs. This seems to be based on their fawning humble qualities which he transposed to men he disliked most ardently, but the odd view does lead him to such remarkable comments as: "I found them [the working classes] to be mostly treacherous; this probably accounts for the growing popularity of dogs in Europe, to make up for the lack of fidelity in servants." (*BR*, 74).

He later tells a fantastic tale of working in Cannes with a gang of
dog kidnappers. Since dogs invariably chased him, simply by walking by he was able to provide a good bag for the thieves. He did not
do more than act as a lure for the dogs, but this was hardly a moral
question: "It was not through any moral scruples that I took no part
in the theft. Dog stealing is an honourable profession, as would be
any form of persecution on these unworthy parasites on the human
family." (BR, 147). This extraordinary attitude is supported with
literary references; he even claims to find antecedents in
Shakespeare:"I share, I notice, with Shakespeare, who never mentions them [dogs] without dislike or as hunters." (BR, 75).

It is easy from remarks such as these to see why Campbell
stimulated such antagonism in the predominately liberal con-
sciences of the intellectuals at this time, especially when he took the
challenge more nearly home, remarking: "For some reason or other
all poets (nearly all poets come of the middle class) consider it their
duty to love workmen, and incite workmen to fight against their
own class; the more bourgeois they are, the more violent 'bolshies'
they become." (BR, 43 - 4). With some curious belief in cultural
time lag he feels that South Africa retains all that is most desirable
in the qualities of western culture, a culture which in Europe has
been surrendered by the "Charlies" and their attendant intellectuals because of their passive denial of that pure assertion of
strength that first forged its qualities: "There is nothing really to
prevent our country from being with South America, the last citadel
and tower of European culture, which we certainly possess and
treasure more than European intellectuals do themselves." (BR, 51).

In case a reader may be a little surprised at the connection between South America and South Africa other than the geographical
hemisphere, one has to recall that in *Taurine Provence* these are
residual "equestrian" nations. It is by the use of the horse—and the
relation to the bull perhaps—that nations show their spiritual
worth. Perhaps the standards are also based on race because "In
European South Africa, we are far less Negrofied than the modern
Europeans."

Other comments move from the outrageous to the deliberately
absurd. Consider the following remarks and their apparent medical
authority: "I don't believe in the spread of microbes to account for
any epidemic so much as in the moral predisposition of human
beings either to catch or reject these microbes; for the latter are
always there in the same quantity." (BR, 143). Such lunatic pon-

tification can even be found in the more debatable world of comparative politics:

> Anyone with the slightest historical sense can see that the dehumanization of Europe is contemporaneous with the currency of these words, "Humanity," "Liberty," "Rights," etc.; but whether they are the disease itself or merely a tardy and impotent remedy is not in question here. *BR*, 144).

There are also extreme religious generalizations including such amazing maxims as "Protestantism is a cowardly sort of atheism," (*BR*, 157), and it must be blamed because "It has even betrayed great minds like Milton's. . . . [Reading *Comus*] makes one regret the wreck of the Armada and the loss of the Inquisition." (*BR*, 157). He has remarks of equal pungency on the subject of women's liberation and the nature of conjugal rights. They are actually rather invigorating: it does not hurt to have one's adrenal glands thoroughly stimulated!

All of these attitudes are linked by one characteristic, and they are specifically aimed at marking his distinction from the people with whom he was forced to mix in England. He was most aware of his differences, and he undoubtedly generated a considerable number of the poses by which he established his deliberate differentiation:

> I speak as "us" only as English critics classify me, since I don't belong either to their time or way of thinking. My ancestors cleared out of Britain at the first whiff of the nineteenth and twentieth centuries, and I only came back to see what made them clear off in such a hurry, which I soon found out. (*BR*, 155).

The indication of underlying attitude is clear, for in comparing himself with the intelligent detachment and gentle calm of William Plomer he remarks, "I always fly off the deep end trying to amuse, startle, impress, charm, or annoy a person."

This determination to provoke is demonstrably what has inspired *Broken Record*. When this is recognized, it is a more amiable and engaging book than one might imagine if one merely selects some of the more wanton comments and erects upon them a philosophy far more politically consistent and therefore more socially frightening than Campbell ever intended. In his own provocative and apparently friendly manner, he is entirely preoccupied with one underlying vision; and I am not sure that one can find it too wrong: the vision that not the meek but the mediocre are beginning to inherit the earth. This possibility offends every belief he has, shatters the sensibility that sees decisiveness and spiritual strength as the great virtues through which man can exert his potential. For this reason, in spite of the shocks along the way, one almost begins to find his views acceptable at the summing up.

Impossible as it must sound, unless the whole range of Campbell's existence is taken into consideration, there is an underlying integrity and simple dignity that the verbal follies will not quite destroy. His support for fascism and his cruel despising of the industrial workers are disgusting, but is there not some part of his vision that is true? Granted that his interpretation of men's potential is, in its physical activism, simplistic, crude, naive, antiintellectual—choose your terms of abuse as you will—but is there not some element that must be admitted, in that last desperate distillation of truth? Even if we despise much of Campbell's judgment, can it be said that what he deplores, the shuffling in the street, the dreary Main Street apathy of consumption based on materialism, is ideal either? Is not this in essence what Campbell draws our attention to? That there have to be alternatives to the conforming and adjusting man if the free and distinctive spirit of mankind is to survive, is a valid enough belief and would certainly be supported by Campbell. If one extracts this general philosophy from his lines, is Campbell not saying much that the left-wing and intellectual antagonists he hated like Orwell, Spender, and Huxley were saying repeatedly themselves? They all saw the degrading threat of uniformity and the mass man although they detected the danger from opposite quarters.

In this book Campbell chooses to end on a quieter and less challenging note. There is the deliberate understated modesty of a view that is none the less immensely true: "As an artist my only use, if any, is to have added a few solar colours to contemporary verse. An enemy of my epoch and time, because I belong to an older, more cultured one." (*BR*, 199). After that he deliberately goes on to define his rationalistic, simplistic creed, I doubt that even his enemies could find his assertion dishonest: "My moral code is the simplest I have met with; never forget a good turn or an injury; and I can recommend it to everybody." (*BR*, 206). After that pedestrian but fine honesty the last lines of *Broken Record* ring with false rhetoric, exotic but merely declamatory:

Shine on you horsemen, holy and divine wheel of swords! And strike as you have already with your azure sword and your golden one, strike the creeping pusillanimous, ridiculous, fiddling black-beetle who tried to abuse them. Singe off his moustaches, sun-strike him through his bowler, increase the paralysis of his shuffle, and crack him through. . . . (*BR*, 208).

This is perhaps Campbell's underlying ambition, yet it is, like the terms he uses of the "Charlies," ridiculous and pusillanimous. There is much in Campbell that makes these terms appropriate for deploring many of the declarations he insists are his considered views and philosophy. But against this provocative stuff must be set what we know of the man and what we can read of his verse. It then becomes very clear that there is posing and that a deliberate affront is intended. He says quite openly: " 'Shocking the Bourgeois' is the silliest thing that we do. I have always preferred to shock the shocker of the bourgeois." (*BR*, 48). He is undoubtedly doing just that in *Broken Record*. The intention is simultaneously a calculated irritation but also an explication of the causation of a work such as this, which is obviously conceived as a deliberate attempt to annoy everybody. In so doing it becomes a further illumination of the strangely virulent, cussed yet impressive, character of Roy Campbell.

CHAPTER 6

Spain and the War: Flowering Rifle

I Mithraic Emblems

CAMPBELL'S 1936 collection called *Mithraic Emblems*[1] was a more extensive and calculated collection of verse than his previous volume *Flowering Reeds*. As indicated earlier, the latter contains one or two impressive and effective poems, but it was a somewhat casual and motley collection of poems that happened to be on hand. There was no overriding theme which justified its gathering more than the accumulation of some dispersed poems. *Mithraic Emblems* has a few poems that might equally be so regarded as a garnering, but it is possible to perceive and pursue more specific lines of writing in the 1936 work. Thematic associations are clearly established significantly linking his Catholicism with his continuing acceptance of the mythic belief of bullfighting.

Throughout the *Collected Poems* the individual poems are divided in two ways. One can conveniently approach this volume of verse through this division between lyrical and satirical poetry, also used for the divisions of *Adamastor*. One may reasonably question the accuracy of the distinctions. One wonders why *Veld Eclogue* or *The Theology of Bongwi* should be considered lyrical rather than satirical, and certain of the longer poems relegated to the satirical section do not exactly maintain that tone throughout their length. But it is a division that Campbell chooses to make, and provides one way in which to look at themes in *Mithraic Emblems*. Similarly, in this collection one might question why *Toril* and perhaps even *The Sling* are not satiric and *A Good Resolution* should be so, but these are quibbles and perhaps demonstrate the difficulty of organizing poems in any such manner. However, in *Mithraic Emblems* there are two other specific sections within the collection which allow the critic to study works grouped around a single theme. First, there are the title series which discuss the significance of Mithras in a long series of quasi-sonnets called *Mithraic Frieze*. Here Campbell's attraction to the bull mythology, the taurine theology, if you will, is debated in a series of poems. The fourth group are those poems which are concerned with the Spanish Civil War which broke out in 1936. They are not in fact identified by a particular title but their affiliation is clear from their subject matter.

A Lyric Poems

One might begin best with consideration of the lyric poems, for here one would anticipate the closest connection with the *Adamastor* poems and so be able to argue for a consistency of intention or technical development. There is still open evidence of Campbell's continuing use of the stylistic devices employed in *Adamastor*. Yet in spite of the similarity there begins to be a much more intrusive philosophical note in the present collection. Even these lyric poems carry their charge of message—a message which was less a question of political identification than an increasingly open affirmation of Campbell's personal belief and intellectual development. Comment upon the qualities of his lyricism would be to some extent a repetition of the remarks about similar poems collected in *Adamastor* and *Flowering Reeds*, so one may concentrate rather on change, the newer qualities that are now so apparent. "The Dead Torero" is compassionate without excessive sentimentality, and "Dedication of a Tree" contains the classic Campbell tone, especially in its last lines. "And burns more sunlight in a single song / Than they can store against the winter snows." (*CP*, 146).

In many other poems, there is more debate than image; evidence of increasing acerbity moving from description to explication and exemplified by the longer poem "The Sling." The poem's title is indicative of Campbell's sense not only of weapons, but of simple, early, humanoid weapons. Through its lines the personal presence of the man is strongly induced. There is the memory of Africa retained in the lines:

> Its tightened thong would jerk me to control,
> And never let the solar memory set
> Of those blue highlands which are Eden yet. (*CP*, 129).

"The Sling" becomes the symbol of a choice of the options for living, the basic apparatus by which man establishes mastery of the
animals, but not at the level of technology represented by the gun,
for the technological power of that weapon forfeits the hunter's individualism. ".The Sling" is also a talisman and so becomes a
measure by which the poet judges all other circumstances. Echoing
the prescient and pessimistic vision of the lines of Wilfred Owen,
"none will break ranks, though nations trek from progress,"
Campbell observes:

> Where none break ranks though down the whole race treks,
> It taught me how to separate, and choose;
> The uniform they ordered, to refuse—
> The hornrimmed eyes and ringworm round their necks. . . . (CP, 129).

"It" of course is again the talisman of the sling which permits judgment. It is typical that the uniform he refuses to wear should turn
out to be that insignia of mediocrity and conventionality, horn-
rimmed glasses.

This is a theme developed to classic extent in another verse,
where repudiation of the shabby and meretricious standards of daily
life is not only total, but done with bitterness and contempt for
those who find such living adequate:

> When stranded on these unfamiliar feet
> Without a horse, and in the Stranger's land,
> Like any tamest Redneck to your hand,
> I shuffled with the Charlies in the street
> Forgetting I was born a Centaur's foal;
> When like the rest, I would have sawn my soul
> Short at the waist, where man mount should meet— (CP, 128).

Here is the vision of Campbell, reduced in London from the fabled
horseman, the free Cossack, to shuffling with the red-necks, a term
which in South Africa is a fairly pungent condemnation of the
English. Besides the emphasis on that fundamental relationship
between man and the horse between his legs, upon which Campbell
loved to enlarge, there is also the indication that cutting off at the
waist removes that crucial part of the man which feels the passions
that counter the cerebral restraint of those shuffling Charlies.
Toward the end there is another revealing aspect, even less tied to
the circumstances of the poem and therefore the more clearly per-

sonal. Two sentiments can be conveniently isolated: "That my worst fortune was to serve me right" and "self-pity is the ordure of the spirit." (*CP*, 129).

To be fair to Campbell, whatever other attitude he took, self-pity was never his tone; anger and antagonism was a more common response to attacks upon his nature, but that particular ordure that marks despair was never his. The slightly more rhetorical assertion of the later rhymes are equally significant: "It taught me that the world is not for Use; / But is, to each, the fruit of his desire—." It is a simple account of the philosophy by which Campbell lived, and as he continues, with strength a little undermined by a hint of defiance, he states: "For him whose teeth can crack the bitter rind— / Still to his past the future will reply." (*CP*, 130). It is typical of his handling of extended images that the rind refers to that fruit metaphor stretching three full stanzas back, but the meaning of the lines is clear enough without that association. The exact language of those teeth penetrating the sour pith stands as a poetic revelation against the mere rhetoric of the last lines, which have a flippancy both false and a little vulgar—typical of Campbell's lapses in taste that affect his judgment of appropriate language at crucial moments:

> Whose home's the Earth, and Everywhere his bed
> A sheepskin saddle to his seat or head,
> And Here and Now his permanent address. (*CP*, 130).

That last line clearly will not do for serious poetry. This is a pity, for there are some interesting and revealing lines in this poem that are deeply expressive of the personality. More than many poets it was the personality that was going to decide the force and direction of all his verse, for the line between writing and living was for Campbell never clearly demarked.

A very similar mood is apparent in the poem "To the Survivors." Though its statement is not readily located in time and place its play with the word "red" and the appeal to the cowboys of the Camargue may indicate the early recognition of the issues that would divide the forces during antagonism "when nations drowse." The last lines derive from these cowboys and assert association with the prowess that they represent, not so much in their exploits as in their attitudes. Campbell again exposes not a general philosophy but his individual feelings.

> Then, like Niagara set free,
> Ride on, you fine Commando: vain
> Were looking back, for all you'd see
> Were "Charlies" running for their train!
>
> For none save those are worthy birth
> Who neither life nor death will shun:
> And we plough deepest in the Earth
> Who ride nearest to the Sun. (*CP*, 136).

In the last lines, there is an unexpected hint of the sentiment of "The Serf," ploughing, in *Adamastor*, but it is undoubtedly mere coincidence. The other sentiments—the sneering and the "Charlies" (well to the rear one notes and hoping to attempt to catch up), the rider image, the man who embraces life and death in a heroism that accepts the threat of fate—these thoughts are the quintessence of Campbell's philosophy. It is later to be exaggerated, thus becoming easy to deride, but its potential excess does not make any less honest its fundamental expression.

In the poem "Faith," dedicated to his friend Wyndham Lewis, Campbell is again the horseman, surrounded this time by white egrets. The anticipated description of the birds' snowy beauty is now soon completed, for there are more intimate concerns that need to be discussed. The birds' feathers make him think instinctively of the quill and its demands:

> And from your slender quills
> Shed me a pen—
>
> That I may write
> All that from here I mark. . . . (*CP*, 139).

This vision that he chooses to "mark" is again of the "Charlies" and the antithetical vision of the world that dismays him. Those who will not face the threat of death that comes to the adventurous, those who count survival as the ultimate virtue, these are the men he deplores:

> For they'll survive
> Who from an offal-leap
> Can feed and thrive,
> Thanking their God for life. . . .

> To be a slave
> Content. (*CP*, 140).

This would be a despicable situation of content to Campbell, who never distinguished ease from apathy. He chose to see himself as part of a significantly superior race, since he exemplifies "The seeded spark / That in the few can spring." Such people represent, he asserts, creatures of "the fiercest appetite / for what we bring." It is a vision that shows at least impressive determination and was specifically designed to challenge those who did not share it.

Campbell adds in *Familiar Daemon* (challenging with a wry dig T. S. Eliot's jaundiced view of contemporary values): "Measuring out my life in flagons / (No coffee-spoon to skim the flood)." (*CP*, 141). If his life was to take on any element of indulgent wastage, it would be marked by the conviviality of Spanish wines and eager carousing, not Eliot's sensitive but ultimately boring life of the intelligentsia, measuring out their life in "coffee-spoons." His chief love, as he remarks, using a verb typical both for its unexpected force and its geographical origin, is "gasconading," "While every cripple's shouldered crutch / Was sighted at me like a gun." (*CP*, 141). In the latter lines the apparently shameless jab at the handicapped has a primarily symbolic association, for it suggests the physical self-destruction of the emotionally cautious, who are equally, in his estimation, the emotionally crippled.

The themes that are to generate into a comprehensive if scarcely coherent philosophy continue to be developed. There is the casual criticism of those "charred mechanic hells" that destroy the spirit of the horseman in "Vaquero to his Wife." There is the same repudiation of mediocrity in "Written in the Horse Truck," in which Campbell remarks:

> Though Life should prove a shunting train
> That rumbles on the wheels of ire, . . .
> There are few tears for us to wipe
> Who travel in the cheapest truck. . . . (*CP*, 148).

There is an intrusive note here of slightly glib phrases, like the sentences in plastic letters that make the platitudinous maxims outside a church or funeral home. For the moment I am less concerned with the adequacy of the tone than the obviousness of the sentiment and its significance as evidence of Campbell's attitudes. Nor is the poem, "Junction of Rails: Voice of the Steel" entirely successful, for it seems to play with the style W. H. Auden utilized to achieve the brash social realism which, it was assumed, ought to be characteristic of contemporary technology. The hint of jazz rhythm, used by Auden, is apparent from the opening of Campbell's lines, with their heavy, syncopated rhythm: "Cities of cinemas and lighted bars, / Smokers of tall bituminous cigars. . . ." (*CP*, 149). Against this despairing vision Campbell sets himself, challenging "this bleak mechanical display" and scorning "progress, the blue macadam of their dream." He despises "what hopes are theirs, what knowledge they forego / from day to day procrastinating woe." As is to be anticipated it is the legendary all-embracing figure of the cowboy (not, naturally enough, the American Marlboro vision) who will make humane restitution of feeling:

> And I have often thought by lonely sidings—
> What shepherd of what cowboy in his ridings
> Forges the Sword so terrible and bright
> That brings not peace, but fury of delight,
> And of whose coming I have had the tidings.
>
> They are the tidings of a world's relief: . . .
> The joy that veld and kopje thrice restored
> To that bleak wilderness the city horde—. (*CP*, 152).

It is South Africa (the nouns "veld" and "kopje" are indicative) that supplies that sustenance that will encounter and challenge the city's malaise, its "joy restored."

One other poem in this lyric collection touches upon the subject of Campbell's philosophy in a way that is obvious, perhaps to the point of being merely simplistic. It is called "Toril," and constitutes a rather contrived debate in the stable between the ox and the bull. The bull begins by describing his prowess and power in typically Campbell diction: "When through the rushes, burnished like its tide, / The lovely cirrus of my thews would slide. . . ." But the bull is preoccupied with the gloom of his inevitable death: "All now to be cut down, and soon to trail / A sledge of carrion at a horse's tail!" (*CP*, 146). The ox can be scorned for not having to face the imminence of this death, but although the ox is living an existence "confederate with pain" he knows that there are worse things than the bull's threatened death. The dialogue is flat and rather thin, but there is some conviction when it is attached to its source as representative of Campbell's vigorous belief:

Bull   But tell me what is blacker than this Death?
Ox   My impotence.
Bull   It was your soul that spoke!—
        More hideous than this martyrdom?
Ox   The yoke! (*CP*, 147).

It is a sentiment upon which Campbell couched his own vital life through his years in Africa and Europe.

B   *Mithraic Frieze*

It has been tempting to pursue the development of Campbell's personal attitudes in this collection of verse, but in so doing there is clear danger of unbalancing critical comment. The major part of this book is the important series of verses that, judged from the title, "Mithraic Frieze," were considered the most significant part of his present volume and make the opening segment of the book. "Mithraic Frieze" consists of a sequence of twenty-three quasi-sonnets. These poems have individually tight, yet not repeated technical structures. They each have the appropriate fourteen lines but each line has eight instead of ten beats, forming four rather than the usual five iambic feet of the common English sonnet. They have a tight and deliberate but not regularly repeated rhyme scheme and make only casual and irregular concession to the octet / sestet division of the common sonnet structure. Nevertheless, in spite of the lack of absolute conformity, either with each other or in comparison with some external structural model of the sonnet, these poems do give clear evidence of a closely and restrictively constructed form. This gives them a strong sense of cohesion and emphasizes the continuity of argument more than a series of varied, blank verse poems would do.

Campbell had long been fascinated with the worship of the bull god Mithras. This was obvious in his extraordinarily revealing study *Taurine Provence*. In describing this bull worship, Campbell was able to bring together his desire for an intense and simplistic sustaining theology: his admiration for the bullfights and the cowboys of the Camargue and his impassioned love for the geography of the regions of the Mediterranean out of which this worship sprung. The poems appear to have originated from a reading of some lines of the poet Mistral concerning the bull worship of the god Mithras. Campbell records some lines, translated into prose, which pose the following conundrum:

In the middle is a bull which a scorpion is about to sting in the belly: a dog also bites it: and a snake undulates at its feet. The bull, stronger than all, has held its own, till a man in a cape, a proud young man, crested with the bonnet of liberty, seizes it by the muzzle and stabs it. Above the dying beast a frightful raven flies. Let him divine the mystery who can! (*CP*, 115).

The poems that follow debate this mysterious question. Perhaps it is premature at this stage to acknowledge that there is no resolution of this conundrum to be elicited from Campbell's series of poems. In fact, it is not at all easy to discover any clearly defined theme in this series. As Harold Collins has remarked in his essay on Campbell, there is little in these verses that adds much information concerning either Campbell or the conundrum proposed. The first poem describes the ritual sacrifice of the bull upon "The Altar." The altar constitutes an association for Campbell with his life, for it is "the shrine / whereon, like flower-fed bulls, are slain / my years, exhaling in their pain / the lily's ghost." (*CP*, 116). The agony of the death serves "to praise His throne of silver fire." The relationship between death and devotion, between the agony of sacrifice and the self-destruction of worship, is made clear from the very beginning.

The second poem describes the power of the sun, for it represents the blue void of the sky to which the dying bull turns its anguished head from its immolation on the altar.

> . . . the stricken beast may view
> its final agony aspire
> to sun the broad aeolian blue—

The description of the sun's rich color is characteristically Campbell at his flashy best:

> . . . against the Bull designs
> the red veronicas of light:
> your cape a roaring gale of gold
> in furious auroras swirled,
> the scarlet of its outward fold
> is of a dawn beyond the world—
> a sky of intellectual fire. (*CP*, 116).

The metaphor Campbell has selected is doubly effective in being not just a palette of mixed colors but linked to an actual happening. The cape of the bullfighter, lined in contrasting colored silk, is swept into a fluid veronica of skillful movement. The bull is pierced by seven swords: "The seven swords that run it through." In order to link this to the sight of the sun Campbell asserts that each of these swords make one of the primary colors. The brilliance of the sun's color is apostrophized in the next poem "Illumination," perhaps a less successful poem, for the declamatory note is heavy and intrusive. There is an echo of G. M. Hopkins in lines such as these. They are hard to mouth successfully, for the resonance is excessive: "O hyacinthal star! whose shining / phasm to film, the flesh will glow. . . ." (*CP*, 117). Following this attempt come seven poems, each one dedicated to one of the seven swords. Combined they equal the perfection of whiteness, as when all the seven rainbow colors are spun on a wheel so that the ultimate visual whiteness is created:

> Of seven hues in white elision,
> the radii of your silver gyre,
> are the seven swords of vision . . .
> the spectrum of the poets' lyre
> whose unison becomes a white
> revolving disc of stainless fire. . . . (*CP*, 117).

Yet although each of the seven swords is identified, it cannot be said that their description adds much philosophically to the solution of the mystery that is the pretended occasion for the writing of these poems. The first is "of lunar crystal hewn" and the "clear spirits of the waveless sea / have steeped the second in their light," and "like moonbeams on a wintry sea / the third is sorrowful and pale." (*CP*, 118). "The flame of ice / the burning cold of death-dealing weapons" is repeatedly offered as a paradox of profundity. Life and death are juxtaposed as they are in the bullring—as they are at any moment where sacrifice is the measure of praise to the living god. In Campbell's simile:

> As arctic crystals that would shun,
> but each become, the living sun,
> where best his image may be sought. . . . (*CP*, 121).

The most characteristic poem is the sixth when the thought of steel blades leads him to thoughts of Toledo and immediately he is back to the significance of Spain and Castile, "of the mad West the sole redeemer."

The next three poems deal with the raven in the carving that Mistral describes. The raven is seen as threatening—"The flesh-devouring bird of time"—and yet the dark contour of his wings also recalls love:

> in those great wings of darkness flare—
> the blue flame that my lover's hair
> trawls like moonrise on the Rhone. . . . (*CP*, 121).

Because of this association with "raven-haired," which is not new in Campbell, the actual bird-raven cannot be as mysterious and apparently frightening a bird as the poem at the beginning of this series seems to require of its symbol. The raven (there seems no antecedent in folklore for this) is viewed by Campbell as a phoenix figure: "That fire is in the Raven's nest / and resurrection in the tomb."

The death of the bull should presumably be the apex of this poetic sequence, but somehow the thrustingly intrusive rhyme forms make the thought seem labored, as in a couplet such as: "As you may hear from one who drank / down on his knees beside the bank." (*CP*, 123). More satisfactory is the poem concerning the strangely symbolic attackers of the bull, "The Snake, the Scorpion, and the Dog." Here there is the more penetrating concept of the relation between ruler and parasite; between triumph and envy:

> Their ancient ruler to deride
> his earthly emanations spring
> like courtiers round a fallen king—(*CP*, 123).

In lines such as these there is appropriateness in both feeling and diction, but they are not sufficiently common. In the next poem the scene moves to "Dawn" with its condemnatory phrase: "Tug, monsters, at the badgered meat / out of whose needs yourselves were born. . . ." Against that savage thought the next poem, which goes on to "The Morning," seems little more than a conventional if pretty idyll: "The woods have caught the singing flame / in live bouquets of loveliest hue—" (*CP*, 124).

The sequence leads, by no particularly identifiable stages of thought, to references to St. John of the Cross. One begins to see how Campbell is linking this Mithraic death into a broader and more Christian view of the religious experience. It has been argued that in the Mediterranean the worship of Mithras was one of the most significant challenges to the increasing acceptance of Christian belief. Campbell now begins to try to bring them back together with his own dual interpretation. It is not the Mithraic screen but Campbell's own intense belief that has become the central element in the poetic explication. By the next poem, "The Meeting," there is a rather casual hint of the importance of this sequence, for Campbell talks of the rare delight of meeting with another rider in a moment of intimacy: "one wedded nimbus our two greetings." Nothing happens, but the contact has set the moment for intense sensitivity, declared in Campbell's beautiful words: "down from the cheeks of Dawn to stroke / and rosy feathers from the sky." (*CP*, 125). This sets the pace for the next two poems which are the actual declarations of the god, appropriately titled "Mithras Speaks." Problems of rhythm again make him offer appallingly unfelicitous phrases such as "We work for the same Boss." His message is one familiar to readers of Campbell: the appeal for action and response; the appreciation of beauty evidenced by reveling in its excess:

> Through the lush lilies as you crash
> and rein horizons in your hold,
> while, baying fire, the aloes splash
> your stirrups with their fangs of gold—(*CP*, 126).

It is a brilliant vision. From that point we are back to the invocations of "Sing Cowboy" and also the last appeal to the sun. The colors that represented the seven-sword rainbow bound into unified whiteness are separated again into their component elements. There is a sense of retraction: blue, green, gold, orange, purple "as Greco saw." This reversion acts as a means of tying off the visual implications of the sequence spectrum, but it does seem artificial and contrived. The poem does not quite work. This is a little unfortunate in that Campbell quite clearly intended a profound statement that would, in searching out the *Mithraic Emblem*, become a way of asserting his own united emblem of cowboy Christianity, linking Africa and Europe, man and his theology.

The whole collection says no more than is achieved in the single poem "The Sling" which expresses, with more urgent poetic tension, the symbols by which the poet counts his days and the threats with which the "Charlies" apathetically negate his priorities. It is probably not surprising that these poems do not entirely succeed. It often seems that the poems that Campbell most urgently wanted to make work are those that give evidence of strain and overtension. In the calm certainty of short pieces his skills do not get pushed by overintensity to the degree that they threaten to destroy the work and themselves. Campbell's more vehement lines are like a highly charged engine being forced to a speed more ferocious than it should be required to sustain. That sense is lost of easy movement and comfort that marks machine, or poetry, working with confident security, well within the confines of its competence and not at that dangerous periphery where the premonitions of disasters are openly apparent even when they do not actually and demonstrably occur.

C   Satiric Poems

There are ten satiric poems in *Mithraic Emblems*, rather longer than the clever quatrain epigrams in which Campbell couches his most acid pronouncements. Again they are very personal to the extent that Campbell's entire spirit—witty, malicious, and indignant—is contained within these verses. "Creeping Jesus" mercifully allows the character who provoked it to remain anonymous. The poem is a vicious attack on the model of some of Pope's more regrettably vituperative character assassinations. He is a person who

> . . . paid mere friendship with his good advice
> and swarmed with counsels as a cur with lice: . . .
> He'd blurt a secret (none so sure as he)
> By hiding it so hard that all could see.
> He'd make men black in everybody's eye—
> Taking their part, so stoutly to deny
> Things they had never done, nor none suspected. . .
> Until his stout defence was interjected! (*CP*, 270).

More general is another of Campbell's attacks on the English critics for their airs and affectations against his good simple assertiveness, a topic that preoccupied dozens of lines in *The Georgiad*. "To a Pommie Critic" begins:

> I cannot voice your hesitations,
> Your difficulties or your doubt?—
> The rictus of your affectations
> Would sprain my jaw and knock me out! (*CP*, 274).

Here is the blunt open soldier-poet who, in a more poetic mood, can expose his soul in "A Good Resolution," declaring:

> I will go stark: and let my meanings show
> Clear as a milk-white feather in a crow
> Or a black stallion on a field of snow. (*CP*, 273).

In "Testament of a Vaquero" he takes on the cowboy persona to declaim his special fortune:

> Thus, on his ancient gelding as he sat,
> From hungry guts ventriloquized alone—
> "At Oxford if I hadn't proved a fool
> (What tragedies my happy face forbids!)
> I'd be a Charlie sitting on a stool
> And teaching mathematics to the kids." (*CP*, 276).

That latter is apparently a disastrous fate if you share the prejudices of Roy Campbell. In "X. Y. Z."[2] he carries the argument forward to the point of establishing an open and averred philosophy. Love is to be measured by its violence:

> No love is worthy to be crowned
> Until its steel is proved,
> And some such monster bites the ground. . . . (*CP*, 275).

Beauty too has to expose the same tough vehemence if it is to be marked by the qualities that Campbell requires of it:

> For Beauty is, like nimble Wit,
> Heedless of causing hurt,
> Yet answers gratefully the bit,
> The rowel and the quirt.
>
> It must be branded like a steer
> And torried with the cape
> Lest in too tame an atmosphere
> It lose its sprightly shape. (*CP*, 275).

"Too tame an atmosphere": it was from this that Campbell continuously fled, feeling himself pursued by the nightmare vision of complacency, mediocrity, and dangerous ease.

These satiric poems then, like the lyric ones, are more revealing of Campbell's idiosyncratic beliefs than the earlier published verse. Campbell is always a close presence in his writing. It rarely takes long to establish the elements of his thought and attitude which are implicit, sometimes very openly so. In these lines there is no need even to probe the implications of the self-exposure. Campbell has decided to speak with open directness of reactions and emotions. What these poems may lack in purely poetic quality they make up in interest, by offering important revelations concerning Campbell's emotion at this crucial time when the issues of the Spanish Civil War were forcing to the attention of all the European intellectuals the realization that they were living under the shadow of an inevitable major confrontation with fascism.

The issue of this war, and Campbell's extraordinary reaction to it, will be discussed at considerable length in the treatment of *Flowering Rifle*. This was Campbell's major work of 1936 and concerns the war, its battles and its political allegiances. On the whole, as I hope I demonstrate convincingly, that is a very poor poem that should be allowed to die mercifully. It does little for Campbell's overall poetic reputation. Even its subject, and its echoes of the intense debates concerning Spain, seem strangely distant history across so many years, and a series of increasingly savage major wars.

D   *The War in Spain*

Campbell's war writing should not be judged only on so tedious and inferior a work as *Flowering Rifle*. Several brief lyrics in the *Mithraic Emblems* collection concern themselves with Spain. In their intensity and conviction they carry a certain poetic merit, no matter the questions that they too often propound concerning Campbell's taste and discrimination, or inevitable hesitations concerning his political attitudes. These poems are at least intensely felt—passionately so. If tending toward the melodramatic, they do avoid mere political harangue. In this 1936 collection seven poems specifically by their titles announce their concern with Spain; particularly with the city of Toledo; a place that became one of the emotive rallying cries during the Spanish Civil War.[3] Some of them are too dramatically declamatory to retain much of an impact, or more accurately, their impact is so hammer-heavy that it causes withdrawal on the part of a reader, who understandably refuses to be beaten into such polemic interpretation of events. Any honest concern with "The Alcazar Mined" cannot survive the ponderous and pompous language in which its praise is propounded.

> This Rock of Faith, the thunder-blasted—
> Eternity will hear it rise

With those who (Hell itself out-lasted)
Will lift it with them to the skies! (*CP*, 154).

In a similar way, "Christ in Uniform" discredits itself by the very journalistic title, let alone the quasi-reportage of: "Close at my side a girl and boy / Fell firing, in the doorway here. . . ." (*CP*, 154). Having set this scene, Campbell goes on to Christ, blood, valor, and fire. "The Fight" begins with a description of a "dog fight" between two planes. This was sufficiently novel to attract the attention of the poets of this war. Certain original reactions are matched in Campbell's vivid, even grandiose language: "The city seemed, above the far-off seas, / The crest and turret of a Jacob's dream. . . ." (*CP*, 156). Such vivid, poetic moments are lost in imprecations of "The Solar Christ" which "zoomed to the zenith."

One has to be very careful here not to be overly snide. It is all too easy to gaze with dispassion upon the intensity of the past; to question its validity from our supposedly objective view of history generated from hindsight. But we are not talking solely of historical validity. One can very defensibly say that these poems do not work as poems, regardless of their topic and intention. Their excess shows in the strained diction and the exaggerated metaphor. One can honestly challenge the technique of the verse as well as the sentimentality of the thought. But there are three poems which achieve a measure of success, where the language is no more intense than the emotion. Their lines blaze with that fervor that Campbell, perhaps alone of his contemporaries, can create, and sometimes control.

"Toledo, July 1936," "Hot Rifles," and "Posada" exemplify the essential qualities of Campbell and his writing and still have a real impact. Their true poetry can be winnowed from among the apparently excessive gush of emotional reaction and the equally exaggerated sense of political responsibility. Perhaps these three poems mark the very best examples of Campbell's strengths and weaknesses in his collection, and disturbingly enough both are found within single poems. As a critic reads Campbell—to generalize perhaps prematurely in this study—the perceptive reader has a vision of a man wobbling at the very edge of a gulf into which it appears at every moment he must fall; then, by some unimagineably acrobatic maneuver he somehow maintains balance, holds his position, and continues his movement forward. That crude metaphor suggests the way in which Campbell's poems constantly totter on the verge of disaster, that disaster being obviously excess, vulgarity, fanaticism—an exploitation of words that drives verse toward being mere flamboyant sound. Repeatedly, to the reader's amazement, sudden instinctive poetic brilliance draws success out of the apparently inescapable disaster of flatulent rhetoric. Of the three poems that one can admire, each exemplifies this near disaster redeemed by a confident counterstroke. The poems have lines of individual brilliance which, though cumulative in their quantity, do not necessarily intensify in their quality to the point where the impetus of the individual metaphors create that final authoritative statement from which a reader's conviction of the validity of the verse must essentially derive. But elements of each speak with a fervor that comes very close to being totally convincing as poetry:

> Toledo, when I saw you die
> And heard the roof of Carmel crash,
> A spread-winged phoenix from its ash
> The Cross remained against the sky!
> With horns of flame and haggard eye
> The mountain vomited with blood,
> A thousand corpses down the flood
> Were rolled gesticulating by,
> And high above the roaring shells
> I heard the silence of your bells
> Who've left these broken stones behind
> Above the years to make your home,
> And burn, with Athens and with Rome,
> A sacred city of the mind. (*CP*, 153).

The first direct manifesto, has power to move: "Toledo, when I saw you die." After that there is a dubious hysteria. The mountain "vomiting" blood and those thousand corpses which "rolled gesticulating by" occasion a regrettable but grotesque grin in the reader who bothers to visualize the actual scene. Yet after all the noisy activity, Campbell begins to tie the poem together. It is not done with entire success, perhaps, but the note of quiet authority of "I heard the silence of your bells" is impressive when set against that fussy activity both literal and poetic in the previous lines. The carefully devised line-break of "And burn," which is effectively rhetorical without being mere rhetoric, leads one to the last line which is straight and tight, linking back to the direct expression of the opening statement. "Toledo, July 1936" is a poem flawed indeed technically and emotionally, but worthy of consideration: intensely felt and sharply expressed.

The reader's reaction to "Hot Rifle" is likely to be very nearly the same. All that movie bravado of rifles too hot to hold is hard to stomach. But again, when the poem is degenerating under him in a plethora of sentiment and swaggering declamation, Campbell draws it together once more with remarkable skill, with that hard, cold, effective image of the rifle: "And the moon held the river's gleam / Like a long rifle to its cheek." (*CP*, 153). It is an image which links, through an effective pictorial vision, the long gunmetal light of water under the moon to the actual rifle's steel blue barrel. Thus man and geography is set in that intense relationship out of which the poet wishes to establish the significance of the scene to man and, more significantly, the essence of Toledo in this geographic and historic context. Then comes the last quatrain. It has a power and authority which I find effective. I admit that the judgment is marginal enough that others might find it excessive. The question is probably to what extent one is prepared to allow intellectual standards to slip a little to achieve the impressive *frisson* occasioned by these powerfully declamatory lines. To allow such lines their momentum to include the reader's as well as Campbell's, I suspect they must be accepted at their verbal level and not pressed with too extreme a visual accuracy.

Perhaps it is "Posada" that is the best exemplar of the dual feeling that is inevitable for any critic who comes to grips with the admirable and yet maddening potential of Roy Campbell's poetry. Again, there is so much to excuse initially, that one almost wonders whether anything can be left for serious discussion. Yet again, and I will admit this is a personal estimate, somewhere within the contents of this poem Campbell brings it off; redeems excess by his sharp eye for the beauty of the landscape which he so devoutly loved. In this poem, the writing exposes concerns which have a strength and validity that finally dominate over the raw material of his scene which so often threaten to dictate to him the tone and quality of his writing.

> Outside, it froze. On rocky arms
> Sleeping face-upwards to the sun
> Lay Spain. Her golden hair was spun
> From sky to sky. Her mighty charms
> Breathed soft beneath her robe of farms

And gardens: while her snowy breasts,
Sierras white, with crimson crests,
Were stained with sunset. At the Inn,
A priest, a soldier, and a poet
(Fate-summoned, though they didn't know it)
Met there, a shining hour to win.
A song, a blessing, and a grin
Were melted in one cup of mirth,
The Eternal Triumvirs of Earth
Foresaw their golden age begin. (*CP*, 158).

There are obviously many things to apologize for in responding to this poem. Surely no one can seriously use the rhyme "poet" and "didn't know it" above the schoolboy level. That woman with her "snowy breasts" recalls one of the more abortive metaphors of "Trees." It is made no more agreeable by the perhaps too realistic extension of the metaphor into detail, there the shape of the mountains as "snowy breasts" is continued with the sun on its peaks whose "crimson crests" presumably refer to the anticipated pink nipples. At an intellectual level one is equally disturbed about that combination of "priest, soldier, and a poet," which draws together into rather dubious association a group representing all that was worst in the reactionary forces that plagued Spain. For some reason these natural questions do not entirely destroy this poem. There is the bare confidence of that flat, bland statement of the opening lines. Somehow the love and enthusiasm allows even the potentially overromantic image of ". . . golden hair. . . spun from sky to sky" to generate a visual power that is unexpected in its ability to resist the crudeness of those "mighty charms." Although one might again have concerns in retrospect about those "Eternal Triumvirs of Earth" because of one's rational experience and association with the conclusion of this particular philosophy, at the end, the poem wins the reader with its conviction and authority that no rational pre-judgments and qualifications can quite invalidate.

Questions must be raised concerning the Spanish poems as they must so often be levied against all that Campbell wrote—indeed all that Campbell was. That in spite of the qualifications and doubts there is certain justification for taking him seriously as a man and a writer, is the obvious assumption of this study. If there could be only criticism and condemnation there would be nothing but a record of that mixed thread of success and weakness, of tiresomeness and integrity, winding together to produce the fabric that makes a man and a poet. Campbell, for all his tiresome absurdities, was heroically and obviously both these things. There is verse in *Mithraic Emblems* which still unassailably proves the truth of that assertion.

II   Flowering Rifle

In 1936 the civil war broke out in Spain. Although its long-range significance can be minimized in retrospect from our present historical viewpoint, at the time it seemed of monumental importance in the history of Europe. The background of the war remains confused. It was not intended to be a civil war in its origin. It resulted from an attempted military coup engineered by right-wing army officers against a government, which, although legally elected, was introducing social reforms at a rate which endangered the status quo of the wealthy landowners. The government was not initially a Communist one; that came later in response to Russian military support; nevertheless its policies were clearly those of the socialist left. The army coup was intended and expected to be an overnight affair. There were to be simultaneous uprisings in each of the major urban centers, and General Franco was to be proclaimed overlord of the country under the weak king, Alfonso. It was anticipated that the government resistance to such a coup would be negligible.

In fact, and perhaps even to the long-range disadvantage of Spain, the steadfastness of the government's supporters, particularly the urban workers and to some extent the loyalty of the air force, prevented the coup from achieving immediate and decisive victory. Pitched battles broke out which finally attracted the attention of the other European powers. Support for both sides was offered and what had been hoped would prove an instantaneous insurrection became more than three long years of cruel and savage civil war, fought upon the Spanish soil with armies augmented by volunteers from other countries. The Germans and the Italians supporting Franco sent in their crack divisions using blitzkrieg devices, tanks and dive-bombing planes. The democracies, including America, nervously and halfheartedly supported the Spanish government through the device of "volunteers" in the legendary International Brigade. The elected Spanish government, seeking for more extensive support, became reluctantly more Communist as it discovered that all major assistance had to come from Stalin and the Russians.

What had started originally as a conflict of national policies became the arena in which the Communists fought the Fascists in an international cockpit, anticipating the battles in Russia in 1941 and 1942. The result was what the American Ambassador George Brennan was afterward to call, in a title of his book on the subject, *A Rehearsal for the Second World War*. During these violent, tragic years, Europe saw all the savagery of the new technological warfare that was to become a commonplace in World War II, the first bombing of cities, the machine-gunning of refugees, augmented by that extra viciousness that derives from embattled internecine political creeds. Concern for Spain and her people became lost in the violence of an ideological conflict.

It is not the purpose of the present author to review in any detail the events of this war. They have recently been recorded with exact and fascinating skill by the British historian Hugh Thomas in his book *The Spanish Civil War*, the first attempt at a dispassionate survey of this conflict. The facts, such as are ascertainable, are available to those who want to read them. We are now perhaps sufficiently distant from the polemical pamphlets of the period to begin to see this war in its historical context. It may be just this possibility of historical balance which hinders us now from understanding precisely the impassioned emotional reaction which Spain provoked during the 1930s. In an age which had seen the virtual destruction of a social system, the great 1929 economic crash lengthening out into the apparently irremediable depression years, it seemed not that the international economy was weakened but that an entire system was breaking down. It was this anxiety plus a very falsely idealized attitude toward Russia, based largely on ignorance, that gave many writers and intellectuals of the period the sense that the Communists had the solution for reconstructing a more equitable and more progressive world out of what appeared to be the debris of the end of the capitalist system.

The intellectuals almost to a man supported the Spanish government in its resistance to the Fascist-backed military coup. Many of them served in Spain; others simply recorded their emotional allegiance from abroad. Most of the major European writers, such as André Maurois, André Malraux, André Gide, Arthur Koestler, and Ignazio Silone, shared this sense of loyalty and identification with the Spanish government. These men joined with well-known English writers like Auden, Spender, and Orwell, and the legendary figure of Ernest Hemingway. They expressed in their writing a romanticized loyalty toward the Spanish government, a loyalty which has been investigated in a recent dual biography of great interest, a book which records the life of two minor poets who soldiered in Spain, Francis Cornford and Christopher Caldwell.

The English poets in particular wrote rather glamorous accounts of the heroics of the International Brigade's Spanish struggle. Spender, as a concerned humanitarian, came very close to echoing the note of the admired Wilfred Owen who had written his laments for the soldiers of World War I. Spender supported the government forces, but his sensitivity was affronted by the destruction of human sensibility rendered by the war. Auden, with his more aggressive, more historical reactions based on a somewhat closer identification with the left-wing political position, wrote his long epic poem, *Spain*, which still, in spite of its weaknesses which are more openly apparent now, retains a clarion power to move.

The right wing had more difficulty in finding its bard because to support Franco was, in clear manner, to support Mussolini and Hitler, and to do this in Europe, even in 1936, was to turn one's eye blindly to their already aggressive, vicious, and shameful governments. The Fascists in general had made very clear the position of the intellectual and the cultured in their society, by the burning of the books, the dismissal of idealists and intellectuals from their university positions, and their imprisonment or enforced exile.

There were writers who chose to remain aloof from the emotional demands of this war. Although condemned at the time, perhaps they are the major poets who do not now have to apologize for their excessively emotional reaction to these events. Two obvious writers who exhibited a dispassionate attitude were T. S. Eliot, with his detached statement of his high-church royalist principles, and W. B. Yeats, lost in his new mystic vision of history. These are at least spared the embarrassment that must come to Cecil Day Lewis who has had to face the perpetuation of an ardent line he wrote which has been so much quoted in ridicule: "Why do I, seeing a Red, feel small?" In fairness to Day Lewis one might recall that belief in the possibility that the Reds were capable of shaping a utopian future was not so patently absurd in 1936 as it seems at present. The Spanish Fascists, the Falange, had only one international bard to sing of their achievement, and that was the South African poet, Roy Campbell.

It is certainly clear why Roy Campbell would be sympathetic to the Fascist regime in Spain, and some of his reasons were not so illogical. To start with, he had become a Catholic, an ardent convert, and the right wing had the support of the Catholic church. Besides the political basis of the conflict, the Madrid government had not been neutral on religious issues. It was violently anticlerical in its assault upon the church. The government felt, with some justification, that the church, with its huge holdings of land, did after all represent a reactionary and mercenary force in the Spanish society. It stood against any social change which interfered with its prestigious position. Campbell writes, "From the very beginning my wife and I understood the real issues in Spain. There could be no compromise in this war between East and West, between Credulity and Faith." (*L*, 317). We also know enough about the development of Roy Campbell's rather simplistic political attitudes to see why he would feel a willingness to support a political creed which set store upon violence, action, work and, if necessary, oppression.

There is, at one level, a sense in which all South Africans, however much they attempt to be detached from their country's policies, do have a certain inherent fascism built into their very natures by the racial experience they derive from within their nation. Even the most moderate and benevolent tend to see the Africans as people who need to be "led." Roy Campbell had developed this attitude into a code of belief. He articulated regularly and deliberately the nature of his political credo. We can pick disturbing yet foolish assertions of his social theories almost at random from his autobiography.

Perhaps Campbell's ideas owed something to the education he received. His autobiography records a teacher whom he recalls as "the finest history master in the world." A man never given to understatement, Campbell insists that this Captain Blackmore "had a really great historical insight." Apparently he made the inaccurate and prejudiced comment, "The League of Nations will bring about the next war. It will be a place for the intrigues of International Masonry and it will probably center around Geneva or Amsterdam. The only good thing that came out of Geneva is the Rhone!" (*L*, 74). There are two comments to be made about the impact this remark had upon Campbell. The first is that Masons joined Jews and Communists in the pantheon of Roy Campbell's ardent hates. The second point is that the very phrase which his history teacher used is repeated verbatim, apparently as Campbell's own philosophy, in another of his books, *Taurine Provence*, in which he talks again of Geneva: "Geneva where peace-mongers sit and peace-makingly prepare the next war. Geneva is the birthplace of Calvin, the home of the 'League' of Nations, and of the silliest schools of psychoanalysis." Campbell goes on, "The only decent thing that ever came out of Geneva is the Rhone." (*TP*, 54). Obviously his teacher's remarks had struck deep into his mind, though who can say whether his teaching initiated or merely confirmed already existing prejudices in Campbell's politically naive thought.

If Campbell happened to fight on the Fascist side, it is certainly not because he had acquired any of the complex political philosophy that a profound understanding of fascism might entail. His beliefs are the result of oversimplifying all the complex issues of contemporary social economics. When he boasts that his grandfather was a working man, he remarks of himself, "I have twice been affiliated with trade union; I could never be a 'labourite.' The labourite is more preoccupied with loafing and striking than working." (*L*, 15). It is a tone that we have heard echoed often.

Campbell in later years came to resent increasingly this stigma of his fascism. He did, with some degree of legitimacy, point out that if he had fought for Franco, at least he had fought against Hitler and the Germans during World War II—a not-so-delicate cut at Auden! He also remarks truly upon the shallow employment of the word "fascist" as meaning anyone who does not agree with the speaker! "Anyone who was not pro-Red in the Spanish war automatically became a 'fascist.' " It is arguable that since obviously all the supporters of the Spanish government, although left-wing in their sympathy, were not Communist, by analogy not all of those people who intellectually chose to support the Franco government were of necessity Fascists. Campbell would reject such hairsplitting evasion. He continues his defense with typical vehemence and exaggeration.

Perhaps as more general evidence of his somewhat muddled political thinking, one might take his curious interpretations of African history in the South African Republic. To describe the explorations of his uncle, he talks of the Matabeles, a branch of the Zulu tribe, and describes the founder of the Matabeles, Mzilikazi, as being "reared in the Communist regime of Tchaka." This African kingdom goes back, of course, well prior to any of Karl Marx's theories. Not abashed, Campbell talks about "a Fascist Beast of Trotskyite in the role of a Tito," obviously trying to make curious and condemning analogies between the unseemly development of the Africans "who deserved their punishment" and the dangerous revolution of Russia, which equally could be accused of "exterminating and massacring thousands." His conclusion of this historical exercise is the remark, "The Zulus were subjected to Communism, which is supposed to be a modern phenomenon, 140 years ago."

The crude lack of competent political insight in remarks such as these may give us a clue to the basis for Campbell's reaction to the Spanish Civil War. Politically and historically, he is too naive to have a comprehensive position any more perhaps than Hemingway did. The basis for his support of fascism at this time derives from purely personal feelings. It was an instinctively emotional, not calculatedly intellectual response that decided his allegiance in Spain. In a sense he is an individualist, carrying individualism to such wild extremes that almost any form of controlled social organization seems anathema to him. If government interferes with his concept of individual man—hunting, riding, making the world between his two hands—it is an organization which, according to him, breaks the spirit of independence and the personal assertiveness of the human being. This explains why later he is just as capable of attacking German Fascists as he was of attacking Spanish Communists.

Such an interpretation at least gives his actions greater personal logical coherence even if they have no political validity and even if they were created out of emotional reaction. His change of sides was not the result of any intellectual conversion, unlike many 1930 Communist believers forced by unpalatable facts into agonized recantation; it resulted from the single objection to government control. When he denounces the Communist dictatorship, it is in fact for the same reason that he would decry any type of dictatorship, for in asserting their identity, he responds to the authoritarianism of both which he despises: "Inexperienced bookworms like Marx and Nietzsche imagined that by such simple expediencies as the elimination of the top dog or the underdog a desirable state of affairs could be attained. As put into practice by Lenin and Stalin the theories of Marx have filled with world with more pitiless top dogs. The theories of Nietzsche as put into practice by Hitler produced a far greater number of piteous and miserable underdogs than they were originally intended to eliminate." (L, 149)

If his reaction to dictatorship as an institution was superficial, he can feel more concern with the position of the poet under either of these regimes. In the larger historical context, Campbell saw things more clearly than the other poets. The idealized pictures of Communism which the fellow-traveling leftists of England in the 1930s wrote into their poetry could not have been written in a Communist country. The generous humanism of their writing would have had little place in Russia where, disbelieved by the liberals, the cruel 1936 purges were going on. There is a justice in his observant accuracy of interpretation when Campbell says, "The poets under Communism were confronted with the same choice: the choice between complete servility, suicide, execution, imprisonment and utter incomprehensibility. Incomprehensibility and servility won."

Campbell made virtually a fetish about being unservile, being completely free in his personal embattled existence. He despised incomprehensibility as style, repudiating the arcane abstractions of symbolism by avoiding them in his own work. It is not often easy to find much sympathy with Roy Campbell's intellectual attitudes. At this present point of history where there does seem to be a more rational balance between political extremes, we might find his assumptions more acceptable than the positions held by the extreme leftists of the time whose work, at least in the 1930s, seemed so much more sympathetic to the human position than Campbell's own. One might as well record at least some sense of identity with his thoughts.

Apart from all this religious and intellectual affiliation with Franco's cause, Campbell's actions were provoked by a deeper emotional commitment, by an intense love for Spain that came through his years of residence in the Iberian peninsula. It derived from the way in which that land permitted him, to some extent, to make a replica in Europe of the free African life which he had once found in Zululand. The life of a hunter, the life of a ·man with a horse between his legs, was what he managed to rediscover in Spain. This emotional connection, this sense of unity, is developed at length in his book *Taurine Provence* discussed earlier. Campbell's philosophy of man's relation to his world shows a spirit like that of Hemingway, but without his defensive and nihilist malaise.

In this discussion of Campbell's motives we have sought the reasonable explanation; but in all his moves there is one other element that must not be neglected, although naturally he is less likely to discuss this aspect in his autobiographical writings. There is in

Campbell's nature an element of what I think must be called cussedness—a determination to remain the odd man out. I have a feeling that if other people finally came round to his intellectual or political position, he would automatically change in order to maintain a degree of separatism in which his excessive preoccupation with individualism, the lone-man concept, could be retained. The previous chapter discussed at some length his reaction to the whole arty society of London. Campbell found it affected to despise and belittle him, and his anger flamed at the rejection even while he pretended to be above any feeling for this pretentious group. His attitude was made entirely clear in his denunciatory poem *The Georgiad*.

Even if Campbell had not been drawn toward the Franco side of the Spanish Civil War by the definable attitudes and connections observed earlier, he might have been driven to it simply because this was the side the others, his hated enemies, the Bloomsburyites were *not* on. The intellectuals of England, virtually to a man, seemed to believe in the humanistic honor of the Spanish government and to see the Franco revolution as an open challenge to western liberalism. The mysterious death of Garcia Lorca, the great poet of contemporary Spain, epitomized the dangers of the Fascist attitude, and became a popular rallying point for the intellectuals.

Campbell, glorifying in his separateness, in his aloneness, was able to go off to Spain and carry on his war. It was not only against the dictatorships represented by the left-wing government of Spain, but a continuation also of his war against the liberals, the Nancy-boys, the Bloomsburyites who had ridiculed him while he was in England. He writes, and perhaps one can detect a slightly hurt note among the apparent bravado:

I'm completely insensible to literary boycotts or unfair criticism either from bull fighting critics, South African political writers, or literary reviewers: things that would break the hearts of other writers only made me laugh! And I can defy public opinion even at its most frantic as in the case of the Spanish War or the Color Bar in South Africa, without turning a hair (*L*, 71).

This defiance of public opinion becomes, I suspect, an increasingly considerable part of the emotional drive in Campbell's life. It helps to explain the curious way in which he could understand Africa so well and yet be virtually racist: that he could fight for Franco in Spain and for the British side against Hitler, in every case feeling confidently above the accusations that were hurled at him.

The Campbells arrived in Barcelona just at the moment when the issues of Spanish politics were generating the controversies and tensions and violence which were to explode in the coup proper. Campbell takes time to describe what is wrong, for Krige, as a Calvinist, had not understood the advantages inherent in a society whose "people have not been amputated from the Church by force of tyrants like Henry VIII, or crooks like Calvin and Luther." Such a simple interpretation of the events of the Reformation is to be expected from Campbell. Unlike his friend Krige, Campbell himself needed no guidance! As soon as he got to Spain he saw, he says:

From the very beginning my wife and I understood the real issues in Spain. There could be no compromise in this war between the East and West, between Credulity and Faith, between irresponsible innovation and tradition, between emotions (disguised as Reason) and the intelligence. . . . Up till then we'd been vaguely and vacillatingly Anglo-Catholic; but now was the time to decide whether, by staying in the territorials, to remain half-apathetic to the great fight which was obviously approaching, or whether we should step into the front ranks of the Regular Army of Christ. (*L*, 317).

In his interpretation he can now see the horrors of the threatening forces of socialism.

Now all those veiled forces of socialism, the base self-seeking greed, which is at the bottom of all modern reform and egalitarianism, began to come to the top. Bombs went off every day, hurting or killing innocent people. Murders were committed in broad daylight. Discontent and hatred seethed everywhere. (*L*, 319).

He moved to Toledo which became one of the great emotive cities of this civil war, and for which he was to write more than one impassioned and moving poem. Toledo was the whole embodiment of the crusade for Christianity against communism, and "I felt it the minute I set foot in the city," he remarks. (*L*, 325). He was arrested and there is the usual bloodshed, violence, and final triumph, surely much exaggerated by the language in which Campbell records his activities. He tells of the famous incident where he fought off an entire clan who had come to repay him for an imagined slight against one of its members. He fights off the whole lot himself, goes to the doctor, and the doctor alas has no anesthetic in the house: "I told him, 'Sew it up without.' 'Anyone would think you are a Spaniard,' he said, as he finishes it off. 'So I am,' I replied, 'in my heart.' " (*L*, 338). This is just an example of the dualism in Campbell's nature.

He is absurdly posturing, and yet simultaneously underneath that pose he is inspired by a real intensity. This feeling is a very different kind of identifying ardor than the false philosophy which he pretends to live by; it is physically sincere rather than theatrical. He finally escapes, not through the aid of the embassy, but by using his own skills and not "caterwauling as Messrs. Koestler and Co. have since done!"

Here is a good occasion to insist yet again upon the extreme difficulty of separating legend from reality in the biographical details of Campbell's life. So little can be verified out of the enormous mixture of exaggerated assertions which he makes. One's natural instinct is to take his stories with a large grain of salt, to diminish his exaggeration by at least half. Some people have claimed that to believe five percent would be excessive, but often they themselves have reason for belittling Campbell's acts. It seems easiest to accept the outline of his existence by viewing the details and incidents with considerable skepticism as facts, but recognizing that the illumination the accounts throw upon Campbell's sense of his own importance is crucial to an understanding of his nature.

As a poet, Roy Campbell's most extensive reaction to the Spanish Civil War was his long, urgent poem, *Flowering Rifle*.[4] This is a lengthy and monotonous epic in rhyming couplets, a style which is at its best a difficult one and too readily becomes the most tedious of all technical poetic forms. *Flowering Rifle* is a poem which Campbell considered his masterpiece; yet it would be better for both his intellectual and his poetic reputation if it were mercifully burned or buried. There are a number of smaller, shorter poems on the Spanish Civil War in *Mithraic Emblems* which, with their own impassioned evocation, are still moving in their earnestness. Unfortunately, we cannot consider this period of Campbell's life without looking at the monstrous poem which exhibits all the worst of Campbell's fallacious, simplistic philosophies, and the most grotesque heaviness and crudity of his poetic technique. Neither theme nor style are leavened by real inspiration.

Ostensibly this poem is a description of the events of the Spanish Civil War, but it is in fact less historical description than a bitter harangue, a political polemic exposing Campbell's vision of a very two-dimensional world. His feeling is as partisan as the old cinema world of good guys and bad guys. His triumph and the success of Franco's troops are entwined, and every success is the source of a jeering scorn at the failures and incompetencies of the government forces. It is not from this poem that we shall gain any dispassionate view of this war; rather, we shall find only evidence of Campbell's spleen and anger and posturing. He sees the whole war in both the human and political terms. In human terms he claims that this war is the war between the "wowser" and the "man." The "wowser" term is accompanied by other abusive epithets of Campbell's: "Charlies," "Rednecks," all words of abuse he reserves for those who do not admire or display the simple strength of the brave fighter which is his human ideal. "Wowsers" not only includes the entire bourgeoisie but somehow manages to incorporate factory workers, intellectuals, and ultimately anybody who does not subscribe to Campbell's viewpoint of the world.

If this personal division in battle was obvious to Campbell, the political-religious one was equally clear to him:

> When on the plains "invincible" was hurled
> The Army of the Peoples of the World,
> The hoarse blaspheming of the godless horde
> Against the Cross and Crescent of the Lord. (*CP2*, 60).

For him it was a frenzied religious campaign. The whole battle is seen as Communist takeover which in truth it became, although historical truth records that the coup was organized by the rightist forces. He describes it:

> In Spain where Lenin thought his way clear[5]
> If anywhere within the human sphere
> Then communism should have triumphed here,
> For through the land for years, it mined and holed
> And trawled the gutters with its seines of gold:
> What was corruptible in all the land
> Was long ago pawn in Moscow's hand. (*CP2*, 178).

He sees communism in Spain at this time as a monstrous disease, a ravening beast that eats up the land, standing as it does for all that is reprehensible in Campbell's world view. He can put together, for example, the line "Slavery, equality, and death," insisting on the equation between equality and slavery. He describes the scene after the Communist takeover:

> And human beings sold worse than shame—
> Far other was to be the wonderous hour

That saw "the people" absolute in power.
But when there was no more to slay or rob
Of whom or what was alien to the mob,
Not all the loot of museums or banks
Could prop that drunken monster on its shanks. (*CP2*, 229).

He blames the industrial system and its attendent urban proletariat for this evil. It does not create the "men," those fine, simple,
honest gauchos whom he saw as the backbone of Spain:

It was the literate lounging class of Spain
That first conceived this Rabies of the brain.
The hardest workers, those that read the least,
Could still distinguish Beauty from the Beast.[6] (*CP2*, 148).

Campbell's final assertion is equally dogmatic: "And all I know is,
communists or germs, / He fares the best who never comes to
terms!" (*CP2*, 212). He is equally vehement in his impression of the
power of the church. He constantly talks of the thundering hammer
of the cross against the pernicious sickle. His opponents are, not
without justice, constantly accused of sacking and looting and rap-
ing in the churches and the convents: "To offal heaps, their
churches sacked or burned, / And some to stables, some to brothels
turned." (*CP2*, 198). The dedicated fervor of his Catholicism shows
itself in that Campbell is actually prepared to reexamine the entire
Reformation period. It seems a little unjust toward the Protestant
position to claim it derives from nothing better than Henry VIII's
lechery. Campbell asserts that it is an age of creeping Tartars in dis-
guise.

For centuries have still been forced to spin
To cover the lewd haunch of Ann Boleyn
And with smug incense to deodorize
Their pimping to a murderous cuckold's sin—
Which gave us first our famous unemployed. (*CP2*, 201).

There are of course numerous attacks upon the hierarchy of the
Church of England, most of whom showed humanitarian concern
for the problems of the Spanish government rather than support for
the Franco regime.

The war allowed Campbell to state most openly and clearly his
political philosophy. It can be seen in the introduction which he

wrote in 1938 to this version of *Flowering Rifle*. One notices the way in which his sneers at the British intellectuals; their concern, their humanity, their intellectual doubts are set off against his proud and easy arrogance: "In this book, naturally, I have still refused to wear the compulsory intellectual uniform of the British "Intelligentsia," however romantic it may seem of me to walk up-right instead of crawling about on all fours in the mental outfit of a moth-eaten beef-eater." (*CP2*, 137). And he continues:

Humanitarianism (their ruling passion) an ersatz substitute for charity in-variably sides where there is most room for sentimental self-indulgence in the filth or famine of others. It sides automatically with the dog against the man, the Jew against the Christian, the black against the white, the servant against the master, the criminal against the judge. It is suicidal form of moral perversion due to over-domestication, protestantism gone bad. (*CP2*, 138).

In the poem he sees himself in an absolutely opposed hierarchy to the liberal pinks, as he would have called them. He sees himself as part of the great triumvirate. In following lines, although he re-fers only to those he admires, clearly there is hope for a self-dentification, a sharing of beliefs and philosophies with these greats:

> But plenty follows still with sumptuous Feast,
> Earth's triumvirs her wise men of the East:
> The Soldier and the Prophet and the Priest.
> Though these are best on fiercest hardship bred
> The snow for blanket and the rock for bed—
> From them the rosy wine, the silver bread! (*CP2*, 177).

Campbell glories in his separateness, in his isolation, seeing himself as the lone single figure of heroism and honesty. His boasting reaches the final accusation.

> As for myself, I glory in my crime—
> Of English poets first in all my time
> To sock the bleary monster in my rhyme,
> At first in arms to face this Prince of Wowsers
> And drive the bullets through his baggy trousers,
> And now to bring, with his bug-eaten head,
> The tidings that Democracy is dead. (*CP2*, 226).

Typical lines alas. It is not only the absurd outrage that he chooses to glory in the death of democracy, but the fact that such an assertion is worded in the language of schoolboy abuse, of baggy trousers and bug-eaten head. There is a constant triviality which inevitably becomes the terminology for such an oversimplified vision of the world. That statement "of English poets first" is highly significant. It is not only a statement of the disastrous individualism which is driving Campbell's character and poetry toward this absurdity of disintegration, but also brings the beginnings of another subject which is constant throughout this long poem, his determination to attack the intellectuals.

The people he attacks can be divided into two groups. They are the contemporary intellectuals and writers of England and those thinkers who have done most to change the twentieth-century vision of the world, Marx, Freud, and Einstein. They have in common a Jewish background, and Campbell is violently and shamelessly anti-Semitic. With the English poet-intellectuals of course, he has been carrying on a lifetime battle, since he first came to London and felt himself rejected by their literary snobbery. He scorns them in general with his accusation against the false humility of intellectuals. In his introduction he scorns them in personal detail, calling them names and accusing each individually. His scornful and bitter nature was made very clear by *The Georgiad*. Now the old Georgian group of poets, of J. C. Squire, was largely forgotten, and a new young left-wing group of poets, sometimes called the Oxford group or more emotively the Pylon Poets, had grown up. It was these men whom Campbell attacked, Auden and Spender particularly. His enemy is in fact the whole group because, as I mentioned earlier, the concern of the intellectuals of England was almost uniformly with the Left. He accuses the whole country:

> In the fat snuggery of Auden, Spender,
> And others of the selfsame breed and gender,
> Who hold by guile the fort of English letters
> Against the triumph of their betters,
> Muzzle the truth and keep the Muse in fetters
> While our hoary sages with white hairs
> Must cringe to them, like waiters on the stairs,
> And few but Wyndham Lewis and myself,
> Disdain salaaming for their praise and pelf[7] (*CP2*, 143).

Only Campbell could be so absolutely sure who are the "betters" of English letters, and be so outraged that he is being kept from his natural destiny. Throughout the poem there are accusations and sneers against these poets, many of whom wrote very tender, moving accounts of the Spanish Civil War. The battle poems of Spender, the great assertive epic of Auden called *Spain*, simply are examples of the way that left-wing sympathies could also inspire verse. Politics aside, nothing in Campbell's poetry can equal those works.

Another poet who comes in for considerable derision is Cecil Day Lewis, whose unfortunate line "Why do I, seeing a Red, feel small?" is constantly referred to: "Day Lewis to the Communist 'feels small' / But nothing's made me feel so steep and tall." (*CP2*, 211). The other intellectuals are equally attacked: Herbert Read, Aldous Huxley, Cyril Joad, John Haldane. There are a series of examples of these abusive references that can be found in the couplets of this petulant poem.

> [his Huxley's, Joad's,
> And Haldanes] skillful in the ways of toads
> And axolotls, as they're helpless boobs
> Outside their world of microscopes and tubes. . . . (*CP2*, 210).

And:

> But Herbert Read
> And Huxley, too, with tender hearts that bleed
> For corpse-defiling Anarchists must plead.
> O world gone imbecile! each way one looks
> Humanitarians slobbering over crooks! (*CP2*, 155).

Finally, the economic principles of deficit spending conceived by John Maynard Keynes which perhaps did more than anything to restore normality during the depression after 1929, is dismissed with the casually simplistic lines: "And honesty can save more time and pains / Than all the theories of Maynard Keynes." (*CP2*, 185). In remarking on the absurdity of such comment one might admit that his remarks have a curious family identity with some letters to the editor published in newspapers in my own region even today!

Since Campbell is concerned with the Communist war in Spain, it is Karl Marx, of his hated trio, who comes in for the greatest abuse. Freud is blamed for the corruption of soul which allows men to be swayed by fallacious political theories. Einstein is less significant in the original poem than in the footnotes; they point out the way in which his theories produced atomic bombs which are ap-

parently the death of true wartime prowess, making war less a thing
of individual heroism than of a mass slaughter. Freud is the
pervert's Bible, and his link with Marx in the world vision of
Campbell is clear:

> As Marx the land, so Freud to blast the mind
> These creeping desert-makers were designed—
> The one by famine to subdue our stomachs,
> The one by formulas the mind to flummox,
> And both to blast our sense of bad and good,
> Reducing life to terms of sex and food. (*CP2*, 186).

He sees Europe preyed upon by this trio as it lay "Vomiting its
spawn of sharks to cough its soul in Einstein, Freud and Marx."
What links these men is the fact that they are Jewish. We know
Campbell's anti-Semitic attitude from the vicious statement he
made about the American contingent of the International Brigade,
the Abraham Lincoln brigade, crudely if wittily saying it was "More
Abraham than Lincoln." The League of Nations, that sadly inadequate attempt to create an international league between the wars, is
seen simply as part of the Jewish International Conspiracy. The
League is that "Sheeny club of Communists and Masons."
Campbell's view of the inspiration for the Communist philosophies
is equally simple:

> No wonder Marx and Lenin worked their New;
> From two old Sheenies harrassed as for their board
> And forced to break their stocking-treasured hoard,
> From time to time against their grudging will—
> That grudge arose that mighty world to fill,
> So easily in Godless men infected
> By any rancour.[8] (*CP2*, 222).

Campbell fights in his poem his urgent battles. He seeks to explain away the death of the great poet Lorca. He defends the savage
bombing of Guernica, the first major air attack in European history
which provoked that magnificent apocalyptic painting of Picasso,
Guernica. He sees nothing but death-dealing cowardice,
viciousness, and bestiality in his opponents, and nothing but flag-
waving heroism and military honor in his allies.

In general the style of *Flowering Rifle* matches the topic; there
can therefore be little subtlety and less distinction. The trouble with

the iambic line for a man who has little restraint is that there is so little control over its continuance. Once you find a rhyming couplet there seems no reason why you should not have another and another. The sentences stretch on. The first sentence, for example, goes on for fifty-two lines. Even there, after a blessed period, it continues with a "who," which syntactically is clearly connected to the preceding phrases, and then goes on for another fourteen lines. This makes for extremely difficult reading, particularly when one is inevitably antagonized by the falsity of the political and moral view which the poet is describing. There is so little restraint in the piling up of phrases. When he talks of "Victory's rainbow! sweetly to inform / The thunder of this harvest-bearing storm . . ." he describes that rainbow in a long series of repetitive images·

> A smile of beauty on the face of power,
> The kestrel moored beside the sailing tower,
> The star-beam anchored on the rushing spate,
> The flower upon the prison's stony gate. (*CP2*, 188),

and so on, and so on, line after line; precisely that syntactic pattern, precisely that rhythm, each line just another variant, as if the really synoptic image escaped him, and a pile of the next best images would achieve as effectively what the powerful impact of a single valid statement should have done.

Another device which also gets out of hand is his use of the extended metaphor. Wanting to talk of Marx's *Capital*, he thinks of Marx as burning the midnight oil. When he gets onto the subject of oil, it has a number of associations for him. He wishes to expand his feeling about it, and so the metaphor is not only extended but set off into a series of different directions. The development does not make a gradually increasing momentum within a single image but is rather a splitting of the one idea into a number of disparate elements which cannot be brought together again. He talks of:

> Torpedoing the Talmud-heavy bulk
> Marx' *Capital*, whose sodden hulk
> (The Apocalypse of hate-hysteric toil)
> Rainbows the waves with tons of midnight oil. (*CP2*, 185).

The rainbow color image obviously is suggested by the idea of an oil slick, a huge, a needless leap from "midnight oil," the conventional idiom. The poet is dispersing rather than concentrating his description by his metaphors. He continues with "Meaningless hieroglyphics, whose oily hues / Enough to brilliantine the world of Jews." Oil has become brilliantine, and this criticism stands upon the curiously British point of view that hair cream is somehow disgusting and European. By the next lines, his comments on oil have become attached to its flammable nature: "Or (as we've seen) to set the world on fire. / Exploded thus, and spilled upon its ire. . . ." (*CP2*, 185-6). Again the oil is seen in a different light, now the base for arson. This is a further continuance of the metaphor, but the connection between brilliantine and burning is a long stretch for a single metaphor to cover.

Occasionally Campbell's comparisons have even a certain easy wit which is alas most often lacking in this poem, although one knows Campbell's capacity in this direction from his little epigrams. He finds an oddly domestic imagery when he talks of the Communists:

> Whatever they would mend they botch the more,
> And aggravate as children scratch a sore:
> As women flog their brats to stop them crying
> To every thud a fiercer howl replying——— (*CP2*, 210).

It is a nice homely little joke which I am sure we have all seen. But such epigrams are too few, and those there are do not bear very detailed intellectual inspection. Whatever other accusations must be made against Campbell, he is not an incompetent man. He is a poet, though one being destroyed by his intellectual vision of the world. But the poet is there, and he shows himself occasionally, even in this poem. Although we may not like the attitudes the poem describes, its power of evocation is sometimes, though too rarely, extraordinarily successful.

There are two areas of poetry which seem to indicate some remaining measure of success in Campbell's writing. One is a rediscovery of the world of color, of beauty; that intensity that he recorded in South Africa, and to which he returned in Spain. These descriptions of the dazzling Spanish landscape are the clear voice of Campbell's immensely impassioned and individual vision.

> The charmed circles of delight she flings
> On every side, with flushed, auroral wings
> Whose spokes, at last, unite their myriad hue

> Till Sight, itself, the radiance must subdue
> To form this stainless aquiline of blue,
> The sky, that veils so rapturous a thing,
> Like sunlight through a passing eagle's wing.[9] (*CP2*, 254).

This fresh, gaudy vision so dazzlingly brilliant seems much closer to Campbell's heart than the political posturing he has chosen to adopt. The authentic voice is breaking through the cant. When he describes the battle march of the Spanish forces, his heroic line takes on a rhetoric of power almost Miltonic in its ponderous strength and urgency. One knows the curious way in which Milton can be so heavy and yet drive his lines on without a sense of their weight dragging at them, simultaneously exhibiting authoritative power, yet pressing forward relentlessly. Campbell, although having little in common with Milton, achieves something like this. The description of the advance of Franco's army has real authority no matter its political quality:

> Unfurled the splendid signal to advance
> When in the stars our sacred ensign shone
> And like a comet through the tempest trailing
> Her stormy hair, along the skyline sailing,
> With red and golden banner waved us on:
> While at the portent blazing over Spain,
> The Heavens seemed with blood and fire to rain,
> And at the sight, the foe, half-dead with fright,
> Fled howling in their Gadarene stampede. (*CP2*, 252).

It seems there has been too little to compliment Campbell upon in this poem. But I fear this is just the beginning of what we shall see of the gradual disintegration of Campbell's poetic skill under the batterings of a political philosophy which was not only sterile in itself, but invited him to demonstrate that shrill anger which had marked his years in London (to the great detriment of his poetry). His next longest poem about Spain, "A Letter from the San Mateo Front," published in his last volume of verse, *Talking Bronco*, can be categorized in exactly the same way as the longer *Flowering Rifle*.[10] There are the same heavy iambic couplets of the style, the same discovery of Communist plots among the English intellectuals to keep them from their admission of Campbell's poetic superiority. There is the same attack on political moderation. Perhaps the tone can be seen most clearly by the way he sets the salutes of right- and

left-wing parties as symbols of the antithesis of their political opposition. This is fairly childish stuff, but there can be no middle
ground in Campbell. He is apparently so fascinated by his discovery
that the device is repeated many times in lines such as the
following:

> And shows the Right hand is the hand of workers
> And the shut Left, of parasites and shirkers. (*FR*, 49).
>
> The fist-shut Left, so dexterous with the dirk,
> The striker, less in battle than from work. . . . (*FR*, 13).

And later, a similar concept: "Nor can a clenched left fist create or
fight / With the calm patience of the open Right." (*FR*, 15). And
yet again: "The Communists whose bungling Left we fight / With
this Right hand,—in every sense the Right!" (*FR*, 18). It is a completely two-dimensional world which allows no subtlety or consideration. These are of course scarecrow figures set up for his attack; the straw men are the liberal writers who apparently conceal
their true Communist affiliations under a guise of humanist sympathy: "From every communist you can unsheath / A snug-fat
"bourgeois" creeping underneath." (*FR*, 14). Against the so-called
"worker" poets, there is the not-unjust couplet: "Since of the
English poets on your shelf / The only sort of "Worker" is myself."
(*FR*, 18). And Campbell goes on to attack the whole ethic by which
these concerned and liberal men attempt to live. "For all their talk
of what is Right and Wrong / What matters most to them is—'Does
it Pong?' " (*FR*, 21). There are personalities to be bandied, attacks
on the Woolf's and the Huxley's and the snide comments of lines
like, "What Auden chants by Spender shall be wept," (*FR*, 20),
which, although acid, has a degree of sharp judgment in its dig at
Spender's excessive emotionality contrasted with Auden's cold
logic. But the attack on Herbert Read is nothing but trivial abuse.

> Till even such a chump as Herbert Read
> Woke up to it that things had gone to seed,
> And chose the next most mouldy thing he could
> That promised nits and jiggers in the wood. (*FR*, 20).

From this assertion of his own intellectual distinction and political
differentiation Campbell continues on to assert anew his poetic
separation and individuality:

> My verse a flaming lariat of Apollo
> See now like filings into its powerful magnet
> Like barbels grasping in its mighty drag-net
> Daring all likelihood of place or time
> To prove my sure trajectory in rhyme. (*FR*, 23).

Political spite, literary anger, and personal vindictiveness meld together into an attack that shows neither good sense, nor moderation, nor reason; Campbell's anger carries him on. There is perhaps a degree of prophetic understanding in his statement:

> And that is why I do not simper
> Nor sigh nor whine in my harangue,
> Instead of ending with a whimper
> My life will finish with a bang. (*CP*, 2, 26).

This was indeed so precisely and cruelly what it did.

When Campbell avoids the crude obviousness of politics, when he looks at the scene around him in this beautiful Iberian land he had come to love with the same excess of affection and enthusiasm which he had felt for Africa, then a note which we recognized in his African poems returns. It is a note that is brilliant, perhaps verging on the excessive, but an excess which is no more than is deserved by the vividness, the exoticism of the country that has inspired his lines. In the cold grey November of England's winter Campbell's description will seem grossly exaggerated or deliberately overflamboyant. In fact, his lines may be nothing less than an exact reflection of scenes which would create just that excess reaction in us if we observed them ourselves, without the intermediary vision imposed by Campbell's brilliant lines.

The thing that strikes the Britisher when he goes to Africa is its excess, the dazzle of its beauty, the almost unimaginable brilliance of color, of the birds, of the myriad of animals. There is so much to comprehend beyond the bland expectations of experience that it inevitably appears intellectually and emotionally indigestible. This is an important idea, because it suggests that when Campbell occasionally appears exaggerated in his descriptions, he may perhaps be more deliberate and accurate than can be recognized by those who have not witnessed the regions about which he writes.

In the turgid poetry of this long epic, however, rarely do you find examples of a successful merging of style and context. Too often the style supplies a shrill, vulgar overlay upon emotions which need restraint and constriction rather than further exaggeration. But for all its rarity, some valid poetry is not impossible to find. In *Flowering Rifle,* it is book five, the section dedicated to Edith Sitwell, which exemplifies his still valid poetic skill. In this section Campbell describes scenes in Spain in a style reminiscent of his early African poetry. The lines demonstrate his characteristic qualities at his vehement best: color terms, action verbs rather than static ones, and the whole concept of a sensual rainbow of description that is so successful just because the lines do not carry us into abstraction but remain locked in the individual vividness of the scene of which he talks.

Lines such as these, from the opening section of the fifth book, show Campbell's remaining qualities, as he plays with the verbalizing of his vision in a staggering virtuoso performance. At any moment among the cadenzas one thinks the technical skill will lapse into bathos; yet somehow the surging authority of his confident physical perception forces us to surge along with his own interpretation :

> The peaks salute the resurrected sun,
> Around whose miracle of death and birth
> Seraphic colours glorify the earth,
> While through the green of an ethereal lake
> To which the palest emeralds seem opaque,
> The trawling vapours, crimson, orange, gold
> Like cherubim their solar King unfold,
> While violent glooms in gorgeous ruin soar
> To surf in amber up the rosy shore. (*CP2*, 232).

Such successful moments are too few and too readily isolated from the total context of this poem to redeem its failure. *Flowering Rifle* remains a poem that exhibits the very worst of Campbell's political attitudes and personal antagonisms in a style that most monotonously sustains the dreary repetitions of its tedious theme. It is not a successful poem with flaws; it is a thoroughly bad poem. Like some old-time prospector a critic can pan through this crude ore for the occasional spark of gold that indicates the true talent and personal and poetic honesty Campbell once had. It is fair also to say that poems in this heroic couplet form can scarcely be imagined to succeed in contemporary times. Readers are perhaps too impatient for the quick dismissive effect, not appreciating the long build-up toward a labored attack. Nevertheless this work cannot be defended easily for either its philosophy or its form. Only its significant revelation of Campbell's personal and technical deterioration at this period in his life justifies the attention it must necessarily receive. Otherwise it would best be mercifully forgotten.

CHAPTER 7

London Years: Talking Bronco

I *Introduction*

WHEN World War II broke out in Europe after Hitler's dismissal of the French-British ultimatum over Poland, the Spanish Civil War had in fact not terminated. Nevertheless, the withdrawal of the Fascist troops of Mussolini and Hitler which had supported Franco, and the disintegration of the International Brigade in the face of the nervous concern of the antiinterventionist democratic governments of France and England signaled recognition that Franco was winning control of a large part of the country. His superior strength brought the termination of the Spanish Civil War into sight, although the last battles were not yet fought. At this time Roy Campbell left Spain, returned to England, and joined up with the British army.

In this way he was rather like Hemingway; the sort of man to whom any action was a lure, and he had no hesitation about volunteering for service. It is to his credit that there was never any question of his supporting Hitler. He was not likely to become an ideological traitor. Nor was he ever in any way involved with Oswald Moseley's British Fascist Party. This sustains the certainty that accusations of Fascism were personally as well as politically unjust. It would be almost not too cruel to say that Campbell was too naive to have any theoretical political philosophy. He could simply see that the very thing which he had hated in the Communist political philosophy, its egalitarian leveling down, was just as inevitably and discreditably present in Germany. A Fascist regime gave no more liberation to the type of human ardor which Campbell admired than did the Communist one. The Fascist creed might, on the face of it, have been more in harmony with his concepts, but in practice it created his anathema, a society of passive uninspired automatons. It was now clear that his support in Spain had been given not to a Fascist cause as such, but sympathetically to the supposed nobility and independence of the Spanish bull-rearing peasant fraternity, as opposed to the apathetic wage-slave proletariat in the industrialized Spanish cities.

In 1939, he joined an army regiment called the King's African Rifles. This regiment was normally recruited from the British colonies of East Africa, particularly Kenya. These flamboyantly dressed, exotic soldiers would obviously appeal to Roy Campbell, and they were his military associates throughout his wartime career. By an irony of contemporary politics, Campbell now found himself on what might roughly be called the "correct" side of the political fence, but the change of side had very little effect upon his behavior. In the poems which he wrote at the beginning of the war, he continues to express two particular themes consistently present in his earlier verse. Unchanged is the boasting arrogance, his vision of himself as the brave, simple soldier always attempting to assert that poetry arises only from the most violent of man's actions.

He also carries on his battle against the left-wing poets who had opposed him during the Spanish Civil War, taking a vicious delight in discovering that for all their toying with the battles in Spain, when it came to the real test of the war which they had talked of for so long, they did not in fact join in at all. Auden left England at that crucial period of September, 1939, and began his residence in the United States. Spender and Day Lewis joined the noncombatant defense forces and took no part in the fighting against fascism which had so provoked them in theory during the conflict in Spain where the Left and Right of politics appeared to be in embattled display. There are perfectly good personal and poetic reasons for their actions, and there is no intention in this present discussion to contrast the lives of other poets with Campbell's. Nevertheless, rightly or wrongly, their apparent defection from a much championed cause gave Campbell extra ammunition to attack these people he so thoroughly despised.

The tone may be seen in the little epigram, not actually a very good one, which he wrote in response to a headline in the daily paper which read "Wars Bring Good Times For Poets." The line was certainly a somewhat cryptic remark presumably intending to suggest the appeal of events to the poet's rhetoric. Campbell's answer is this:

> Lies! Let the Left-wing Muse on carrion prey
> To glut her sleek poltroons, the vulture's kin.
> My only pickings were a ranker's pay,
> With chevrons on my sleeve, and on my skin. (*CP2*, 72).

What this lacks, of course, in comparison with those earlier sardonic epigrams of his is their driving force. For once the rhyming couplet would no doubt have been a more effective format, and the verse would be more memorable if its iambics had been more resonantly regular. A reading aloud indicates its unusual lack of incisiveness.

As far as the development of Campbell's personality at this time is concerned, the most significant issue is his delight in his noncommissioned officer's status. He could not be a private; that would require the humiliation of kowtowing to authority. He would not be an officer; that would smack to him of the despised public school superiority associated with the establishment. He had to be a leader of men, and to be a leader of men one became a sergeant. This was precisely the rank which he set out to obtain, the role we could have diagnosed as fitting with his urgent feeling about his relationship to men, to war, to fighting. He glories in a particular type of rather rough resistance to established authority. A little poem, almost an epigram, called "Snapshot of Nairobi," written at this time when he was in the King's African Rifles, goes:

> With orange-peel the streets are strown
> And pips, beyond computing,
> On every shoulder save my own,
> That's fractured with saluting. (*CP2*, 282).

One notices how he effects to despise the officer class, indicated by the pun on "pips" (the British term for officers' star insignia), and how he scornfully suggests that rank is only achieved by fracturing a shoulder by saluting everyone; an interpretation which usually is put in much more vulgar terms in army parlance.

The poem which discusses most fully his feeling at this time about his life and his political ideas is called "Monologue." It is true that much of Campbell's writing is a kind of monologue, since he was never a man to allow much dialogue. But this one is more intimate by being less public and less rhetorical, although he still makes the same rather painful and pointless boasts. There is the same confidence in simple strength, the same accusations about other people. Others, he claims, avoid their responsibilities and profit from not undertaking their required duties in this war. He has remained true to his sense of personal allegiance. The opening lines indicate exactly, not necessarily what Campbell was but how he wished to appear. We all have our defenses, masks, to put forward to the world. In Campbell's case this particular "mask" is so common and so obvious that this is merely one further statement of the assertive vision that he always wished to demonstrate. Here are the opening lines:

> No disillusionment can gravel,
> A mercenary volunteer
> Who joins an alien force, to travel
> And fight, for fifty pounds a year.
> A grizzled sergeant of the pommies,
> A gaunt centurion of the wogs,
> Can fall for no Utopian promise
> The Bait of grasping demagogues. (*CP2*, 67).

The picture is of the firm, simple but strong man completing the duty for which he volunteered, in spite of his inadequate pay. He is not the prey of false idealism but shrewd and pragmatic, unlike those others, who avoided the challenge:

> The Left-Wing Prophet, Bard, and Seer,
> Sleek Babbits of the Age to be,
> Who farm this carnage from the rear
> Have yet to find a fly on me. (*CP2*, 67).

Like all professional soldiers, he has few illusions about this war. It is a curious fact that Campbell, just as many other poets, reserved his illusions for Spain. Somehow World War II did not allow for idealism and illusions in this sense. That war was a functional job, necessitating sacrifice—essential, grim, and hardly picturesque. When Campbell writes about this war, he writes more in the tone of the angry dissatisfaction of the poets of 1916 - 1917, closer to the verse of someone like Siegfried Sassoon than to the rhetorical glory he claimed to find in Spain. It has a straightforward anger, reminiscent of Day Lewis' comment that he was required to "defend the bad against the worse":

> I'm fighting for a funk hole-warren
> Of bureaucrats, who've come to stay,

> Because I'd rather, than the foreign
> Equivalent, it should be they.
> We all become the thing we fight
> Till differing solely in the palms
> And fists that semaphore (to Right
> Or Left) their imbecile salaams. (*CP2*, 68).

This seems to be a political advance in a sense: Campbell is now condemning the follies of ideologies meeting in battle, a folly which might have been just as grossly apparent in Spain. He even uses his well-worn Left and Right salute symbols again, but revealingly at this time both sides are condemned. It is a view that better fits in with his declarations about his attitude to politics and his denial of any Fascist ideology in his partisan support in Spain. There had been a very clear dichotomy between his assertion that he was not politically involved and the joy with which he celebrated only the defeats and hardships of the one side, and that, of course, the Left.

What may be happening is that his Catholic religion is becoming a more predominant motivation. In the continuation of the lines just quoted, he talks about his inability to distinguish between the extreme ideologies of Right and Left. Later he avers that when what he calls "the daft illusion fades / One thing remains intact, the Cross." Here it is theology not politics that decides a man's obligation. Seeing himself as a poor honest soldier of the ranks, he produces a statement that comes curiously close to the genuinely humane and seems particularly touching coming from the belligerent Campbell:

> I know that all ideals miscarry,
> That cowards use the blows we strike,
> That liars aim the guns we carry
> Screeching their hatred on the Mike. (*CP2*, 69).

Somehow that "Mike" is an unhappy word in this form, but except for that, these lines seem to be sophisticated. Their thought is carried by rhythm and rhyme which are very much a consequence and not an awkward adaptation to the diction. Could there be evidence here of a breakthrough, a possible change in Campbell's attitude, recognition coming through delusion? One would like to think so, but there is too little subsequent evidence of this. As we read through the other poems in this last volume, *Talking Bronco*, we rather see the same shrill note, the same petulance, the same personal, individual assaults.

The somewhat vindictive attacks are now particularly directed at Auden and his Oxford group of poets. When Campbell so violently battled against the neo-Georgian poets of the 1920s when he first came to England, his bitter satire was reserved for J. C. Squire and his etiolated bunch of minor countryside verse-makers. Curiously, although the Oxford group was conceived as a deliberate reaction against the earlier mode, that reversal was extreme enough that it still did not bring the accepted voice of the period any closer to Campbell's poetic and political attitudes. Again, Campbell finds he is unable to receive the appreciation which he considers his due. Again, he is unfashionable; and even now when history has changed so much he is not acknowledged as the poet of the age—a role he so desperately sought. It is certainly extraordinary how fashion can swing from one extreme to another politically and stylistically and yet leave Campbell, who never himself trod any cautious middle ground, still finding his own legitimate concepts of poetry neglected and scorned.

There are new poets now, and he indicates the direct continuance of his anathema: "Squire was the Auden of those days / And Shanks the Spender of our trade."[2] It is these poets who are stigmatized in such stanzas as:

> Like Left-wing Poets at the hint
> Of work, or danger, or the blitz,
> Or when they catch the deadly glint
> Of satire, sword play of the wits. . . . (*CP*, 282).

Equally objectionable are the new critics, who had as little appreciation for Campbell as any of the earlier litterateurs, for Campbell's verse fits no comfortable critical appreciation:

> Collective writers at my name grow raucous,
> And pedants raise aloud indignant cry
> Like the New Critics and the Kenyan caucus—
> Or poultry, when a falcon cruises by. (*CP2*, 113).

Occasionally in these later poems he remembers the beauty of the Spain which he loved so well. It appears in a poem called "Heart-break Camp" whose rhythm is heavy and unvaried, and its content includes a number of typically army-humor portraits of officers: Sir Dysentery Malaria and Lord Tremens (of the Drunks). But there is more than this mediocrity. When Campbell goes on in this poem, pensively, to talk of his memories of Spain, quite a different, more ardent, more tender note creeps into his verse. It is almost as if Campbell finds it impossible to write of Spain without being inspired, or if that is too strong a word, without being moved to an extra intensity and an extra feeling. He is never neutral about Spain any more than he was ever neutral about Africa. The verses which concern themselves with that country have the same old evocative, exotic appeal:

> Our vineyard and the terrace
> By the Tagus, they recall,
> With the Rose of the Sierras,
> Whom I love the best of all!
>
> My heart was once her campfire
> And burned for her alone,
> Fed with the thyme and sapphire
> The azure days had grown. (*CP2*, 71).

This looking backward was purely nostalgic, for it could give him little consolation now. Ahead lay a future which held little hope for someone of Campbell's beliefs and disposition. His vision is of terror: "The east is conquering the west / The future has a face to flee." (*CP2*, 75). Characteristically, he supports this powerfully apocalyptic vision with his opinionated political assertion that Yalta was another Munich. What is this future vision which he confronts with open despair? It is the whole world of welfare states, the whole structure of liberal socialist economics applied to human welfare in the debasing egalitarian way that appalled him. In the simple social terms of Campbell's ideology, such social organization only created men without ambition, without urgency, lost in the comforts and lack of responsibility that government handouts and welfare bring. He sees these changes in terms very close to those of the right-wing pamphlets which are occasionally circulated in this country. With the ironic title of "How It Works," he attempts another epigram:

> Salute the free Utopian State
> We fought for. Feed but do not look;
> For each free tuppence worth of Bait,
> They charge a dollar on the Hook! (*CP2*, 96).

Even in a welfare state, observes Campbell, "you don't get anything for nothing."

More grotesquely, he continues in a poem called "The Ancient Horsebreaker" (not printed in *Talking Bronco*) to separate his own view of life from those who exist within the security of a social welfare system:

> Incertitude my easy norm,
> Thought to Security conform
> A Nation whose Collective Denture
> Grins ghastly as the Barrier Reef:
> Each leaf is my Insurance Form
> That whirls before the rising storm.
> It is to Hazard and Adventure
> I go for Unemployed Relief. (*CP2*, 116).

A very obvious dichotomy is set up here: he wants "Incertitude," "Hazard," "Adventure"; others only ask "Unemployed Relief" and "Free Dentures." The capital letters add their touch of irony. For some curious reason the availability in England of free false teeth has provoked the largest amount of semicomic criticism of the welfare medical services.

In yet another little epigram he assaults the basis of Britain's welfare state, the Beveridge Plan. The generous social legislation initiated by the old statesman, Beveridge, now becomes reduced to this:

> Through land and sea supreme
> Without a rift or schism
> Roll on the Wowser's dream—
> Fascidemokshevism. (*CP2*, 283).

Even in this brief epigram there are many features of Campbell's attitude. "Wowser," which has appeared before, is a vision of the despicable man, the man without honor, without valor, without integrity. But we note where Campbell has now mounted his political opposition: he is embattled against a combination which includes fascism, democracy, and bolshevism, all in one absurd compendium word. To despise all political systems is the natural place that Campbell would reach, since he is so utterly individualist in all his attitudes. Nevertheless, it does not make for any responsible judgment to lump together all varieties of contemporary political structure into a single enemy that you can assault. If you attack everything in this way, you really attack nothing, because there is no positive against which you can measure your opposition. There can be no effective antagonism unless there is something against which you measure your dislike. If you despise fascism and bolshevism and democracy, then only anarchy, which Campbell would equally despise, is left.

Obviously, Campbell is wandering farther from any possibility of sober, considered belief, and his condemnations are responses to nothing more than a series of words which cause the same inexplicable emotional reaction as a national flag. Yet—and how often in commenting on Campbell's writing does such a balancing coordinate clause come at the point where one nears complete condemnation—for all the absurd exaggeration as a social philosophy, this vein in his own personal terms does carry a kind of quixotic grandeur. I believe in the Campbell of these next lines, for they only record the distinction of his actual life. I respect and admire him for this kind of assertion, which has the added honesty of being precisely the code by which he chooses to live:

> Rather than mechanized enslavement
> I'd crawl a cripple on the pavement
> Or die a beggar in the drains
> Of Barcelona or Madrid. (*CP2*, 117).

II *"Talking Bronco"*

The longest poem in this final collection of Campbell's work is the title poem "Talking Bronco." It is a very Campbell-like decision to use as his poetic persona the wild, untamed, independent horse. He is thus able to speak quite literally, if one will excuse the pun, from the horse's mouth. In this poem all the attitudes we have come to realize with some despair that Campbell has accommodated to himself are paraded for a last vindictive, spleenful, childish presentation. All the themes which one has deplored in his other poems are here; the anti-Semitism, the virulent anticommunism, the attack on the intellectuals, the assertion of simple physicality as a more valid way of life than cogitation. All these stands converge in yet another long series of sharply rhyming couplets.

The opening lines state the attitude: "In human history, and rightly so, / The Final Word is with the knock-out blow." (*CP2*, 84). Orwell, with much more compassion, made a similar assertion about the nature of history and the inherent violence of man when he described the horrifying nightmare of the future as "a jackboot stamping on a human face forever." The attitude is very different in

Campbell. He adds confidently that this is "rightly so." There are fewer generalizations in this poem; rather, it is a vindictive personal attack on those left-wing poets, Auden, Spender, Day Lewis, and MacNeice. To represent them he invents the great composite guy, MacSpaunday, and this caricature is assaulted with all the vehemence and schoolboy scatology of Campbell's nature. There are attacks like this:

> Quote to me any phrase you ever uttered
> Excepting on the side your bread was buttered,
> And cite one single case where you were found
> Save where the cash and comfort most abound,
> As a fifth column and a trojan horse
> In Left-wing ranks to neutralize the force
> Of Socialism. (*CP2*, 90).

He contrasts his own military record of which he is so defiantly and naively proud, saying,

> Then go and ask the Billy goat at Brecon
> Who broke the record of his I.T.C.
> With rifle, tommy gun and L.M.G.?
> And on the targets wrote his number, name,
> And unit with an autograph of flame? (*CP2*, 86).

He contrasts these impressive successes of his military training with an attack on those poets who had warned most sharply of rising Fascist power:

> While joint MacSpaunday shuns the very strife
> He barked for loudest, when mere words were rife,
> When to proclaim his proletarian loyalties
> Paid well, was safe, raked in the heavy royalties,
> And made the Mealy Mouth and Bulging Purse
> The hallmark of Contemporary verse. (*CP2*, 87).

There is very much more in this vein which it would be tedious to cite in detail. The accusations are that only conscription would bring them to fight, that every impassioned line they had written had been motivated by greed for money: "Where Briddish Intellectuals made their pile / And Book-Clubs flourished in prodigious style." (*CP2*, 88). He contrasts with their cowardice and failure his own proud valor:

> And now today I'm fighting for the Jew
> (Since Poles or Finns subsided out of view
> Though once the pretext for this war, it's true.) (*CP2*, 93).

There remains some poignancy at that interpolated ironic comment on the Allies' war aims. The two countries for which the war was declared both received no support during the awkward bargainings of the 1945 peace conference. Campbell continues to exhibit his prowess, asserting his Christianity as an underlying belief that held together his apparently changing allegiance:

> So I have fought for Christians, and my steel
> Is always pointed at the tyrant's heel,
> Whether from Right or Left he dares to clout
> His Maker's image with a butcher's knout.
> For Blacks I've done as much, and risked my life,
> As since for Jews or Christians in the strife;
> When others jumped the liner for Japan
> I stayed and faced the music I began. (*CP2*, 93).

The latter reference, of course, is to those intellectuals who went to see China during the time of the Japanese invasions.[3] It is typical of Campbell that in these lines where he proudly and legitimately displays his courage he can simultaneously expose it alongside terms of contempt. He can employ such a noun as "blacks," a most offensive term at that period, and indicate a feeling of arrogance and superiority at the very time he is insisting that he is in support of them.

In "Talking Bronco" he goes one stage further. Besides contrasting the validity and nobility of his beliefs and actions with those of the "Pylon Poets," he also praises his poetic technique, comparing it to what he asserts is the inferiority and incompetence of his literary enemies. In fact, of course, there could not be a more embarrassing issue on which to demand an open comparison. Campbell has many lines of moving, even momentous poetry, but he is rarely a superior conscious technician. When he is successful, the verse almost appears to run away with him in an ecstatic flow, a flurry of brilliance. His thoughtful technique is painfully intrusive. When he tries to bind his violent pictorial concepts into the strict limitations of a narrow syntax form, his style is often jarring. This difficulty is particularly noticeable in his rhyming couplets, for he is regularly unsuccessful in his drearily obvious heavy handling of this particular poetic style. It ill becomes him, in lines such as the ones in this poem, where the couplets themselves are so grossly mismanaged, to accuse other poets of incompetence. His accusation has to stand against the evidence of our ears as we read his damning lines. Nevertheless, Campbell was never one for modesty in any field, and consequently, he decided to go into battle on this issue as well as on the usual ones of political and social belief.

His real concern, as in the poem *The Georgiad*, is that people who do not respect his competence and capacity are in powerful positions in the world of letters; prominent editors and influential literary critics reject his abilities. Such people act as a barrier to recognition and form a hierarchy that expresses contempt for his achievement. He assumes he is being deliberately shut out from his destined position in the world of letters only by the envy and ignorance of his opponents, for he cannot conceive that it might be any lack of skill upon his part. He very determinedly separates himself from the others who wrote of Spain when he remarks:

> As many philistines, plus all the Jews
> Who ran the jet-Black Market of the News
> When in the greatest racket of the ages
> Commercial greed conscripted bards and sages
> And every scribbler hired his raddled muse,
> For Profit in the Barcelona stews. . . . (*CP2*, 85).

That denunciation is, of course, absurd, but like many generalizations of this sort it can hardly expect to be seriously tested; it remains just a piece of general invective. Where, however, he gets on to the exact details of writers, the accusations may be so much less tenable, since we can offer a defense from our own literary knowledge.

He takes this persona, the "Talking bronco," seeing it as the racehorse winner, while the Bloomsbury and Fleet Street writers are doubly also-rans, for not only is Campbell the poetic victor, but he cannot resist reminding them that "their" side was defeated in Spain. He writes:

> So History looks the winner in the mouth
> Though but a dark outsider from the South,
> A Talking Bronco, sharked from ear to ear
> With laughter, like a running bandolier. . . . (*CP2*, 85).

He now supplies a deliberate and exact analogy of those beliefs we have already observed as general attitudes in the auto-biography—the meritable consistency between poet and soldier, between man of action and man of letters. He actually goes so far as to utilize the military forms as the words, as the metaphor to express his poetic invention. Continuing the image of the rifle bullets above, he says:

> Ejecting from the breech, in perfect time,
> The shells of metre and shucks of rhyme,
> Yet drive the thoughts with perforating aim
> Like tracer-bullets on their threads of flame. (*CP2*, 85).

He goes on to assert the significance of this most mechanical inter-pretation of the rhyming couplet form and his feeling about its value.

What he says has its own reasonableness and truth. It is simply that there is a clear contradiction between the advantages he pre-tends to derive from it and what is, in fact, achieved when we read the crude rhythmic form which he utilizes:

> Free verse and prose are slippers for the dons
> Unfit to clang this marching age of bronze:
> The true vernacular a thorax throws
> And leads the rhyme and meter by the nose;
> It takes the gradients at a marching tread
> Alert, for all the ambushes ahead,
> And when it finds some wild romantic dream
> Has broken loose, with tousled hair astream,
> It's easy to collect it on one's pen
> As passing troops collect a wayside hen: (*CP2*, 91-2).

There is something slightly touching about Campbell's attempt to find in this grey uniformed world of war "a marching age of bronze." It is obviously the world element which would please and satisfy him. It is the search for this ideal which is purely myth that doomed him to such predestined failure. He will not accept what the world is now; rather, he seeks this legendary vision which is his hoped for, longed for, concept of the world of individual men, of bravery and action. In refusing to conceive an element of illusion in this search he becomes almost a latter day Don Quixote, simulta-neously as magnificent in concept as absurd in fact.

The poem continues this crude sense of parallels, using a long and awkward metaphor to explain the clinching effects he hopes to derive from his couplet. The metaphor is a homey military one, picturing a soldier rolling his cigarettes from pieces of paper and tobacco:

> So you can back the couplet every time,
> With its ten fingers twirling thumbs of rhyme,
> To seize and clamp the trailing thoughts they fray
> And scatter like tobacco by the way,
> And in iambic fold them, neatly set,
> As nimble fingers scroll a cigarette,
> For memory to case them in his breast
> And smoke at leisure, as it suits him best. (*CP2*, 92).

The trouble with those lines is that there is no connection between the metaphor and the fact. We know the structural effect of the couplet form. We can remember its effect most obviously in the clinching termination of the Shakespearian sonnet form. We can equally see how effectively it was handled by Pope and Dryden, whom Campbell would be most happy to call his masters. We can also see its sharp effect occasionally in the most confident, and equally the most brief, of Campbell's epigrams, which have been quoted earlier. But your couplet form does not become tightly efficient because you liken it to a neatly rolled cigarette. In fact, contrary to Campbell's assertion about the lax effect of *vers libre*, the couplet form, unfortunately, most encourages the lack of discipline and restraint that allows Campbell to produce these wretchedly long, repetitive poems with their automatic stress patterns. So untenable is Campbell's view of his technical skill that we are not really surprised to find that when he finally finishes his praise of the couplet form, he has actually got to the stage of linking it to his political viewpoint, too. The failure of the left-wing poets to use the couplets which Campbell recommends is evidence that left-wing poets do not have the correct political, let alone poetic attitudes.

The verse goes on like this:

> For what poor Spaunday never understands—
> The couplet is a verbal pair of hands
> With a two-handed punch, more clean and deft
> Than his one-armed and butter-fisted Left. (*CP2*, 92).

One recalls the number of times in *Flowering Rifle* that Campbell uses the concept of the left hand as being awkward and, by analogy, offers "evidence" of the lack of competence in left-wing philosophies and politics:

> The stumps and bunions of our modern prose
> And of free verse, will never pluck the rose,
> Or lace the boot, or prime the hand-grenade
> That sinks their pink Utopias in the shade. . . . (*CP2*, 92).

He is now back to where he was at the beginning of this section. He despises free verse and prose as being unsuited to the themes of this time. It is intriguing, though, that Campbell puts together, as only Campbell would, the concern of poets with plucking the rose and priming the hand grenade, demonstrating again the mixture of the conventional romantic poet and the new romanticism of war which he so constantly advocates. The "pink Utopias" is a comment on all that idealistic socialist vision that Auden once appeared to advocate:

> My verse was nourished by Toledo's sun
> In whose clear light Ray, Sword and Pen are one,
> One in his soldier-poets of the past,
> And here again united in her last:
> The Pen a sword, prophetic in advance. . . . (*CP2*, 92).

He seeks that lost double accolade in the title "soldier-poet," and with it he will drive out the hypocritical poets of England. Campbell's last couplet is revealing indeed: "So will my verse propel you to your doom, / And give you to the vultures for a tomb!" (*CP2*, 94). It is so clear how he conceives his verse as a weapon for political battle. He also exposes a total lack of charity in letting the vultures eat the poets for standing against the philosophies which he embraces; and one notes that Campbell takes his last violent image from his memory of the cruelty of Africa.

III   *Conclusion*

If this is the material of this last collection of poems, what can be said for Campbell as a writer at this terminal phase in his poetic life? After 1946 there was to be no other volume of poetry during the last eleven years of his life. While he lived in Portugal there was a series of translations, and Volume II of his *Collected Poems* was published in 1957, the year of his death. This collection offers one or two new poems in a section called "Later Poems, 1939 - 56," but in view of the range of the dates, it is not easy to see which of them were from any later period than *Talking Bronco* selection of 1946. One can point out only two aspects of poetry from this last collection that are worthy of any serious note. Even now, even after all these petulent, bad-tempered attacks in his sharp couplets, one can still occasionally discover true evidence of Campbell's skill as a lyric poet. He is a poet whose lyricism is undoubtedly founded on a somewhat excessive note; he employs a style which verges on the opulent. Occasionally these verses seem, as I have indicated earlier, mere dazzle, mere extravagance of words and colors; yet at other times there is masterly power, and examples are apparent even in his last collection, among the snappy petulant harangues. There are verses which flame across the page, fill the eye and the tongue with that power and passion that is Campbell at his best, but which must be searched for. One is forced to seek out the true ore of poetry buried among the crude mass of his total verse output.

In his last collection, he dedicated a long poem to David Wright and his wife Poppa, a poem called "The Rodeo of the Centaurs." This was a poem of Campbell's old tradition, a poem of exultant strength, of brilliance, of color, a poem which does not bother itself with childish political battles, does not fight out the old intellectual arguments. The poem simply responds urgently and beautifully to a strange vision which in a sense incorporates all of Campbell's emotional involvement, in that both rodeo and centaurs are brought together, uniting the present-day bullring battle with those legendary creatures of the past, the half-bull centaurs. We are reminded of the constant preoccupation which Campbell expressed for the Minotaurs and the whole background of bull worship and bull life, by which he attached a sort of religious fervor to the ethics of bullfighting. This poem, then, is another which displays Campbell's most exotic but powerful achievement.

It is not necessary to discuss the theme fully. It is a fantasied re-creation of the ancient rites of the centaurs. It derives its ardor from the meritable sense of identification with this lost eagerness: "As if / Our breed had not departed long ago, / I hear a voice, and one that I should know—" (*CP2*, 106). The inclusive "our" and the assertive auxiliary verb "should" make clear the intimacy Campbell feels with his construction. Imagination, now freed from the literal reference of actual event, escalates into mythic history and flourishes brilliantly in the words. Lines such as these occur throughout the poem:

> Loud flutes the oriole in the berried ash;
> White on white sands the dark-blue wavelets flash;
> The great wood-pigeons hurl to left and right
> The clattering whinny of their headlong flight
> Through milk-white poplar-trees that colonnade
> Beside the stream, an aqueduct of shade,
> Then, as they near the sea-cliff, slack their stride
> Of silver places, falter, and divide,
> And let the stream fall sheer, like powdered snow,
> Or a white horsetail, through its six-rayed bow,
> Till with the kindred whiteness it can mingle
> Of sister-foam, and salt, and creaming shingle. (*CP2*, 106).

One notes the features that link this work to Campbell's earlier African poems. There is the constant color reference, white, dark blue, milk-white, silver; the active verbs, hurl, fall; and the other energetic words and phrases, "clattering whinny," "slack their strides," "falter," "divide." They all stress that activity which lends the vehemence to his descriptions.

Perhaps even more powerful, and certainly more brilliant, is a similar example a little later in the poem. His constructions here, as elsewhere, are simply too long to quote in entirety, and I have to begin this extract partway through. His introductory "or," in fact, begins a sentence as though in spite of the continuing drive of the idea some punctuation seems unavoidable:

> Or as the sacred aloe skyward rears
> That flowers but once in every hundred years
> Stirs the dead lava through its crust of snow
> Reviving fires that long ceased to glow,
> Resolving these in living sap to run
> And rise erupting to the noonday sun,
> Till, white without, but red within as blood,
> To rift the pod with its explosive bud,
> Smoking its pollen forth in fumes of gold
> As though the fleece of Colchos were unrolled,
> The bloom whose yawn is redder than a panther's,
> With snarl of fire and slash of golden anthers,
> Gashes its great glory from the blue—
> So from the brutes the goddess burgeons through. (*CP2*, 109).

This is, typically, one long extended metaphor, almost irrelevant in actual function. It is hardly necessary to make your simile at such length to communicate a comparison. Quite clearly these are set pieces seen as much for themselves in their poetic effect as for the precise analogy that is being made. Such devices are common enough in English poetry; nevertheless, the remarks about the previous lines remain equally true here. The colors and the effects are even more violent: there is not only the blue and white of the sea image, for now we have red, gold, and the colors become fire. The verbs of action are still more intense. The scene is an erupting explosion and becomes quite vicious.

It is characteristic of Campbell in high gear that even the opening of a bud is seen in a term as noisy and expansive as an explosion. The likening of the pink-throated center of the plant to the yawn of a panther is another of these images where Campbell's vision is so much more violent than the conventional and obvious one. It is comparisons like these that take us beyond the expected into an intensified reaction which gives Campbell's lines their extraordinary impact, especially their immediate force. After consideration we may inquire of ourselves whether you can make an appropriate analogy between the opening center of a plant's petals and the deep red, fleshy throat of a panther, or whether this is not a disconcertingly extravagant metaphor, inappropriate if you visualize its elements too clearly. In other words, as elsewhere in Campbell, while his impact convinces us at the nonrational level with the urgency and intensity of his emotional impact, if the reader's brain rules his reactions, the excess becomes questionable; the images are surely seen to be strained. It may be only in the first reading of these lines that one does succumb to this feeling of the brilliance and reacts to the violence as appropriate to the context.

There are further examples of Campbell's power in this poem, as in others in this last collection, which demonstrate the same sensitive awareness of the pictorial scene rendered into intensified description. An example can be taken from a single stanza of the poem "Twin Reflections." In this brief verse, Campbell writes:

> If you had seen an almond-tree in bud
> Sprayed on the dawn like Biscay on the piers,
> Flushed from within, as if with conscious blood,
> Yet glittering with dew, like chandeliers— (*CP2*, 119).

Here again is his extending metaphor, the vivid color, the sharpness of his verbal forms. But again there is the confident intensity that brings effectiveness. The image dazzles us, almost literally, for Campbell succeeds in blinding us to his inadequacies with the exultant brilliance of his color. Here we have the success of Campbell's type of verse: it is not the only possible effect in poetry; it is not even one that necessarily has to be rated highly in the order of the significant functions that poetry performs, especially to an age that makes increasingly cerebral demands upon verse; it is, however, a very real effect, and it is the one that is the mark of Campbell's successful poetic achievement when he manages to induce this conviction in us even temporarily.

There are several moments like these, but Campbell was not now the eager young man of *The Flaming Terrapin* days. For all his extreme energy and ardor he was a man who had fought many wars—and had been humiliated and belittled. Although he still carried his violent battle against the "Charlies" and the "Wowsers," he was a man for whom the original vision was perhaps becoming a little soured. It was a little more difficult with every passing year to maintain this excessive energy when physical youth was fading. Perhaps it would not be too much to say that he had not developed the poetic maturity that could replace the daily sense of muscular loss. For the moment he only recounts, with a sadness both impassioned and wry, his aging body.

> From Notting Hill to Prince's Gate
> I'd started breaking-in my stick
> And of my new, three-legged gait
> Acquired the quaint arithmetic.
>
> No more to canter, trot, or trippel,
> Where dandies prance along the Row,
> I coaxed the strange unwieldy cripple
> I had become yet feared to know. . . . (*CP2*, 100).

There is a strange responsibility in the foregoing poem, "Rhapsody of the Man in Hospital Blues." Campbell has changed; he looks at London now with an eye that sees rather deprivation and loss than a challenge which invites him to battle. He makes a comparison of himself with the street cleaners. For some inexplicable reason, the street cleaners of London used to wear a broad-brimmed hat, rather like the hats of the Boy Scouts or Smokey the Bear, pinned up on one side. By an irony, this hat style is also that worn by both Australian troops and by Campbell's own regiment, the King's African Rifles. This ironic accidental identification becomes the basis for a bitterly revealing comparison: he suddenly sees himself reduced to the scavenging ranks of the street cleaners. He needs a walking cane, and they too, have sticks in their hands; sticks with spikes which they are using to pick up the small pieces of trash out of the London street:

> In the same action were our talents
> Employed, though in a different stead,
> Since I was prodding for my balance
> And they were prodding for their bread. (*CP2*, 101).

There is a special and new note in this bitterness of Campbell. It is no longer the cold bitterness of confidence that despises others. Here we begin to see that chink in the armor, the man who, like Hemingway, lived by his physique and begins to die as he loses his prowess and strength and finds no substitute in the intellectual world for the daring action which he can no longer perform. In this doubt we see evidence of Campbell's humanity and begin to recognize how Campbell's nature could have earned the respect and affection of men when he allowed more of them his friendship. Previously we have seen too much of that side of his life that centered on enmity. There is almost a sense of tragedy as he goes on, contrasting his present position not only as a limping man, but also as a person who has now to contemplate the potential failure of a career which was launched with such meteoric zeal more than twenty years before. It is not for nothing that the metaphor he chooses to express this loss is one from his Africa, the Africa of his youth. He returns to a recognition of what that past could have induced for him:

> Gone was the thunder of great herds,
> Lost as the lilt of marching men,
> And void the bandolier of words
> That feeds the rifle of my pen. (*CP2*, 101).

The image of the rifle as the source of poetic construction echoes back to *Flowering Rifle*. It is a reminder of the bad things that Campbell could produce. But that sense of loss, those "great herds,"

the animals of his youth in Africa are so very different in the way
they influence his past. He goes on:

> Amongst the leafless trees that froze
> The wind struck up with flute and fife
> The regimental march of those
> Who've fallen out of step with life. (*CP2*, 101).

How much more does it hurt the fiery-tempered Campbell remem-
bering his youthful strength, to record:

> We must be silent when men mutter,
> And keep calm when tempers rise,
> And when we're shoved into the gutter
> It's we who must apologize. (*CP2*, 101).

He looks again at the London scene, and I think it is extremely
revealing that at this moment he sees it through the images of the
past, the images from Africa he once used so successfully. The images are now employed to record something that no longer has the
urgency and the beauty which he knew in his youth. They are as
hollow as the emotion they describe; the image literally shows the
degeneration in its very association. Even his desire to describe
cosmic maneuvers has become reduced to the driving power of a car
as is indicated in the brief metaphor in "The Moon of Short Rations"
where he says, "And Boreas opens out his throttle / Down
speedways chevroned by the storks." (*CP2*, 74). The throttle image
and the speedways are very modern ones to apply to this legendary
movement of the wind, unlike the similes he would previously have
used.

The native force of the decline may not be entirely clear or obvious at first. But one can support the critical reaction by many examples of similar metaphors in poems from *Talking Bronco*. The
way in which he is now bringing the disconsolate images out of his
present, unsatisfactory, limited experience becomes cumulatively
clearer. We see the hollow remainder of the old style. There is
enough similarity to document most obviously the emotional declension. Perhaps it is only a light exercise when he uses this style in
"Washing Day," an amusing little poem about the clothes drying on
the line: "Pyjamas, combinations, and chemises / Inflate themselves
and dance upon the line." (*CP*, 283). Yet he carries this style
forward, and the point to notice in this poem is the way in which the

old forms, the extravagant verbs, the urgency are not used any more in a direct way. They have become a sort of ironic statement, as though what he calls the "dizzy choreography" can only be used for something as prosaic as clothes on the line. He can see the irony of this himself, when he writes: "They argue, or embrace with kind persuasion, / And parody our dalliance or our strife." (*CP*, 283). The link between human actions and fluttering pyjamas allows little heroics concerning human emotions.

This mood can be seen most obviously in one of the most interesting poems from *Talking Bronco*, "Dreaming Spires." Campbell has apparently borrowed a motor bike, and he goes driving in the country: I notice that he calls his vehicle a "hardware bronco." It is quite clear that he wishes, in a sense, to recapture his old horseriding days. Unable to do this in the context in which he is living, he now can only get this past excitement out of driving a motor bike, which is a somewhat less heroic cavalier act than his earlier horse riding. He wants to imagine that he really can be one of the "Centaurs of an age of steel." As he drives his motor bike he apparently has a vision that seems to incorporate Africa and England. He describes again the African animals which he wrote about so warmly in his early poems:

> With kicks and whinneys, bucks and snorts,
> Their circuses stamped by;
> A herd of wildebeest cavorts,
> And somersaults against the sky. . . .

He continues this with a description of the zebra:

> Across the stripes of zebras sailing,
> The eyesight rattles like a cane
> That's rattled down an area-railing
> Until it blurs upon the brain. (*CP*, 279).

We remember Campbell's interpretation of the zebra movement from the most famous and perhaps most beautiful of his African poems. It is extremely indicative of the present declension of the elation of his poetic vision that when he now thinks of zebras, he thinks of the rather prosaic iron railing outside the house along a London street. In fact, this is not an unacceptable metaphor, as such. The similar stripes make a clear liason between the two visions. But it would never have occured to Campbell before this to liken the zebra, who have stood in his mind for the fire and freedom and movement of the open African bush, with the railings of London streets. Somehow the clear vision that he once had of Africa is being merged with the dismal London environment, within which he is now so reluctantly existing. These two once separate existences come together again within a single line as he talks of how "both wart and road hog vie together."

This merging is made even more explicit in a later stanza where Campbell writes:

> Or so my fancies seemed to sing
> To see, across the gulf of years,
> The soldiers of a reigning King
> Confront those ghostly halberdiers. (*CP*, 282).

Campbell has crossed his gulf of years; and he is seeing fantasies as memory, and the memory goes back to Africa, to the past. The remembered past is now denied in his life as he has increasingly denied it in his poetry. It is this detachment that created for him the empty relative failure of his last years after so much brilliant promise in his youth. He concludes in a tone of loss: "Into the dusk of leafy oceans / They fade away with phantom tread. . . . (*CP*, 282).

There is little left for Campbell to contemplate. In these last poems we derive some further sense of his autobiography. One of the more serious poems of this nature from the *Talking Bronco* collection is one entitled "Reflections." In this poem he now sees himself as a reflection, and it is most revealing that the reflection is of that other self, of that kind of man whom Campbell has always despised and has totally denied in himself. Campbell discovers the existence of the self that encourages people to indulge in the comforts of warm beds, safety, and good beer, resisting lazily all those demands for self-sacrifice and self-denial:

> Of many selves we all possess
> My meanest has the most persisted.
>
> A shifty, and insidious ghost,
> Of all my selves he is the one,
> Though it's with him I meet the most,
> I'd go the longest way to shun. (*CP*, 284).

As he recognizes this other character, he admits the weakness that comes upon him. The old physical strength which had been such a major part of his psyche is yielding to age, and the decline is emotional, too:

> When manhood crests the full red stream
> Of comradeship, and breasts the surge,
> Dreaming a chilled, amphibious dream,
> He haunts the shallows by the verge. (*CP*, 284).

There is still one dangerous belief that persists with Campbell, that if only he would sell out, prostitute his muse as he believes the other false bourgeois poets have done, there would be for him the later dramatic equivalent of their popular success. He still imagines that he is being denied fame and wealth by his integrity, as he would have it, or by his obstinacy, as others would judge:

> Within his heart, so chilled and squamous,
> He knows I've got to sell my pride
> To make him safe, and rich, and famous;
> And he would fatten if I died. (*CP*, 285).

"His" here refers to that sneaking part of Campbell that tempts him toward popularity. There is a certain courage in this determination not to surrender, except that we cannot have Campbell's sense of the established virtue of that position which will not yield.

This unquestioned confidence that he is right, that his position is the only one for a man of honor and respect, shows much more in the autobiographical elements in the two last poems, "Autobiography in Fifty Kicks" and "Dedicatory Epilogue to Rob Lyle." "Autobiography in Fifty Kicks" is exceptionally bad. It has a rhythm that is lacking in subtlety even by the worst Campbell standards; there are driving anapests. The deliberate use of "kick," that cliché of the inarticulate, sets the level. Its theme is the assertion that all his life was attended by a series of kicks. He got his kicks out of life so that his lot was like a football, the kick of the rifle, the kick of a bronco, a dozen or more kicks of life. Finally, in what may be the most absurd analogy, even in Campbell, he likens death to the final kick upstairs into the heavenly place:

> For I've tried all the kicks out of life, except one.
> It's a two-booted kick, to whose impact aglow,
> Clean over the goal-posts to glory I go. . . .

The last line is: "I say to my Life 'Come and kick me once more!' " (*CP*, 115). If this has any analogy in English literature, it is with these dreadfully hearty boy-scout sort of poems of encouragement, such as those by Rudyard Kipling. It is hardly the work of any responsible writer.

It may be unfair to talk of a poet's accidental failures. Nevertheless, the point with Campbell is that so often his failures are revealing of what is wrong with his total poetic attitude. It is the lack of taste, the lack of ability to distinguish between poetry and this ludicrous doggerel of popular verse, the lack of the capacity to judge and evaluate with any degree of accuracy and honesty, that inhibits Campbell from becoming a truly significant poet. His life never allowed him to develop the judgment of taste which would have permitted him to encourage those qualities in his poetry which represented his most significant potential. Not being able to recognize what was characteristic of his best work, he could not discover and eliminate those qualities which made it degenerate into spleen and silliness.

Not much better than the previous poem is the "Dedicatory Epilogue," because it still employs the same old arguments. Now as he approaches death, he cannot recognize its implication with more accuracy than to say what he so aptly calls "Couplets, my old customary tandem":

> In self-defense of our forbidden gender
> To band together, rather than surrender
> Our manhood to the All-Castrating Knife
> Of London and its literary life. (*CP2*, 133).

He is back to the constant attacks again on the literary intelligentsia of London, the hierarchy of letters. The last line of the poem has a phony heartiness that is highly distasteful in every way, especially if read aloud: "From your ex-sergeant, still your comrade too, / My Captain and my Godson, here's to you!" (*CP2*, 133).

CHAPTER 8

Last Poems

IN 1949, a single volume of "Collected Poems" was published in London and Chicago. Though less comprehensive than the subsequent three-volume *Collected Poems* it remains the most available and conveniently comprehensive edition. It is for this reason that I have often referred to this publication in the footnotes throughout this book. The collection is dedicated to his wife Mary, whom he had married in such romantic circumstances in London in 1920, and whom he had loved so deeply for so many years until his death in Portugal.

Most of this collection consists of published work from the major volumes of verse in which his poetry had previously been printed. But the book was introduced by two poems of dedication to Mary, one in the lyric mode to introduce the lyric poems from the earlier books and one satiric verse to introduce the section of poems of satire. It seems possible that these were among the last verses actually written by Campbell—for there was no later collection after *Talking Bronco* in 1946. Therefore one might contemplate these works in order to attempt a summing up of the verse of this man; to use them to perform some kind of assessment of his poetry at these latter days of his life. Certainly, they are unabashed examples of his work. There is not the least evidence that toward the end of his life he was in any dramatic way willing to modify his stance, either personal or poetic. Thus they become heroic, perhaps rather defiant last reassertions of his principles, his beliefs, and his determination of what poetry ought to be.

The satiric poem, in rhythm, diction, and theme, is much as we have come to anticipate. There is the adulation of the open-air way of life—the point made with a deliberately selected South African word: "Folly in towns, like maggots in a corpse, / But wisdom breeds with leisure in the dorps. . . ." (*CP*, 175). There is still the

mixture of the exotic diction and the sloppy, both compounded in a
phrase such as "the daftest butterfly of spring." There is the unhappy overcolloquialism of "I'm the sort of guy that. . . ." There is
the constant and crucial association of writing with activity, with
hunting, riding:

> My pen the spur, my rhyme the jingled rein,
> My hand the downswung stirrup of my brain,
> Although I've had to spurt to save my hide
> A canter is my ordinary stride. . . . (*CP*, 175).

There are the same old violent and unselective attacks on "the
Bolshevik parade," for such people do not know, apparently, the
virtues of sacrifice and hunger personified as "That sterling chap
sham bolshies do not know." There is the same, perhaps consistent
would be a kinder word, interaction between the Catholic belief
and the worship of Mithras: "Luck on our side, we play at pitch and
toss / Christ for our king and Mithras for our boss. . . ." (*CP*, 176).
There is the continuous assertion of his own ardent determination to
seek the solution of living. "To live comes first with me—to them a
crime." There is the boastful "Against a regiment I oppose a
brain / And a dark horse against an armoured train." (*CP*, 177).
We know the identity of that "dark horse" from the published
autobiography, and it does not take very long to perceive that the
opponents are more human than mechanical, particularly when the
idea is developed into the neat pun: "This age is broken ground on
which we ride, / Fatal to heavy troops, this great Waste Land."
(*CP*, 177). Eliot's poem, which was such a seminal influence in the
arty twenties, is castigated because it represents everything both
philosophic and literary which Campbell gave his life to assaulting
and rejecting. In Campbell's long poem, with its rhythmic and extending couplets there is little new; little to suggest that a more
significant and important work was potentially possible in this vein.
It may well be that simply the entire style of satiric couplets had
been played out in the earlier verses. Certainly, there is here not
even the acid penetration of the better selections of the earlier
poems, only the rather drab repetitions of tired battles and familiar
forms.

But if the satiric form is getting even more tired with passing
repetition, the introductory poem to the lyric section is an interesting and valid poem which indicates that it is still the lyric

mode that suits Campbell best, the style in which any continuance of his superior skill would rest. It is true that it is a typical Campbell poem, which at the most petulantly critical level is to say that it exhibits somewhat tired and repetitive aspects of the devices which we have learned to recognize as characteristic of his work elsewhere. But even if one begins by nodding a casual recognition of the characteristic Campbell qualities, the colors of "the peacock's flaunting pride," the gold and the gorgeous dyes and the crimson and white which inevitably mark the polychromatic element of Campbell's intensity in verse, there is still a good deal more. There is a more urgent and individual declamation. Even if one perhaps holds in reserve qualifications of approval of Campbell's attitude, there are nevertheless lines that are honestly indicative of qualities that Campbell chose to sustain throughout his life. They are not entirely unadmirable:

> Firing a golden fusillade of words,
> Lashing his laughter like a knotted scourge,
> A poet of his own disdain is born
> And dares among the rabble to emerge—
>
> His humble townsfolk sicken to behold
> This monstrous changeling whom they schooled in vain,
> Who brings no increase to their hoard of gold,
> Who lives by sterner laws than they have known
> And worships, even where their idols reign,
> A god superbly stronger than their own. (*CP*, 15).

This is all typically Campbell, not only the assertion of the "golden fusillade of words" but even the very diction in which that announcement is couched. How characteristic too is the arrogance in that word "disdain" and indeed "rabble" as he sets his experience against those unworthy and negligible "Charlies" who surround him. He calls himself later "the matador of truth." There is not only the deliberate image, appropriate enough as he charges the recalcitrant bull, but it becomes a convenient shorthand for all the associations with the tauromachy that he has developed throughout his life. After this in the poem, he begins to move beyond the self-declaration, the self-assertion, into the dedication proper. In lines of immense passion and most touching and deep commitment of emotion he talks of his wife:

> But when the Muse or some as lovely sprite,
> Friend, lover, wife, in such a form as thine,
> Thrilling a mortal frame with half her light
> And choosing for her guise such eyes and hair
> As scarcely veil the subterfuge divine,
> Descends with him his lonely fight to share—(*CP*, 16).

This verse shows tender, intimate, and impassioned sentiment, and the diction which contains the emotion matches it in appropriate tone. The lines go on to more crucial declamations of adoration and appreciation with: "He knows his gods have watched him from afar, / And he may take her beauty for a sign. . . ." (*CP*, 16). There is the more intimate response to her nature and the loving that she brought to him:

> When my spent heart had drummed its own retreat,
> You rallied the red squadron of my dreams,
> Turning the crimson rout of their defeat
> Into a white assault of seraphim
> Invincibly arrayed. . . . (*CP*, 16).

Without stopping at this point to speculate upon the very deliberate symbolism of that red and white, there is a handsome and honest devotion here, making appreciation into a poetic energy, and leading up to the more intimately personal assertions of the last stanza, which begins:

> Sweet sister; through all earthly treasons true,
> My life has been the enemy of slumber:
> Bleak are the waves that lash it, but for you
> And your clear faith. . . . (*CP*, 16).

Which is a dedication that verges on the sublime; and later, necessarily, when the circle is drawn, Campbell returns to himself and admits:

> . . . I am a locked lagoon
> That circles with its jagged reef of thunder
> The calm blue mirror of the stars and moon. (*CP*, 16).

We have heard before of that reef with its explosive thunder of breaking waves, but this is hardly the question: recognition does not disavow the image. Novelty is not required if it is not so much fresh comment as deliberate affirmation that is sought. The colors are here, and the explosive intensity of these lines are in a manner of those effective if excessive early poems, but now it is all set to the service of something else, a dedication primarily and initially to a woman loved deeply and constantly throughout many years and to a creed that has sustained him. There is certainty rather than brashness in the line "my life has been the enemy of slumber." Somehow in this context it seems to have a little less bravado, to be a little jaunty, though no less true for its relative calm.

This poem brings together several aspects of Campbell's writing. It includes the old devices not necessarily refreshed by repetition, but they are now at the service of something serious and important in his life and as such they are marshalled to the service of a more profound pronouncement. In this sense the dedicatory poem to the *Collected Poems* becomes both a summing up and a kind of microcosm. It is not entirely effective, there are moments of tension in it that a different and perhaps less extreme poet might have resolved with more cautious professional skill. Yet it exhibits too those features that make the poet worthy of attention and make the man capable of winning the affection and friendship of many admirable people when aspects of his life might make one imagine that there could only be scornful enmity. That ardor of truth really does speak with an honest and open voice. When he speaks of true and intimate and constant affection that was demonstrated through a devotion that was measured throughout the long years of an intense and loving relationship, there is a harmonious confidence that makes the introductory dedication of this important collection of his work a fitting statement of the man's work and his passionate sentiment. That in itself marks important evidence of what Campbell was and what his poetry may be deemed to have achieved at its points of success.

CHAPTER 9

Translations

R OY Campbell made a considerable reputation as a translator. In fact, Volume III[1] of his collected works is devoted entirely to his translations from French, Spanish, Portuguese, and Latin. According to Mary Campbell's preface, these are only a selection of the large number of translations that he undertook throughout his life. She observes, "The first poems my husband translated, when he was eighteen years old, were from Rimbaud and Baudelaire, and he continued translating all through his life." (*CP3*, 13).

It is outside the scope of this study to attempt to undertake the extremely complex task of discovering whether Campbell was a "good" translator. This would require consideration of many issues: a fundamental discussion of what constitutes good translation, a stylistic analysis of the diction of the author in the original, accompanied perhaps by an analysis of the attempts by other translators to render the material into English, and so on. For the present purpose, the important thing is to see what light these translating activities throw upon Campbell's overall accomplishment as a poet. In this regard there are two specific questions: the motives for the particular choice he made of the authors he chose to work from, and the degree to which his translations show evidence of his own thematic and stylistic qualities—the degree to which his translations become in a measure a part of Campbell's own creative activity.

I   *Baudelaire*

Several of Campbell's early poems admit antecedents to be found in the poetry of Baudelaire, but his full translation of *Les Fleurs du Mal* was only published in 1952. It was deliberately not given its established English title, *Flowers of Evil*, for Campbell cavils accurately that "mal" in this context rather includes the attributes of sickness, anguish, pain, than mere "evil."

His declared reasons for undertaking the translation make intriguing reading. They are typical of Campbell in the affectionate and very personal associations that motivate him:

Having had considerable success with my translation of a Saint, St. John of the Cross, I determined to translate a fellow sinner who is hardly less of a believer, even in his rebellious and blasphemous moments than the Saint himself. I have been reading Baudelaire since I was fifteen, carried him in my haversack through two wars, and loved him longer and more deeply than any other poet. I translated St. John of the Cross because he miraculously saved my life in Toledo in 1936. I am translating Baudelaire because he lived my life up to the same age with similar sins, remorses, ostracisms and poverty and the same desperate hope of reconciliation and pardon.[2]

One notes then the motives, affection, and understanding of the French poet. But above all, Campbell declares his sense of identity, the concept that Baudelaire is expressing in his verse precisely the concerns that he has encountered himself. Obviously, the overlap discovered in the experience is likely to generate a similar overlap of expression in the translations. Such an identification does not easily generate any dispassionate detachment toward the work. Campbell borrows the sentiment of another of his translations to comment on the Baudelaire task:

> And though in shame and all precarious shifts
> You were my Model—mine's the crowning sorrow,
> To share your luck, but lack your towering gifts.[3]

In a concluding paragraph of his introductory note he sets out the principles he has established for his task. He attempts colloquial translations, avoiding the false poeticisms of "o'ers" and "mids." He senses that he has "erred on the slangy side" but defends himself on the grounds that he "feared to offend the great original who had a horror of the pompously poetic."[4] He is thus obviously referring the judgment to the general spirit of the original rather than the literal accuracy of the lines—a distinction between intention and result that often preoccupied Campbell as a man and as a writer.

The selection from this Baudelaire volume in the third volume of the *Collected Poems* may be enough to give some sense of what Campbell achieves with that poet, and the original complete

volume will be difficult for many readers to obtain. The first verse
of the opening poem "To the Reader" ("Au Lecteur") indicates
that Campbell will be fairly arbitrary in his translation. The original
reads:

> La sottise, l'erreur, le péché, le lésine,
> Occupent nos esprits et travaillent nos corps,
> Et nous alimentons nos aimiables remords,
> Comme les mendiants nourissent leur vermine.

Of these lines Campbell makes:

> Folly and error, avarice and vice,
> Employ our souls and waste our bodies' force.
> As mangy beggars incubate their lice,
> We nourish our innocuous remorse. (*CP3*, 95).

"Mangy" is a Campbell addition but not a disagreeable one and
"incubate" is a good strong Campbell verb, verbs always being a
notable quality in Campbell's lines. But why the curious alteration
of the rhyme scheme? Baudelaire has *a b b a;* Campbell *a b a b.* It is
a particularly noticeable arbitrariness in that it is achieved only by
equally reversing the meaning, inverting two lines to place the beg-
gar simile before the statement. It would make an accurate translation to reverse the order of the last two lines. More significantly, it
would require no change whatsoever in Campbell's own version.
This makes the decision even more indicative of his own poetic
preference, since it cannot even be justified by specious appeals to
convenience or difficulty.

The same reordering occurs in the second verse, which inverts
Baudelaire with just as little syntactic or semantic reason: "Trusting
our tears will wash away the sentence. / We sneak off where the
muddy road entices." (*CP*, 3, 95). The original reverses these lines
and their rhyming order. In these lines, "Sneak off," in fact, is a
Campbell invention, for the literal phrase is "we return gaily," a
concept that Campbell does not render but rather reverses in meaning. Perhaps his own sense of guiltiness is better matched by that
than Baudelaire's wry irony.

"The Albatross" is an example of Campbell's successful translation of Baudelaire. Baudelaire's crews are not "loafing" like
Campbell's with his scorn for the idle. "Vastitudes" is a Campbell
neologism for "gouffres" while *ce voyageur aile* ("winged trav-

eler") becomes "this soarer of celestial snows." That is a typical
Campbell phrase and the subject here is pure Campbell though
quite needlessly magnificent. The identification with the poet— the
actual term "stranded on the earth" recalling his "stranded on this
unfamiliar street"—reminds us precisely of his London experience,
reacting similarly to what he now calls "those jeering crowds."

There are similar intrusions in "Elevation." Campbell's spirit,
"Like a strong swimmer with the seas to fight," includes that note
of vigorous battle common to Campbell but not present in
Baudelaire's words, *comme un bon nageur qui se pame dans l'onde*.
The measure of "ineffable" happiness matches exactly Campbell's
own philosophy, his often expressed yearning for places "beyond
where cares of boredom hold dominion." There are even direct
echoes of earlier verse. "The Giantess" employs again an image that
Campbell used in "Posada," where the Spanish mountain scenery
was also seen as a female at rest "make her stretch out across the
land and rest. . . ." (*CP3*, 98). "Her Hair" also has that rich
Campbell roll of verbal line:

> O fleece that down her nape rolls, plume on plume!
> O curls! O scent of nonchalance and ease!
> What ecstasy. . . . (*CP3*, 98).

Some sense of the relationship of these translations from
Baudelaire, comes from another direction, not from a painstaking
inspection of the accuracy which Campbell achieved, but from a
more generalized reaction to the verse as a work of poetry. As one
reads through the translations from Baudelaire in the *Collected
Poems*, many would appear at a reading to be Campbell's own. This
is not only because he does impose his own rhythms and diction
upon Baudelaire's works, but because he so obviously shares by disposition some of the basic concepts and attitudes of the French
poet. Notice the extended urgent rhythms of lines such as this simile
in "The Possessed": "Like some bright star from its eclipse
emerging / To flaunt with Folly where the crowds are surging—"
(*CP3*, 100). The overall situation of "Spleen" is again so applicable
to Campbell:

> I'm like the King of some damp, rainy clime
> Grown impotent and old before my time,
> Who scorns the bows and scrapings of his teachers. . . . (*CP3*, 104).

In "Meditation"· there is that recognizable apparent arrogance of attitude that occasionally intrudes elsewhere in Campbell:

> While the lewd multitude like hungry beasts,
> By pleasure scourged (no thug so fierce as he!)
> Go forth to seek remorse among their feasts—
> Come, take my hand, escape from them with me. . . . (*CP3*, 114).

Or read "The Owls," which, like "The Cat" has that curious intimacy with which Campbell always writes of animals, plus his common insistence on the symbolic implications of their actions. In this poem, the palpably autobiographical element appropriate to Campbell's own life is implied in the following section:

> Men, crazed with shadows that they chase,
> Bear, as a punishment, the brand
> Of having wished to change their place. (*CP3*, 103).

That "wish to change" was so precisely what drove Campbell into his special exile.

In Campbell's hands Baudelaire comes out sounding a lot like Campbell. But this fairly obvious truth is part of another issue. From the very beginning, Campbell chooses to translate Baudelaire just because he feels that very deep affinity that goes with a sense of shared attitudes and experiences. To this degree the similarity is both understandable, even desirable, in a version that makes any pretense to be living poetry and not literalistic prose. These Baudelaire translations will not necessarily prove to be the most careful and subtle presentations of the linguistic and cultural nuances of the French poet, but they are vigorous and imaginative verse. It is possible that Baudelaire would recognize himself in Campbell's highly individual lines, and find something of his own authentic voice in a style quite different from his own.

II *Rimbaud*

Comments made about the Baudelaire translations must surely apply equally to Campbell's fine version of Arthur Rimbaud's longer poem *Drunken Boat*. It is a poem that had long attracted him, and indeed close examination will indicate a very strong resemblance between "Le Bateau Ivre" and *The Flaming Terrapin*. The influence is quite obvious. A general observation of Campbell as translator begins to be apparent. Just because he is a poet and not a professional technician with language, his success is going to be measured substantially by the degree of identification he feels with the author. There is some equation between what Campbell has tried to achieve elsewhere in his own writing and how he makes the poet speak in his altered language. Campbell would feel an identity with Rimbaud; the truth or accuracy of such feeling is, as so often in Campbell, beside the point, for there is some deeper level than obvious fact at which Campbell finds it essential to function.

With Rimbaud, Campbell would share many things. Equally, though this would be set aside for the purpose of translation, Campbell would reject with most vigorous scorn and disgust a number of elements in Rimbaud's character. Rimbaud's homosexuality, his deliberately contrived personal squalor, his simplistic adolescent determination to shock the bourgeoisie would antagonize Campbell totally if there had been a contact in person. But there are other connections that would emphasize not opposition but identity. Most essentially, there is the link between the poet and the man of action they both share. It is true that in the chronology of his biography, Rimbaud, unlike Campbell, separated his period of creating poetry from his time as a man of action. His living in Africa occurred later in his existence when his poetic achievement was behind him. One does not, however, have to determine specific measurable overlaps, merely those overall similarities which generate a sense of affinity, even affiliation. Rimbaud's later life as the white man among the tropic savagery of Africa, his sense of isolation and alienation, and the challenge of his vigorous and dangerous life that offended many—all these things would exert an appeal.

There is also a mystical element in Rimbaud. Neither of these poets can in any general way be considered "mystic" in a specifically religious sense. Their lives were perhaps too uncontemplative for that, but there is a kind of mystical fervor of spiritual being that infiltrates a number of their lines. More specifically, *The Drunken Boat* contains evidence of that sense of the purification of the sea, that sense of mystical repose that Campbell also describes in relation to the ocean. It was through the sea that Campbell sought his independence and sensed his isolation. He would share these elements in Rimbaud's nature, admiring his rejection of his society, his vigorous self-discovery in his travels. But personal identification would not be enough: there also would have to be a warm response to the nature of the created poetry itself; its diction and harmonies. *The Drunken Boat* is a youthful poem as brilliant as Campbell's own early writing and charged with the same qualities; excess, passion, color, fervor. Brian Hill's well-known translation of *The Drunken Boat*[5] comments in its introduction on Rimbaud's style, discussing its impact: "his early work is mainly derivative, but at the same time it shows an astonishing command of language and an imaginative scope that are rarely found in a boy of his age."[6]

That could well be a summing up of Campbell in those early Durban years of writing culminating in *The Flaming Terrapin*. Rimbaud's experience was more limited than Campbell's, not in internal intensity of course, nor in its psychological fervor, but in its geographic extension. Brian Hill reminds us of the necessity of Rimbaud's imaginative force, for *The Drunken Boat*, which he rightly calls "that superb poem of the sea," describes a sea that Rimbaud could "know only in books and pictures." This is a far cry from Campbell's knowledge, his infant and juvenile involvement with the Indian Ocean that washed the harbor of his Durban home and his young manhood period of seamanship after he left South Africa. There is an identifying sense of isolation among men in Rimbaud's lines: "J'etais insoucieux de tous les equipages . . . / Les Fleuvres m'ont laisse descendre où je voulais. . . ." rendered by Campbell as "I cared no more for crews of any kind / The rivers let me rove as I inclined." (*CP*, 3, 17).

It is perhaps merely overstraining the details to notice that Campbell's translation indicates his recognition of Rimbaud's self-centeredness. Rimbaud at least starts his poem with "As I," with "I" as the second word. Campbell boldly and instinctively begins with the pronoun in his version! "I felt no more the guidance of my tow-men," a rendering of the line which has the literal meaning "As I went down impassive [impassibles] rivers."

Another moment of interest is obvious in the curiously revealing (though, at the same time, not inaccurate) rendition of Rimbaud's concept in his translation of these lines: " . . . Et les Peninsules démarrées / N'ont pas subi tohu-bohus plus triomphants." In Campbell these become "Nor have the unmoored headlands on their sides / Sustained so proud a buffeting as I did." (*CP*, 3, 17). The last phrase, although perfectly in keeping with the overall tone, is, in fact, a complete addition by Campbell. It emphasizes two things, his own identification with the situation and his exaggeration of his positive role as a man heroic, defiant, and victorious.

If one reads verses from this translation even at random one can recognize immediately two aspects of the writing that remind us of the hand of Campbell: the overall virulence and energy of the rhythms across the lines as a whole, and the deliberate selection of vivid and visual words. His sixth and seventh verses read:

> Since then I have gone bathing in the hymn
> Of a sea sprayed with stars and whitely creaming:
> Devouring the green depths where, flotsam dim,
> Sometimes a drowning man descends half-dreaming.
>
> Where with slow-pulsing and delirious fires,
> To flush the blue, while day blazed white above,
> Stronger than wine and vaster than your lyres,
> Ferments the crimson bitterness of love. (*CP3*, 18).

The rich color imagery is common enough in Campbell's work. "Flushed" is typical of Campbell's deliberate choice of energetic verbs even though it is a reasonable enough translation of "teignant" (though "tinged" would be the most obvious dictionary version) as are "sprayed" and "ferments" made verbs from weaker present participles. Particularly reminiscent of Campbell's own driving color-filled lines is such a verse as the fifth:

> Sweet, as to children the tart flesh of apples,
> Green water pierced my shell with juicy shudder,
> Spewing a wine of azure blots and dapples
> That rinsed me round, dispersing helm and rudder. (*CP3*, 18).

The urgent verb "spewing" is Campbell's reference to the phrase "des vomissures," and that nicely chosen noun "dapples" is totally Campbell's invention.

There are other indicative aspects in these verses. Rimbaud writes *Je sais les cieux cervant en éclairs . . .* which Campbell deliberately renders as I *have known*, indicating his union with the experience of the original poet who wrote merely the present form "I know." Campbell's "with breakers I have charged the reefs and screes" recalls his own earlier poems of the coast especially, because of that verb "charged" where Rimbaud has in fact the noun *assaut* ("assault").

This translation has a magnificent vigor and energy in its lines. It is true that Campbell's inevitable iambics so natural in English do not match the rhythms that Rimbaud attempts, but one thinks that that old sinner himself might have enjoyed the extraordinary power and color of Campbell's version of his masterpiece.

III   *Horace*

In a way one might wonder why Campbell turns to that learned Roman gentleman Quintus Horatius Flaccus—Horace—for another of his major translations. Yet it is to be remembered that besides the impassioned Campbell of the lyric verse, there is the didactic Campbell of *The Georgiad*, with its long series of critical couplets.

In translating Horace's *The Art of Poetry*, Campbell employs the rhyming pentameter couplet, "heroic verse." This is a form that he has often used in his poetry anyway, but for this particular purpose he can reasonably point to an extensive neoclassical tradition for such a format. Pope and Dryden both employed such line forms. Campbell can then appeal as much to custom as to his own palpable determination to use this heroic line. Certainly, the modern reader's ear has grown attuned to find it a desirably familiar style for such subject matter, even though it is not in fact in any measure close to the Horace original. Some have legitimately attempted to avoid the pressures of this general expectation and seek a more exact rhythmic equivalent of Horace's Latin measures. In a fairly well known translation by John B. Quinn,[7] this scholar has employed many meters "especially the anapestic tetrameter" and has fallen back on heroic verse "sparingly." Again, one can recognize the pressure of certain of Campbell's preferred forms; such characteristics prominently displayed are better seen in the light of Campbell than explained by reference to common neoclassical norms.

If there has been some attempt to evaluate Campbell's personal sense of identification with his coexistent author as one measure of his ability to translate, the argument might be thought to break down with his work on Horace. Identification of a personal nature might be the last thing one would anticipate in the Horace poetry in contrast with his reaction to the work of Rimbaud. But even here, there is some sense that Campbell occasionally recognizes that he shares part of the experience which Horace records. Here is Campbell when the theme touches, simply in passing, on the topic of exile:

> . . . when in common prose
> Peleus and Telephus recount their woes

> In exiled poverty: they must discard
> The thundering bombast that they spout so hard,
> And in plain simple language play their part
> In order thus to reach the hearer's heart. (*CP3*, 28-9).

Compare this energetic, even somewhat crude, but enthusiastic language, with a prose version by Edward Blakeney:[8] "Often too in a tragedy Telephus or Peleus utters his sorrow in the language of prose when poor and in exile he flings aside his paint pots and his words a yard long in eagerness to touch the spectator's heart with his lamentable tale."[9] Or again with John Quinn's ludicrous attempt at verse:

> And so, often do Peleus and Telephus grieve
> In a prosy discourse when poor exiles they leave
> Their majestic, sonorous, grandiloquent art
> Not unmindful of moving the spectator's heart. . . .[10]

To judge accurately whether Campbell's version is pure Horace is difficult. It is certainly vigorous and readable verse, and perhaps its success owes something to our recognition that comment on the suffering of that "exiled poverty" and the lines "to reach the hearer's heart" establish Campbell's personal identification and sympathy.

As has been observed earlier, Campbell's style in the heroic couplet mode owes something to Pope and Dryden, but they are incomparably more skilled technicians, and can introduce apparently limitless variants in the ostensible regularity of his iambic pentameter rhyme. Campbell lets his lines press on until they dangle, as it were, to an end, to be concluded by the inevitably dropped voice of the breathless speaker/reader:

> One Bard grows turgid when he would seem grand:
> One, fearing thunder, crawls along the sand:
> One who attempts too lavishly to vary
> A single subject, if he is not wary,
> Will make. . . . (*CP3*, 26).

There is a kind of weariness in such writing that rapidly communicates that sense to the reader as well.

Campbell's indignation about flatterers and the hangers-on of letters is transposed here from his denunciations in *The Georgiad*. Many of these lines, reputedly of translation, sound very much like this poem:

> The poet, if he owns a rich estate
> Or leases property at a high rate
> Collects his flatterers, as meat does flies
> By flashing golden bribes before their eyes. (*CP3*, 41).

In the less imaginative accuracy of prose the lines have been interpreted "As a crier collects a crowd to buy his wares so a poet, rich in
land and rich in investments, bids flatterers flock to him for their
profit." This line indicates that the source of that powerful metaphor of disgust with the syncophants—meat attracting flies—is
Campbell's not Horace's.

There is evidence of Campbell everywhere in this translation.
The interpolation of the devil in "crazy poets like old nick" is one
example. The vigorous colloquialism of "hell for leather" is a phrase
he likes so much that he is forced into utilizing the extraordinary
term "blether" to match his rhyme, which he would not have needed if he had remained close to the original. It is also Campbell's
phrase to say "lets rip." The lines have all Campbell's rejection of
the power brokers of literature:

> If some poor devil falls into his grip
> He hugs him to his heart and lets rip
> And will not cease till death. So leeches suck
> And, 'till they're gorged, will never come unstuck. (*CP3*, 43).

It is a good distance from Horace in many ways. Yet the Roman's
views have a fundamental ring of good sense about them which
may be matched in some degree by Campbell's energetic denunciations. The Horace translation also matches those qualities we are
familiar with in other poetry of Campbell's, where he employs the
rhyming couplet. Most prominent is the heavy, often intrusive, end-
stopped lines that hammer at the clinching rhymes.

In spite of the inhibitions imposed by Campbell's sense of structure and style, he is not especially rigorous in following Horace's
form. Although his version gives the superficial impression of being
a close translation he avoids the agonizingly stilted forms of a line-
by-line translation which would seem a likely consequence of his
style. As he remains even less immediately close to the original than
with Rimbaud, the fidelity to the actual meaning can only be
measured across a substantial segment of the lines of Horace's
didactic poem. Again, one can examine this translation in familiar
patterns. First, there is the overall sense of identification without

which Campbell would not begin such a task. Second, there is the intrusive though not poetically less admirable choice of words that mark Campbell's own taste and judgment, that diction that tends to override the original just as, in a similar way, overall rhythms of the lines are intrusively his, not the original author's. Last, bringing these specific elements together one can recognize the particularly personal tone that Campbell always establishes in his translations, which then become virtually poems of his own. With Baudelaire and Rimbaud there is some sense that no matter the details, his tone is about appropriate for their work. With Horace one is less confident of this, because the dry detachment that Horace retains even at his most formally vehement is lost.

IV *Lorca*

It is likely that Campbell attempted his translations of Lorca as much as a political as a poetic gesture, for Lorca was deeply involved, as was Campbell, in the events of Spain's tragic civil war. The commonly accepted theory of Lorca's death has been that he was executed by the Fascist Falange in July, 1936. This still seems the likely truth, but the initial simplicity of the explanation concerning this event that so angered and incensed men who admired him and supported the government cause in Spain has been challenged. In the cooler dispassion of historical distance certainties have been replaced by a sense that the events of this period were too confusing both politically and personally to make a deliberate martyrdom out of this distressing assassination. Political blame and guilt may be beside the point. Rather than seeking association with Lorca in spite of his own allegiance to the Falangist cause, Campbell may simply have identified with Lorca's Spanish ardor, his passion for poetry and bullfighting, and his overall love and appreciation of the beauties of this Iberian region that both poets found so compelling.

The well known paperback, *Selected Poems*, of Frederico Garcia Lorca[11] actually includes some of Campbell's translations in its pages as part of an attempt to demonstrate the most effective endeavors to render Lorca's Spanish verse into English. The American editor of this selection, Donald M. Allen, writes in his introduction of "the several obstacles in the way of successful translation of much of Garcia Lorca's verse."[12] His own criteria for selection included "being faithful to the text of the Spanish poems and, more often than not, to the spirit as well, insofar as this is possible in the incredibly difficult matter of translating poetry."[13]

The difficulties, and they are many, raised by Lorca's style, make a significant impress on the work of a translator. As one reads Campbell's versions of some of Lorca's lyrics one thing is clear: here at last, is a poet whose individuality is powerful enough to press through Campbell's lines. The Lorca poems do not become that kind of translation that is merely thinly disguised Campbell, which offers lines that would seem to be Campbell's own verse if one were not familiar with the background and did not know that he was rendering the work of another poet. In the Lorca translations, Lorca still speaks firmly and directly in his own tongue and Campbell pays him the ultimate homage of a good close rendition. This evidence of Lorca's style is obvious even in the very simple optical aspects of a first reading. The brief and broken lines, as in "Fable and Song of a Horseman," for example, are quite carefully followed by Campbell. Accuracy is by no means total. He will still deliberately play with rhyme order. In "Adam" Lorca's *a b b a* becomes that rhyme scheme of *a b a b* that Campbell regularly prefers in his own work. The ardor of Campbell's words matches the intensity of Lorca, particularly in the concluding lines, and here in this triplet the rhyme scheme matches Lorca's exactly:

> But a dark other Adam dreaming yearned
> for a stone neuter moon, where no seeds bud,
> in which that child of glory will be burned. (*CP3*, 80).

In spite of the relative care with which Campbell follows the original lines, there are still certain elements of his own style that are persistently apparent. In "Somnambulistic Ballad," for example, the opening line commonly and fairly literally rendered as "Green, how much I want you green" (*Verde que te quiero verde*) is translated by "Green, green, how deeply green!" This, in an uncommonly defensive and explanatory intrusion, is then justified by a footnote explaining its secondary association as the literal. Lorca's second line reads *Verde viento. Verdes ramas* ("Green wind. Green branches"). In Campbell it becomes "Green the wind and green the bough." That inclusive conjunction "and" reminds us that Campbell could rarely accept punctuation except at the end of his lines.

In the second stanza after the repeated "Green, green, how deeply green!" Lorca has *Grandes estrellas de escarcha*. Campbell's line begins with an assertive verb "See": "See how the great stars of the frost. . . ."

Because Campbell's style is marked by more verbs than many writers employ, those elliptical verbless lines of Lorca will not fit with Campbell's own poetic line and so he adds verbs and conjunctions extending these phrases into double clause sentences. As a further example, exactly the same effects occur later toward the end. "Green her flesh and green her tresses" (*CP3*, 69). (*Verde carne, pelo verde*) has the additional conjunction, while there is an extra verb in "An icicle hung from the moon" as a version of *un-cárambano de luna*. Another area of modification is found in the same skillful verb choice so common in Campbell's work. *Mil panaderos de cristal / herian la madrugada*," more literally "A thousand crystal tambourines / were piercing the dawn," is adequate. It is Campbell's own need as a poet that motivates him to seek out a more vigorous verb "wounded the dawning of the day."

In a similar way "San Rafael" is altered to set it in keeping with Campbell's conception of the poem. The opening line of Lorca of "the closed coaches" is reversed with the second, referring to "the edge of the rushes": "Along the river of reeds / Closed carriages assemble where. . . ." Besides the absolutely arbitrary and at one level indefensible inversion that curiously truncated "where" is dragged back from the third line of Lorca. It stands there because Campbell needs that for his rhyme with "bare" to come. This could be explicable by appeal to the insoluble problems of finding English rhyme, but in fact the whole concept of the rhyme scheme in this piece is Campbell's own. It has no existence in Lorca's poem.

Precisely similar observations taken from one of Lorca's most famous poems, "Romance of the Civil Guard," will amply confirm this particular diagnosis (Ballad is the common usage, but Campbell is for once literalistically rendering Lorca's *Romance de*.) The opening lines in Campbell are: "Their horses are black as night / Upon whose hoofs black horseshoes clink. . . ." In these lines the simile "black as night" is somewhat of a cliché in English and is totally invented by Campbell. Ideally, invention should improve the original, not render it banal and commonplace. The verb "clink" is another intrusion of Campbell, again indicating his own determination to find the provocative verb. Lorca has nothing more than the blunt statement of "The horseshoes are black" as one in a series of his firm sinewy statements. In the same way the verb "shine" is introduced in line four. The rest of the verse is relatively close to Lorca in spite of Campbell's deliberate rhyming, although there are odd moments where accuracy wavers without logical justification. Lorca's *una vaga astronomia / de pistolas inconcretas* becomes an oddly doubled up armory of "A blurred astronomy of pistols / and shadowy six shooters." But to set aside for a moment this tiresome nit-picking, let us select lines virtually at random. Here is the respectable and accurate translation of A. L. Lloyd:

> Naked, the wind turns
> the corner of the surprise
> in the silver-dark night
> the night benighted by nightfall. [14]

The last line apes Lorca's repetitive rhetoric of *noche que noche nochera*, but in so doing the flow of the Spanish becomes a teeth-exposing tongue twister in English. Examine Campbell's version.

> Around the corner of surprise
> The wind bursts naked, on the sight,
> In the night, the silver night-time
> In the night-time of the night. (*CP3*, 61).

There is calculated repetition here too, but it conveys that sense of ominous tension that Lorca generates with his own rhetorical device. There is the feeling in these poems of Lorca that Campbell knows the experience of living in Spain as well as Lorca does. His verse does not very closely match Lorca's precise, spare but throbbing diction which is, in some ways, the antithesis of Campbell's vigorous lines. But the translation in its own way achieves an equal intensity and function. In this unexpected way the tone is transmitted, albeit the words can be shown to be inaccurately translated.

CHAPTER 10

The Critics' View

E VERYTHING that has been written in this book indicates
the division of opinion that will be found in the critical reviews
of Campbell's work. It is not only a division between
critics—between those who find his poetry admirable or intolerable—but a division within the attitude of the single critic who
finds that Campbell and his work both exasperate and enthral.
There is considerable truth in the comment of C. J. D. Harvey when
he points out the underlying problem inhibiting any dispassionate
assessment of Campbell's poetry: "He is one of those writers (Byron
and D. H. Lawrence, perhaps are two others) whom it seems impossible to discuss on literary grounds without including a great
deal about his personality, his philosophy, his politics and other
seemingly irrelevant matters."[1] Even in this explanation, Professor
Harvey finds it necessary to qualify "irrelevant" with "seemingly."

Although one would certainly agree in the abstract that such concerns ought to be irrelevant, there remains a disturbing sense that
with Campbell it is not so easy to keep these irrelevancies at arm's
length. In the criticism of Campbell's poetry, the old political
battles are often refought. Prejudice colors the reactions even when
there is the pretence of academic evaluation. It is for this reason
that the assessment of person overlaps with judgment of *persona*.
Invariably, there is the recognition that Campbell is a phenomenon
particularly remarkable in this age that does not expect so vehement
and flamboyant a man. It is useful to quote Professor Harvey again,
because he so well expresses one's exasperated bewilderment: "The
personality is so strong that we have lost sight of the poetry. Confu-
sion of critical criteria rationalizes objection to ideas by finding artistic faults. We accept Hardy's atheism, Hopkins' Catholicism—even without sharing them—why do we find it impossible to
make that discrimination in Roy Campbell's case?"[2] One general
reason may well be that in this age we do not take religion seriously

enough to be provoked by its controversies any more, while issues of politics and race now provide the sharpest impact on the sensibilities. However the question of "Why," is, in this case, both rhetorical and insoluble. The critics continue to attack and praise the poetry because of their reactions to the man. Some estimation of these responses may be perceived from the reviews given to Campbell's work.

From the very beginning, the reviews of Campbell's first publication, *The Flaming Terrapin*, exemplify the duality of opinion that was to pursue Campbell throughout his productive life. There is admiration, invariably of his energy and power. The *Boston Transcript* review comments that "Campbell's verse has a wild unrestrained vigor and strength about it such as has recently not been seen in modern poetry."[3] There are also reservations about its extravagance and excess. "*The Flaming Terrapin* is not a poem to be observed with a microscope"[4] and "Unfortunately the poem as a whole is not quite so impressive as it is in its parts"[5]; or, "Terrific image after terrific image astounds the mind, and the impact gradually disintegrates it."[6] But there is always some concluding admiration even in the face of the doubt at the extremes. A typical example of such a viewpoint comes from the review by Hamish Miles: "Even if he seems now and then to be lashing himself forward with his thongs of epithets, one is left justifiably amazed. It is something after all to have the power to amaze."[7]

Lengthier quotations from two major critics will confirm this view and establish the first reactions to the poetry of Campbell in 1924 when he appeared as a young prodigy. Babette Deutsch produces a dauntingly extended list of deficiencies which still culminate in comment of praise: "One may neglect obvious flaws: the facile allegorical passages, the unnecessarily confused mythology, the crowding metaphors, too heavy for their frame, the abuse of the meter. One dare not neglect the gift of a man who sees the waves mounting into the night."[8] In a similar tone, Garnett exposes his own reluctant admiration.

It would be easy for me to pull the poem to pieces, to quote passages inspired by extravagance of manner and it is true that a cold and correct taste may be repelled by the poetic rhetoric and by the naive inconsequence of the Argument. But the beauties are so many, the poet's imagination so daring, his descriptive powers so fresh and triumphant, his imagery so strong and often so delicate, that the very immaturity and wildness of his Muse will interest the discerning.[9]

The shock effect of Campbell's work was reduced with passing time, and the obvious strengthening of his poetic technique nullified some of the common accusations of immaturity. By 1931, with the publication of the first collection, *Adamastor*, the faults are demonstrably less evident and critical praise is more uniform. For once there is less cleavage of opinion. In some cases the praise may be considered almost uncritical. The *New York Times* was unqualified in its admiration: "In *Adamastor* Campbell proves that he is a poetic force for the rejuvenation of poetry, abundantly alive, starkly individual and cyclonic of utterance."[10] Bernice Kenyon simply asserts, "Roy Campbell is a genius—one of the very few to whom that misused term can safely be applied."[11] Even more declamatory in its appreciation was the vehement comment of Richard Church: "Today we are privileged to hear, clearly and indubitably that eternal miracle, a great word master, a Merlin, a Lavengro. Mr. Roy Campbell has found our English language weary with intellectual age and drawing over the close fire of education. He has stung it to life, to rebellion and has made it proud, eloquent and young again."[12]

This question of "youth" and "young language" refers of course to the South African inheritance from a "younger" land, an interpretation which Campbell was later to scathingly satirize with splendid force. Only in *Poetry* was a discordant note of retraction evident. Its theme could be anticipated: concern whether Campbell's admittedly fervent rhetoric could always be as convincing to the reader as it apparently had been to its creating writer: "Instead of being swept along by a poetic tornado, I listened coldly to much over-rhetorical oratory."[13] The critic here puts his finger on one thing that is invariably fatal to appreciative enjoyment of Campbell's verse. An overscrupulous discrimination must be reined in, so that it is not dominant when the impact should overwhelm the intellect and substitute feeling for thinking in the Dionysian mode of art. In spite of this complaint there is considerable measure of agreement in kind if not degree in the initial assessment of Campbell. He is seen as an original and exciting poet, his potential threatened by his own excesses both technical and personal.

When one looks ahead and reads the reactions of critics to his last works it is easy to find confirmation of this original initial evaluation. But by this time, particularly with the publication of the American collection *Selected Poems* in 1955, the sides are drawn up ready to wage war over Campbell's personality like dogs skirmishing for a bone. The comments at this juncture, if conceivably justified in their basis by the principles of literary criticism, are regularly couched in a language that exhibits snideness, arrogance, and cruelty. If these attitudes, as often asserted, are mirrored in Campbell's own, they are no more becoming for that reason. Campbell's petulance and spleen are, in fact, simultaneously their cause and reciprocation.

Randall Jarrell in the *New York Times* was scathing in his summing up of Campbell; "It is a very bad tempered Byron who writes these poems; his heart no longer bleeds but only barks and bites. Never was there an angrier poet."[14] There is no particular advantage in offering counters to such views, so bad-tempered in themselves; but it is at least worth remarking that there have been vastly angrier poets than Campbell even at his most ferociously splenetic. The proportion of anger by any definition scarcely makes a majority of the contents of this particular collection, and such an opinion can only be derived from external information concerning Campbell's public life.

There is some similar snideness from Robert Graves who admittedly had personally suffered from Campbell's poetic satire, yet his remarks here are at least connected with the quality of the poetry rather than the personality and do have some wit to commend their acid tone: "As a poet Campbell slowly polished his provincial and therefore Tennysonian style—until he developed a grandiose gasconading manner which has its charms in short quotations but soon fatigues. (Unfortunately he went in for very long poems)."[15]

In the left wing *New Statesmen* a critic exposes his own snobbery and exemplifies the unfairness of the assaults on Campbell when they bore so little upon his art: "Campbell's political and social views are either trashy or slapdash in an open-air way; something is due, I suppose, to the colonial chip. . . . "[16] More noticeable than the political grievance here is that inability to avoid reference to the ever-to-be-expected inferiority of the colonial that derives from the self-satisfied aesthetic of the British intelligentsia. That "I suppose" is a masterly example of English condescension in its languid indifference.

There is of course substantial truth in the fact that Campbell was a colonial poet. That was his very strength, although he was too often disloyal to his true recognition of that inheritance. Snobbish put-downs by effete, British intellectuals are hardly adequate measures of the significance of this fact. Perhaps these reactions were partly a product of the times. In 1960, a younger writer, John Wain, himself an inheritor of the postwar years with their liberating destruction of British colonial and class confidence, was able to discourse in a more balanced and reasonable way on the importance of this foreignness which Campbell brought to English poetry in his ideas, language, and technique, making it a cause for admiration rather than shallow scorn: "As a poet he isn't 'English' in the least; his lines evoke glare and shadow, dramatic Southern Cities, bare parched mountain sides, sun-dazzled coasts. He never succeeded in capturing the cool tones at which English poets excell and perhaps never tried very hard."[17]

More honest critics, even when writing for the left-wing papers such as the *Nation*, which were so antagonistic to all Campbell's professed social philosophy, occasionally appreciate that Campbell's skills will not be argued away by any facile attacks on his political beliefs. There is a profundity in the honesty of John Ciardi's comments when he reviews the *Selected Poems* in 1955, because in his response he struggles with his own prejudices:

No poet writing in English has equalled Campbell's violence. None has presented a mind—to me at least—more despicable, a mind compounded of storm trooper arrogance, Sieg Heil piety, and a kind of Nietzschean rant, sometime mixed with ponderously uncomical sense of satire. The center of that mind—and its poetic style—is all sledgehammers. It would be comforting to one's sense of liberalism to report that the result is merely thud-thud. What must be reported instead is that the sledgehammers are sometimes magnificent.[18]

In spite of the concluding note of reluctant admiration, this review provoked an equally obstreperous exhibition of retort by epithets from Campbell's American publisher, Henry Regnery: "I consider Mr. Ciardi's remark not only stupid and libellous but extremely cowardly."[19]

There has to be a balance between snide remarks and the malice that has engendered them, and any rational evaluation of the poems that remain as the justification for Campbell's life and work. No one better expressed these divisions and the painful personal reassessment that they require than Edwin Muir who, in a few lines, establishes the thesis that this book has attempted to substantiate through a number of chapters: "Comparing *Flowering Rifle* to *Talking Bronco* with Campbell's early poetry, one has the feeling of looking on while the partisan and the man of action kill the poet. Campbell's name will live by such poems as 'The Golden Shower' in this volume and by a number of poems in the first. But it is sad to think of his journey from his pagan paradise to this rowdy corner of the inferno."[20]

From the standpoint of the formal historian, rather than the literary critic, Bergonzi makes another attempt at evaluation. Although his version is more specifically political, it largely repeats the agitations of these critics. Particularly, he attempts to assess the extraordinary persisting virility of the antagonisms Campbell engendered.

Why do people still react so violently to this abrasive personality across the years? With the passing of the years it should be possible to see Campbell's total achievement and the myths that he inspired in some kind of perspective. On the one hand his admirers should recognize that Campbell, however much he liked to appear as a simple apolitical poet, was an ideologically committed writer, many of whose attitudes were dangerous and sometimes vicious. On the other hand, those who refuse to do justice to Campbell's poetry because of their dislike of his ideas—even though the best of his work was written before 1936—should recognize that a writer can be important despite reactionary and illiberal attitudes. The problem has to be faced with Pound and Celine and Drieu La Rochelle. Unlike them Campbell did at least bear arms against fascism.[21]

Of course if Bergonzi's position is correct, it no more matters that Campbell fought against the Fascists than that he has supported Franco. No responsible literary argument can be based upon the nonpoetic activities of a writer. But he does go on to note that it may be Campbell's relative rarity in English letters that has caused such a specially controversial reaction. The writer as a politically active intellectual, deeply involved as a spokesman for international and domestic events, is part of a continuing tradition of the radical artist in Europe, but it is a far less common phenomenon in Britain where almost by definition the artist exempts himself from day to day concerns.

Just because Campbell was capable of engendering animosities, he was equally capable of establishing very deep and fervent friendships. One of the most determined and long lasting was his relationship with that consistently berated and underrated man of letters, Wyndham Lewis. Several fictional characters deriving much from Campbell's personality are found in his novels. In *The Apes of God*, there is the character of "Zulu Blades" and in *Snooty Baronet* the major figure McPhail is clearly drawn from Campbell's life and philosophy. In a touching letter written in 1932 after a visit with the Campbells in Martigues, Lewis wrote appreciatively, "Always remember this, at a point in my career when many people were combining to defeat me. . . . you came forward and with the most disinterested nobleness, placed yourself at my side and defended my book in public in a manner that I believe no other work has ever been defended."[22]

Lewis was always willing to reciprocate. The strength of this friendship remained warm through decades. In 1951, in another letter the same affectionate response is clear: "To find you still at my side is a matter of the greatest satisfaction to me and I hope that we shall always remain comrades in arms against the forces of philistia. I learned from you that 20 years ago I was described as an 'old volcano' [by W. H. Auden]. Let me say I shall always be prepared to erupt and pour out a stream of lava on our foes."[23]

Even the correct attempt to discriminate between man and poet sometimes brings out a bitter tongue from the critic who turns from attacks on the poetry to assault on the personality. Seymour Smith in *Encounter* makes a legitimate judgment rendered false by the intemperance and shallowness of the language in which he chooses to couch his complaint: "Many speak warmly of Campbell's generosity as a boon companion; and it existed. But should we allow ourselves to be deterred from pointing out his failure to fulfill his potentialities as a poet on the strength of a few beers?"[24] There is a great deal more to Campbell's personal friendships than the ability to sup convivially a few beers. Wright has confirmed his generosity and kindness. Russell Kirk remarks in his affectionate or admiring memoir, "the union of the seer and poet, scald, troubador, saga singer, once was taken for granted. Now Roy Campbell stands alone."[25] He goes on to epitomize the qualities of the man, and his list is a long one:

A faithful lover and a hot hater, a soldier, a sailor, a hunter, a bull-fighter, a horse-breeder, a critic, a translator, a champion of religion, a great brawny Carlyle-hero of a man, a South African and a Scot and a Latin rolled into one gigantic frame, a singer of sea chanties, a master of pencil sketching, a High Tory, a great drinker, a great talker, one of the fiercest and kindest beings alive—this adventurer is one of the few modern poets likely to be read a hundred years from now or two hundred. It is his power of loving and hating that gives his verse its invariable strength and its frequent splendor.[26]

For all the attempts to contradict or defend the amiability of his personality, it is undeniable that his reputation will live by several of his early poems. Edith Sitwell, a loyal and lifetime friend, commends with unanswerable accuracy the distinction and caliber of certain poems by which Campbell will always be remembered: "If 'To a Pet Cobra' is not a great yet terrible poem, then I do not know one when I see it. It is truly magnificent."[27] In her moving memoir written for *Poetry*, Edith Sitwell asserted Campbell's greatness in words that carry their own conviction, even if, in the last resort, they must be deemed exaggerated: "On Easter Monday the 22nd April 1957, the English speaking people lost one of the only great poets of this time, a poet whose every line conveyed vigor and fire. . . . The great poet was Roy Campbell."[28]

Opinions of Campbell vary, except that they are always opinionated. There is vicious attack, and occasionally excessive defensive admiration. The responses are based on many irrelevant reactions that add little to our experience of the poetry. When there is a serious and sincere effort to appreciate the work, the prejudices inevitably fade away. There remains the awareness that here, in the work of this South African, there is a verse of the highest order; perhaps within its particular form, it is as fine as any engendered in the twentieth century. If Campbell could never achieve the humane profundity of Yeats, the intellectual prowess of Pound, or the masterly technique of Eliot, there are poems of such irresistible distinction that no shallow condemnations of his person can ever negate the consequence of his lasting poetic achievement.

Perhaps as accurate an assessment as any comes from another South African writer who knew him so well—Uys Krige. Again, the comments are purely assertive, but in spite of that they convince because of their confident authority: "Of his poetry I should like to say finally, that whatever its faults . . . when all the cliques, claques and coteries of our time have settled into their rightful little grooves, Roy Campbell will stand out as one of the finest lyric voices of his generation."[29] There seems little to add to this unchallengeable and satisfying summation.

Notes and References

Chapter One

1. Roy Campbell, *Light on a Dark Horse* (Chicago, 1952): hereafter cited in the text as *L*.
2. David Wright, *Roy Campbell* (London, 1961), pp. 40-41.
3. When the authorities were repatriating wounded troops they somehow got the impression that Campbell's place of origin was South Africa rather than England from which he had in fact enlisted, and they shipped him back to Durban briefly.
4. Roy Campbell, *Collected Poems* (London, 1949), p. 293: hereafter cited in the text as *CP*.
5. Robert Armstrong, *Critic* 20, no. 4, pp. 18-21.
6. Ibid., p. 20.
7. Alan Paton, "Roy Campbell: Poet and Man." *Theoria*, no. 9, (1957), p. 19.

Chapter Two

1. Roy Campbell, *The Flaming Terrapin* (London, 1924).
2. Roy Campbell, *The Wayzgoose* (Cape Town, 1928).
3. The *OED* speculates inconclusively about the antecedents of this term. It was applied originally to an entertainment given by a master printer to his workmen about St. Bartholomew's Day. In more general later use, the term refers to "an annual festivity held in summer by the employees of a printing establishment, consisting of a dinner and an excursion into the country."

Chapter Three

1. Roy Campbell, *Adamastor* (London, 1930).
2. In the original *Adamastor* version, "Parachute" replaces "Catapult."
3. Technically although from the *Adamastor* publication, this poem appears in a preliminary section labeled "Early Poems" not from the *Adamastor* group itself.
4. "Mazeppa" is another poem in the "Early Poems" presection of the *Adamastor* collection. Campbell admits them to be "lifted" from the Provencal poet Mistral, and there are similarities; nevertheless much derives simply from Campbell himself.

5.   G. S. Fraser, *New Statesman and Nation* (December 17, 1949), p. 738.

Chapter Four

1.   Roy Campbell, *The Georgiad* (London, 1931).
2.   It is significant that the original *Georgiad* line has France, not Spain, as the country of allegiance. Politics and history had altered his priorities.

Chapter Five

1.   Roy Campbell, *Taurine Provence* (London, 1932): hereafter cited in the text as *TP*.
2.   Roy Campbell, *Flowering Reeds* (London, 1933).
3.   Roy Campbell, *Broken Record: An Auto-biography* (London, 1934): hereafter cited in the text as *BR*.

Chapter Six

1.   Roy Campbell, *Mithraic Emblems* (London, 1936).
2.   This poem was almost totally rewritten after its first printing in *Mithraic Emblems*.
3.   In *Mithraic Emblems* ten poems concerning the Spanish Civil War were deliberately grouped in a section entitled "Toledo, 1936."
4.   Roy Campbell, *Flowering Rifle* (London, 1939): hereafter cited in the text as *FR*. This poem was substantially revised when it was published posthumously in 1957 in *Collected Poems II*: hereafter cited as *CP2*. The major difference besides changes in individual lines is that the whole first book of the 1939 version is broken from the main work and printed as a separate poem entitled "A Letter from the San Mateo Front."
5.   Line added in revised version.
6.   These lines are found only in the revised version.
7.   Appears in the first book of revised version only.
8.   Page 118 of *Flowering Rifle* has similar sentiments expressed in completely different words.
9.   Lines added in revised version. The earlier version has a tongue twisting conclusion: "Her stormy hair, Aurora: borealing."
10.   The original *Flowering Rifle* includes a fifteen page introductory section. Book I in *Collected Poems II* is Book II in the original publication (1939).

Chapter Seven

1.   Roy Campbell, *Talking Bronco* (London, 1946).
2.   *Talking Bronco*, p. 35. These lines do not appear in the *CP2* version.

3.   See W. H. Auden, *Journey to a Frontier* or, Andre Gide, *Man's Fate*.

Chapter Nine

1.   Roy Campbell, *Collected Poems III* (London, 1960): hereafter cited in the text as *CP3*.
2.   Roy Campbell, *Poems of Baudelaire* (New York, 1952), unpaged.
3.   Ibid.
4.   Ibid.
5.   Arthur Rimbaud, *The Drunken Boat*, trans. B. Hill, (London, 1953).
6.   Ibid., p. 8.
7.   Horace, *Odes, Epodes and the Art of Poetry*, trans. by John B. Quinn (St. Louis, 1936).
8.   Horace, *Complete Works*, edited by C. J. Kraemer, Jr. (New York, 1936).
9.   Ibid., p. 400.
10.   Quinn, p. 164.
11.   Frederico Garcia Lorca, *Selected Poems* (New York, 1955).
12.   Ibid., p. viii.
13.   Ibid., p. viii.
14.   Ibid., p. 87.

Chapter Ten

1.   C. J. D. Harvey, "The Poetry of Roy Campbell," *Standpunte*, October, 1950, p. 53.
2.   Ibid., p. 53.
3.   *Boston Transcript*, September 27, 1924, p. 4.
4.   *New York Tribune*, September 21, 1924, p. 4.
5.   *Spectator*, July 19, 1924, p. 98.
6.   *New York Times*, September 14, 1924, p. 14.
7.   H. Miles, *Dial* 77 (November, 1924), 423.
8.   B. Deutsch, *The Literary Review*, September 6, 1924, p. 4.
9.   E. Garnett, *Nation and Antheneum*, June 7, 1924, p. 323.
10.   *New York Times*, January 25, 1931, p. 2.
11.   B. Kenyon, *Outlook*, April 15, 1931, p. 536.
12.   R. Church, *Spectator*, May 3, 1930, p. 745.
13.   *Poetry* 38 (May, 1931), 98.
14.   *New York Times*, April 17, 1955, p. 4.
15.   *New York Times*, January 5, 1958, p. 6.
16.   *New Statesman*, November 30, 1957, p. 736.
17.   John Wain, *Spectator*, March 4, 1960, p. 328.
18.   John Ciardi, *Nation*, December 10, 1955, p. 515.
19.   H. H. Regnery, *Nation*, February 11, 1956, p. 128.

20. E. Muir, *New Statesman*, January 11, 1958, p. 49.
21. B. Bergonzi, *Journal of Contemporary History* 2 (1976), p. 147.
22. W. Lewis. *Letters,* ed. W. K. Rose. London 1963, p. 206.
23. Ibid., p.543.
24. M. Seymour-Smith, *Encounter*, November 1957, p. 38.
25. R. Kirk, *Sewanee Review* 64 (Winter, 1956), 164.
26. Ibid., p. 166.
27. E. Sitwell, "Roy Campbell," *Poetry* 92 (April, 1958), p. 42.
28. Ibid., p. 4.
29. U. Krige, *Poems of Roy Campbell* (Cape Town, 1960), p. 31.

Selected Bibliography

PRIMARY SOURCES

1. Poetry
The Flaming Terrapin. London: Cape, 1924; New York: Dial Press, 1924.
The Wayzgoose. London: Cape, 1928.
Adamastor. London: Faber, 1930; New York: Dial Press, 1931; Cape Town: Koston, 1950; London: Faber, 1954.
The Gum Trees. Drawings by D. Jones. London: Faber, 1930.
Poems. London: Hours Press, 1930.
Nineteen Poems. London: Benn, 1931.
Choosing A Mast. Drawings by Barnett Freedman. London; Faber, 1931.
The Georgiad. London: Boriswood, 1931.
Pomegranates. Drawings by J. Boswell. London: Boriswood, 1932.
Mithraic Emblems: A Poem. London: Boriswood, 1932.
Flowering Reeds. London: Boriswood, 1933.
Mithraic Emblems. London: Boriswood, 1936.
Flowering Rifle. London: Longmans, 1939.
Sons of the Mistral. London; Faber, 1941.
Talking Bronco. London: Faber, 1946; Chicago: Regnery, 1956.
Collected Poems. Volume I. London: Bodley Head, 1949; Chicago: Regenery, 1955.
Nativity. Drawings by J. Sellers. London: Faber, 1954.
Collected Poems. Volume II. London: Bodley Head, 1957; Chicago: Regenery, 1957.
Collected Poems. Volume III. London: Bodley Head, 1960.
Selected Poetry. London: Bodley Head, 1968.

2. Prose
Robert Burns, A Critical Essay. London: Faber, 1932.
Wyndham Lewis. Poets on the Poets Series. London: Chatto and Windus, 1932.
Taurine Provence. London: Harmsworth, 1932.
Broken Record: An Auto-biography. London: Boriswood, 1934.
Light on a Dark Horse: Autobiography 1901 - 1935. London: Hollis and Carter, 1951; Chicago: Regenery, 1952.
The Mamba's Precipice. London: Muller, 1953; New York: Day, 1954.
Portugal. With Campbell's own illustrations. London: Reinhardt, 1957; Chicago: Regenery, 1958.

3. Translations

Helge Krog. *Three Norwegian Plays.* London: Boriswood, 1934. Includes "Happy Ever After," "The Trial, and The Copy."

Saint John of the Cross. *Poems.* London: Havill Press, 1951; New York: Pantheon Books, 1951; London: Boriswood, 1952.

Frederick Garcia Lorca. *Poems.* Cambridge: Bowes and Bowes, 1952; New Haven: Yale University Press, 1952.

Charles Baudelaire. *Les Fleurs du Mal.* London: Havill Press, 1952; New York: Pantheon Books, 1952.

Six Spanish Plays. After James Mabbe. New York: Doubleday, 1959; Toronto: The Mayflower Press, 1959.

4. Selected Essays

"Decade in Retrospect." *Monthly Reviews* 52 (May, 1950), 319 - 33.

"Epitaph on the Thirties." *Nine,* no. 5 (Autumn, 1950), 344 - 46.

"A Note on the Waste Land." *Shenandoah* 2 - 3 (Summer, 1953), 74 - 76.

"Dylan Thomas, The War Years." *Shenandoah* 5 (Spring, 1954), 26 - 27.

"Poetry and Experience." *Theoria,* no. 6 (1954), 37 - 44.

"Memoir of Dylan Thomas." *Poetry* 87 (November, 1955), 111 - 14. B.B.C. Talk.

"Concerning Dylan Thomas." *Poetry London* 1 (March, 1956), 35 - 36. A Correspondence.

SECONDARY SOURCES

1. Books

DAVIS, V. *Bibliography of the Works of Ignatius Roy Dunnachie Campbell.* University of Cape Town: School of Library Studies, 1954. An attempt at a comprehensive bibliography of Campbell's work.

KRIGE, U. *Poems of Roy Campbell Chosen and Introduced by Uys Krige.* Cape Town: M. Miller 1960. A lengthy personal and critical appraisal along with a selection of Campbell's best verse compiled by a lifelong friend.

SMITH, R. *Lyric and Polemic.* Montreal: McGill-Queen's University Press, 1972. The first full-length study subtitled "The Literary Personality of Roy Campbell." This biographical-critical study draws heavily on unpublished letters.

TEMPLE, F.J., and LYLE, R., ed *Hommage à Roy Campbell.* Montpellier: La Licorne, 1958. A series of personal reminiscences and eulogies by many major writers including Richard Aldington, Lawrence Durrell, Wyndham Lewis, Alan Paton, and Edith Sitwell. In French.

WRIGHT, D. *Roy Campbell.* London: Longmans, 1961. A brief study by a young South African poet that combines excellent criticism with personal reminiscence.

2. Articles

ABRAHAMS, L. "Roy Campbell: Conquistador-Refugee." *Theoria*, no. 8 (1956), 46 - 65. A South African writer argues that not only did Campbell's poetry deteriorate after he left South Africa but his exile cost him his rightful central role in the development of South African literature.

BERGONZI, B. "Roy Campbell: Outsider on the Right." *Journal of Contemporary History*, no. 2 (April, 1967), 133 - 47. An historical assessment of Campbell's political beliefs viewing him as a writer in the context of the Fascist-Communist struggle in Europe.

CIARDI, J. "Muscles and Manners." *Nation*, December 10, 1955, p. 515. An example of the virulent personal and political antagonism Campbell engenders.

COLLINS, H. "Roy Campbell: The Talking Bronco." *Boston University Studies in English* 4 (Spring, 1960), 49 - 63. Substantially a review of criticism. Analyses Campbell's principles and poses, and defends him against many unjust attacks.

KENNER, H. "Narcissist of Action." *Poetry* 82 (June, 1953), 169 - 75. A rather cruel personal article insisting that Campbell's motivation was his "awe" of London society.

KIRK, R. "Last of the Scalds." *Sewanee Review* 64 (Winter, 1956), 164 - 70. An extended review that becomes lusty, rhetorical, affectionate praise for the man and his verse.

KRIGE, U. "Roy Campbell as Lyrical Poet: Some Quieter Aspects." *English Studies in Africa*, no. 1 (September, 1958), 81 - 94. A sensitive discussion of the early poetry, similar in tone to Krige's later extended introduction to *Poems of Roy Campbell* (see above).

MONROE, H. "On a High Horse." *Poetry* 38 (May, 1931), 95 - 100. A classic review by a distinguished critic that exemplifies the divided response to the early poems.

PATON, A. "Roy Campbell: Poet and Man." *Theoria*, no. 9 (1957), 19 - 31. An enthusiastic and affectionate memorial essay by South Africa's major writer.

POVEY, J. "A Lyre of Savage Thunder." *Wisconsin Studies in Contemporary Literature*, no. 7 (Winter, 1966), 85 - 102. An essay foreshadowing the critical argument of this book, that exile undermined Campbell's poetic gift.

REGNERY, H. "Rejoinder to Ciardi." *Nation*, February, 11, 1956, p. 128. An indignant personal counter to Ciardi (see above) by Campbell's publisher and friend.

SCOTT, T. "Impressions of Roy Campbell's Poetry." *Western Review* 14, no. 3 (Spring, 1950), 214 - 24. A general review arguing somewhat glibly that Campbell's career declined from "first major poet of a great and youthful continent" to "a big angry colonial."

SERGEANT, H. "Restive Steer." *English Association Essays* (1957), 105 - 122. A shrewd and sensitive critical analysis of Campbell's poetry that is the better for avoiding any personal judgments.

SEYMOUR-SMITH, M. "Zero and the Impossible." *Encounter*, no. 9 (November, 1957) 38 - 51. A memoir filled with snide remarks and casual spite, typical of London left-wing critical reaction.

SMITH, R. "Campbell and His French Sources." *Journal of Comparative Literature*, no. 22 (Winter, 1970), 1 - 18. A close and convincing analysis of the influence of French poets (Rimbaud, Baudelaire and Valéry) on Campbell's own poetry.

SITWELL, E. "Roy Campbell." *Poetry* 92 (April, 1958), 42 - 48. An elegy on Campbell's death by a longtime loyal friend, herself a distinguished poet.

WEIGHTMAN, J. C. "Pedant Finds Fault." *Twentieth Century* 153 (February, 1953), 135 - 41. A scornful dismissal of Campbell's competence as a translator in a review of his translation of *Les Fleurs du Mal*.

Index

231